The Wall and the Bridge

THE
WALL
AND THE
BRIDGE

FEAR AND OPPORTUNITY
IN DISRUPTION'S WAKE

● ● ●

GLENN HUBBARD

Yale

UNIVERSITY PRESS

New Haven and London

Yale University Press books may be purchased in quantity for
educational, business, or promotional use. For information, please e-mail
sales.press@yale.edu (U.S. office) or sales@yaleup.co.uk (U.K. office).

Set in Gotham & Adobe Garamond types by
Integrated Publishing Solutions.
Printed in the United States of America.

Library of Congress Control Number: 2021939970
ISBN 978-0-300-25908-7 (hardcover : alk. paper)

A catalogue record for this book is available from the British Library.
This paper meets the requirements of ANSI/NISO Z39.48-1992
(Permanence of Paper).

10 9 8 7 6 5 4 3 2 1

Contents

Preface   vii

Acknowledgments   xiii

1 Introduction: Economists and Real People   1

2 How We Got Here: Falling Walls and Missed Bridges   19

3 Mass Flourishing: The Unknown Adam Smith   39

4 Adam Smith Schools Today's Commentators   58

5 Why Walls Are Still Attractive   84

6 Bridges   105

7 Business as a Bridge Builder   134

8 Governments and Bridges   151

9 Mass Flourishing Requires Bridges   178

Notes   199

Index   221

Preface

When I began my study of economics in the 1970s, the United States was already undergoing significant changes on account of structural shifts in technology and globalization. Industries, firms, and jobs were being upended. While those experiencing business failures or job losses felt these changes acutely, economists and political leaders were slow to pay attention. Eventually, waves of populist fears of change became a groundswell, and elites began to notice in earnest.

My own journey as an economist actually unfolded at the same time as the deindustrialization of Youngstown, Ohio, which I note in the book. My first college economics course in September 1977 introduced me to skills that became more valuable over time, thanks to both technological change and globalization. Youngstown's steel closures began in earnest that month, and it suffered heavily from those same changes—a cautionary illustration of losses from economic forces that benefited many others, including me. While I worked hard and had the blessing of great teachers and mentors as an undergraduate at the University of Central Florida and a Ph.D. student at Harvard University, I also found significant public support for gaining the skills of an economist. Without assistance from the federally funded National Merit Scholarship and the National Science Foundation, I could never have become an economist and benefited from these structural changes.

This book is about "noticing" and, more important, about ideas to address those structural, disruptive changes accompanying economic progress. From the dawn of modern economics, thinkers like Adam Smith, a central figure in this book, knew that progress and disruption were inseparable, like the two sides of a coin. Smith articulated rules of the game for a successful economy and championed mass flourishing, in which individuals broadly were prepared to compete in a dynamic economy.

Contemporary economics in the Smithian spirit often embodies the classical laissez-faire traditions and modern neoliberal perspectives more completely than Smith himself. Smith, who wrote *The Theory of Moral Sentiments* almost two decades before writing his magnum opus, *The Wealth of Nations,* saw the economy as a moral system of flourishing, not just an economic system for generating incomes. The narrow neoliberal, laissez-faire take has led to a strained political debate between "capitalism" and "socialism." More ominously, neoliberals take public support for the dynamic competitive economy for granted. Recent political events, with the resurgence of populism, suggest otherwise.

The all-too-common political challenge to the increasingly flimsy laissez-faire defense of the economic order is the *wall.* A wall can be physical (from Hadrian's ancient structure in Britain to President Donald Trump's border barrier), but it is generally a metaphor for barriers against change—like changes in technology or global markets. Walls of protection often come from nostalgia, a desire to restore the economy to the way it was, the good old days. But the economic tinkering that wall building requires is self-destructive for the economy as a whole and even for those supposedly protected. Smith saw that; he wrote *The Wealth of Nations* in response to such tinkering by mercantilists.

The antidote or counterargument to a wall is a *bridge.* Bridges prepare individuals for, and reconnect them to, participation in a dynamic economy. In an economic sense, they are required for mass flourishing. Politically and socially, we need bridges in order to regain public support for the economic system.

Populist leaders and commentators often blame economists for not noticing real economic pain from change, or for handing out laissez-faire pieties as band-aids. While there is some truth to this, economics is not the problem and offers many solutions. Such solutions are familiar in spirit both to Smith and the Econ 101 course you may have taken in college. Those solutions—bridges—are the only realistic alternative to destructive walls; they can sustain popular support for openness and dynamism.

Populist pressures have shifted politics from accepting change toward building walls against change, as opposed to building bridges of adjustment. Walls and bridges have thus become the new counterpoints in policy debates, with walls too often winning the debate because of a failure of economists to fully engage.

This book follows my own journey of noticing the problems and assessing walls and bridges in the light of classical and recent economics. It begins with Chapter 1's description of the key structural economic changes of technological change and globalization. I draw on my experience as President George W. Bush's chief economic advisor in 2001, and the pain that my Columbia students and I observed on recent visits to Youngstown.

Chapter 2 chronicles the irony that our present tensions came about from a lack of readiness when walls *fell*. Without the Berlin Wall, trade barriers, and transportation and communications costs, among other limitations, we gained opportunities for many industries and communities, while others suffered painful adjustments. We were ready to cheer on the "gainers," but had little to offer the "losers."

Chapters 3 and 4 turn to economics, beginning with the father of modern economics: Adam Smith in *The Wealth of Nations* gives us a concept of prosperity due to openness and competition, while the Smith of *The Theory of Moral Sentiments* reminds us of the value of "mutual sympathy." Together, these combine economic rigor with a moral foundation for mass flourishing as the economy's goal. Chapter 4 chronicles three departures from Smith's (and most contemporary economists') views—protecting particular jobs, protecting particular products or industries, and protecting workers and communities. These might seem like relatively modest walls, aiming to strengthen society at the small cost of lost efficiency—but they risk the economy's dynamism. Smith's vision remains correct against these soft walls, but the punchline is less laissez-faire than a call for bridges.

Chapter 5 traces modern populist calls for walls to elites'— economic and political—neglect. Walls are again in vogue because we have failed to prepare individuals for, and reconnect them to, participation in the evolving economy. This preparation and reconnection require bridges, the subject of Chapter 6. That chapter outlines an economic approach to bridge building, marrying Smithian mass flourishing to the modern economy. It suggests supporting training and rebuilding social insurance to focus on structural, not just cyclical shifts. Abraham Lincoln's land-grant colleges, Franklin Roosevelt's unemployment insurance, and the G.I. Bill offer lessons on partnerships between federal support and local needs and inclusion.

While individual agency in bridge building is important, business and government have major roles to play. Chapter 7 highlights the roles for business in advancing preparation and reconnection and the need to preserve broad public support for the open and competitive economy championed by Smith and contemporary economists. Government's role is the subject of Chapter 8. Federal funding for bridges is certainly important, but previous successes also show the gains from public–private collaboration and from tailoring assistance to local needs.

Chapter 9 concludes with three summary observations. Mass flourishing is a moral as well as economic imperative; it requires bridges, not walls; and it depends on intentional business and government action.

The novel coronavirus pandemic beginning in 2020 only amplifies the need for bridges. Sadiq Khan, the mayor of London, tweeted on November 7, 2020, in response to the election of President Joe Biden and Vice President Kamala Harris, that "it's time to get back to building bridges, not walls." Yet the developments so far in 2021 are not yet reassuring. The Biden administration is relying on another kind of wall, transfer payments, that will likely leave disadvantaged communities worse off in the long run. This book makes the case for designing and executing bridges to mass flourishing.

New York, New York
August 2021

Acknowledgments

I fell in love with economics early in my education and never let go. One reason for my disciplinary ardor is my belief that economics offers powerful ideas to generate both prosperity and broad participation in it—mass flourishing. Two tours in Washington, in the George H. W. Bush Treasury Department and then the George W. Bush White House, exposed me to both the complexity of policy design and the powerful sway of neoliberal economic ideas. Over the past decade, my research into contemporary American populism pointed me toward the wide-open space for walls left open by popular dissatisfaction with neoliberalism.

The idea of a "wall"—dramatized especially by former President Donald Trump—calls for a counteridea. I centered on a "bridge," a way to connect two points otherwise difficult to traverse. That metaphor allowed me to build on the mass-flourishing ideas of Adam Smith with potent reforms of social insurance to make that flourishing possible.

This book's subjects have been in my thoughts for some time. My long-standing interest in reform of social insurance traces to conversations over many years with my brilliant teacher, the late Martin Feldstein. Another brilliant teacher, Benjamin Friedman, gave me both an interest in these subjects and the critical point that economics is, in part, a moral study. My Columbia colleagues Charles Calomiris, Kent Daniel, Michael Graetz, Bruce Greenwald, Ray Horton,

Tano Santos, Joe Stiglitz, and especially Ned Phelps have heard me out on many of the arguments here, and I have learned much from those discussions. Washington colleagues Chris DeMuth, Robert Doar, and Michael Strain have also been kind in offering feedback on ideas.

Editorially, I have benefited from sponsorship and suggestions by Seth Ditchik at Yale University Press. Harry Haskell also offered strong editorial advice at Yale University Press. I received ace proofreading and copyediting assistance from Jennifer Brailsford, Lyndsay Clark, Deborah Crowell, Beth Miller, Clara Miller, Emily Webster, Ellen Wolf, and Elena Zeller. John Landry has been a superb editorial partner over the course of this project, brimming with amazing suggestions and thoughtful criticism. Rimjhim Dey and Tunku Varadarajan have been generous with thoughts and comments.

I am grateful to Columbia University and its Chazen Institute for Global Business for the time and intellectual community to pursue the project, and to the American Enterprise Institute for intellectual and financial support when I held the John H. Makin Fellowship during the 2019–2020 academic year. Will Baird at AEI provided excellent research assistance. My longtime assistant at Columbia, Wilhelmina Sanford, patiently shepherded the manuscript through many iterations.

My greatest debt of gratitude in this project and all others is to my wife Constance. Her insights, suggestions, and patience with my constant juggling were the bridge from ideas to book. This book is dedicated to her.

The Wall and the Bridge

1
Introduction: Economists and Real People

The Wall in Washington

I first came up against wall thinking in 2001, as the recently appointed chairman of President George W. Bush's Council of Economic Advisers. The council is a small but significant organization within the executive branch of the U.S. government. Since its founding in 1946, it has brought economic analysis to bear on policy questions of interest to the president—effectively a small consulting firm with one client. I had been an economic advisor to Governor Bush during the 2000 presidential campaign, and I knew he was genuinely open to advice and ideas on complicated political questions.

One of our first questions was whether the federal government should assess tariffs on steel imports. President Bush summoned me and other advisors to offer views on the question. As an economist, I believed the tariffs would hurt the economy as a whole. The steelmakers, their employees, and other groups would get relief. But users of steel—far more businesses and consumers—would be worse off. Their harm would demonstrably exceed any short-run gain for the steelmakers. Worse still, the tariffs seemed an attempt to blunt the forces of technological change and globalization that could transform the future of American productivity and wealth.

I knew the politics were tough here, and not on my side. During the campaign, now Vice President Dick Cheney had voiced sympathy for steel protection in remarks in Wheeling, West Virginia. Steel workers were geographically concentrated in politically important states. And their concerns were real: Firms, workers, and communities were demoralized and hurting economically—and they not unreasonably turned to elected officials for help.

Before going to the meeting, I recalled one of my wife Constance's favorite sayings, which reflected her ability to take the clutter around her and turn it into clarity. She believes that individuals fall into two groups—economists and "real people." Economists have special ways of thinking about most things, and they often communicate that thinking poorly. But real people are in charge. President Bush was definitely—proudly—a real person.

I went to the meeting armed with my Econ 101 arguments, but hearing my wife's admonition, I took along two maps. The first showed job losses and the transition from one sector to another. The president acknowledged it and observed that he wanted to limit those job losses. Then I explained that the map represented the transition from agricultural to manufacturing employment from 1900 to 1940. Surely, the president did not want to put Americans back on the farm. Of course he did not. So far, so good.

I then showed him a map illustrating projected job losses by county in the U.S. heartland as a consequence of higher steel prices. That map, which showed total job losses would exceed the number of jobs the tariff advocates sought to protect, was Econ 101 brought to life. The president took notes. Progress.

Yet I lost the argument: The president chose to impose steel tariffs. I knew he had to make a complex political call—economics was only one factor. I had not made the sale.

Calls for protection are familiar and appear to offer attention and help. I continue to be convinced that Econ 101 is right, that such calls end poorly. (And in fact the tariffs were just a temporary bandage.) But the economic reasoning so attractive to economists just didn't quite make it with "real people,"—even the smartest, most engaged real people.

It hit me only later: I had used good suggestions from Econ 101, but had I used *all* the good suggestions?

No, I hadn't. And that's what this book is about. And today, these arguments face much higher economic and political stakes than in 2001.

The battle over steel tariffs was part of a steady stream of policy arguments about handling the side effects of two tectonic economic forces—technological change and globalization—that buffet American workers and businesses. Those same forces have driven economic and political debates in the United States (the election of President Trump), the United Kingdom (Brexit), France (the Yellow Vests protests), Italy (the Five Star movement), Greece (the rise of Syriza), Brazil (the election of President Jair Bolsonaro), and elsewhere.

"Real people" versus economists, the tussle continues. When confronted with structural, disruptive forces like technological change and globalization, real people—or, more accurately, their political leaders—have pushed back throughout history. Change is hard, often intolerable. The common response is *walls*—physical or metaphorical barriers to change or the unknown. Like the steel tariffs.

By contrast, economists, since the dawn of their discipline, have emphasized *bridges,* helping individuals prepare for change and celebrating the economic gains from change and disruption. I could have done a better job at explaining bridges that afternoon in the White House.

The case for bridges is now all the more important. To overcome the present and historical popularity of walls, economists need to do a better job of showing that walls are misguided.

The fundamental problem is that we economists have let the public debate drift to the opposite extremes of building walls and a laissez-faire optimism about change and markets making everything OK. After multiple decades, we know that market forces by themselves are not enough to revive dislocated industries. But bridges—informed by economics—can revive them, far better than walls.

To explain how, we need to go back to Adam Smith, the father of modern economics. His *Wealth of Nations* promoted not just openness to change, but also *mass flourishing*. He believed economics could make everyone better off, not just the elites or clever entrepreneurs. We need to restore that spirit.

Smith lived at a time when walls were a matter of course. Since ancient Rome—think Hadrian—walls have been simple to explain and play to the concerns of elites and ordinary people. Smith opposed walls with a radical idea: The "wealth of a nation" was not an inventory of assets like gold, silver, land, or trade surpluses, as many leaders then (and now!) seemed to believe. It was, instead, the economy's ability to generate income for people to spend.

That was good news, because this ability could improve over time. Growth over time could come from openness to new occupations (specialization within the economy), openness to foreign trade (trading with others to take specialization a step further), and openness to new ways of doing things (technological and organizational change).

Openness was therefore essential for growth and prosperity. Crucially, Smith also argued that openness by itself wasn't enough to ensure future success. To turn those gains into *mass* prosperity and flourishing required bridges—paths for connection and reconnection to the dynamic economy—not walls.

The idea that change, even chaotic change, was essential runs through economics from David Ricardo (on trade), Joseph Schumpeter (on creative destruction), and Friedrich Hayek (on gains from uncoordinated discovery) to Edmund Phelps and Deirdre McCloskey today (on dynamism). Change, even disruptive change, is good, as long as the economy works with the change for a better result—rather than tries to fend it off with walls.

Today's big economic changes are two: *technological advance* and *globalization*. From computers to artificial intelligence and robots, new technologies have created entirely new job categories (in programming and data analytics) and industries (such as social media), boosting productivity and incomes. Globalization has generated enormous benefits for consumers, with gains from trade in lower prices (think Walmart) and greater variety (think of the range of clothing and smart devices at reasonable prices). Businesses gain from greater efficiency—from competing against other firms abroad and from cost-effective global supply chains. Globalization, too, has increased purchasing power and bolstered productivity. The effects of these forces on growth, on possibilities, and on prosperity illustrate well Smith's idea of the wealth of a nation.

Many political leaders embrace this change, noting that it increases prosperity on average for people. The big gains on average can be used to compensate those who suffer major losses from change. In this view, there's much gain—and there needn't be much pain. This conclusion propelled innovation and openness with American business and policy leadership for decades, with a sunny, laissez-faire approach of letting change unfurl with as little interference as possible.

Unfortunately, the pain turned out to be real—and worse than expected. In econ-speak, it is *structural*—whole types of jobs and businesses can wane for a very long time. Investments in one's own human capital (careers) or in business capital (companies) can suffer large and continuing losses. These losses can happen more quickly than in days gone by (think of the decline in newspapers) and with geographically concentrated effects (steel and auto industry employment in the Midwest). These losses are much larger than those experienced in a recession or a business-cycle downturn, in which a person might lose a job only to regain it some months later when the economy recovers. These are lost jobs that likely will never come back.

With economic policymakers at a loss in dealing with structural declines, the historical attraction to walls has returned. If foreign steel is cheaper (especially with government subsidies abroad), why not impose tariffs to "level the playing field"? If companies are phasing out some job categories to boost efficiency, why not tax them for doing so? If robots are replacing jobs, let's make it more expensive to use them. And let's end our merchandise trade deficits, not transfer our wealth to other nations. Let's protect the jobs and businesses Americans are used to having. Let's build walls.

Adam Smith understood this dynamic. He argued against mercantilist contemporaries who wanted to manage trade and guilds that sought to preserve their current privileges. Nor did he ignore the pain with the gain, because he sought mass prosperity, indeed mass flourishing.

Smith and other Scottish Enlightenment thinkers understood that *economic* constructs were in part *social* and *political* constructs. Kings and princes had not interfered with openness simply because of economic ignorance. They had done so because walls against change were appealing and facilitated the mercantilist orthodoxy of the day. Smith was not a dogmatic free marketeer—he wanted prosperity spread around. People understand the free market best when they can feel some of its benefits.

Continuing in this vein a century and a half after Smith, the British economist Nicholas Kaldor argued that openness improves overall incomes and that the *gainers can compensate the losers*. Again, we can get much gain and not much pain. This became the Econ 101 prescription.

But *do* gainers compensate losers? How would they?

I love economics, and I am proud to have cowritten a market-leading textbook titled *Economics,* the fabled Econ 101 course.[1] As a result, I often guest-lecture on economics. Invariably, I encounter students who themselves, or through their parents, neighbors, or communities, have suffered from technological change or globalization. And seemingly, that hardship has gone unaddressed by elected officials.

Closer to home for me are the not-infrequent questions about whether Econ 101 is just wrong or inapplicable to today's concerns. And if Econ 101 is wrong, why not try walls to block the pain of change? Why not elect leaders who do so?

It's not just students. A spate of recent popular books has gone after economics and economists as lost in a laissez-faire fog, mistaken in their protests against protecting jobs and businesses. Some critics have even called us the captured handmaidens of gainers from change in a contest against the losers from change.

But Econ 101 isn't just right about the source of the wealth of a nation; it has better answers for alleviating the grief from change. As Smith desired, it has answers for mass prosperity, not just prosperity on average.

The answer is *bridges.* While walls have an intuitive appeal, bridges take us somewhere. The journey somewhere is about *preparation* and *connection* to new opportunities. How can we prepare individuals for these opportunities? What can individuals themselves do? What can business do? And governments?

Preparation involves training workers for the jobs of today and the future, among other skills. But there's more to assess than preparation for new things. Disruptive change separates individual workers and businesspeople from the dynamic productive economy that is delivering great gains on average. How do we reconnect them? For economists, this inquiry is about *social insurance:* temporary transfer payments to help individuals cope with forces beyond their individual control. When you or I feel unable to control or influence our situation, fear is a natural feeling, and walls are on its heels. Rethinking social insurance can offer valuable reconnection to the economy, yes, but also to noneconomic factors like individual control and dignity.

Connection and reconnection—bridges. Not walls. As we will see, Econ 101 has answers here. And economists need to spell them out, better than we have in the past. Increasingly dangerous conversations about walls, on the political right and left, risk killing the golden goose of our dynamic economy. Economists—and real people—have the same fight.

Youngstown's Predicament

The burgers arrived, and they were tasty. We sat rapt in The Federal restaurant in Youngstown, Ohio, listening to a reporter from the local newspaper, *The Vindicator*. I was with another professor, Ray Horton, and two dozen MBA students from Columbia Business School in New York.

Horton and I thought our students would benefit from a trip to America's industrial heartland, in addition to their usual haunts of London, Silicon Valley, and Singapore. It was November 2017, a year after President Trump's election victory focused policymakers on the damage wrought by economic disruption.

We'd had a busy day. In walking across the historic Mill Creek Park Bridge, Horton and I remarked about what a useful and attractive connector it was for the city. We then struggled for the rest of our walk with the question that framed the journey and frames this book: Are there economic bridges for Youngstown and similar communities to carry them to renewed opportunity?

Youngstown, nestled halfway between Pittsburgh and Cleveland, was for decades a heartland center of manufacturing success. But then change played out both fast and slow. Horton and I had taught our students the benefits of openness and trade for innovation and efficiency, and this story touched on the other side.

On "Black Monday," September 19, 1977, before the students were born, the Youngstown Sheet & Tube Company announced it was shutting the Campbell Works. Dating back to 1902, this was the larger of the company's two mills in the Mahoning Valley in northeast Ohio. Five thousand individuals were suddenly out of work. More closures followed, with ripple effects through the steel industry's supply chain in the local economy. Within five years, 50,000 jobs left the Mahoning Valley. Those jobs would not return. It's not that local business leaders did not try to help. The mills were simply not economically viable.

The community looked to politicians and switched out the local congressman. Six years later his successor lost to Jim Traficant, who served the district for eighteen years before a federal conviction for corruption. National politicians came every four years to talk about protecting jobs. The steel tariffs of 2001 failed to resuscitate local industry.

In 2016, GOP candidate Donald Trump came to Youngstown and called for walls to restore Youngstown's jobs. His Democratic opponent, Hillary Clinton, likewise promised to bring back past glory, as had her husband, President Bill Clinton, in the 1992 campaign. After his election and a few months before our visit, President Trump had repeated the familiar reassurance: "We're going to get those jobs coming back, and we're going to fill up those factories."

Yet the continuing U.S. economic recovery and the large cut in corporate taxes after the president's speech, both promising developments, were still missing the mark in Youngstown. Graig Graziosi, the reporter who spoke to us, pointed to a clear sign of decline: The median house price in Youngstown in 2016 was just $43,000. More than one student, coming from the ultra-expensive New York City housing market, sat up and took notice. A median household income of $24,000 per year, 29 percent below the national median, offered one explanation.

Trump's rhetoric in 2016 had revived the community's hopes for political change. Clinton barely won in Mahoning County, in contrast to President Barack Obama's crushing defeat of GOP challenger Mitt Romney there four years earlier. Trump actually carried nearby Trumbull County, the first Republican standard bearer to do so since President Richard Nixon's national reelection sweep in 1972. He also won Ohio as a whole. His popularity in the midwestern industrial states was crucial to his surprising victory; he would also carry Mahoning County and Ohio in 2020.

That forty-year odyssey from Black Monday to the election of President Trump stimulated our journey for lessons amid disruption's losers. The stark difference between Youngstown's struggles, and the forty years of success from openness that I taught my students, should have had me thinking harder earlier. We got from our visit a lesson in community from businesspeople, educators, and social service leaders trying to address consequences of economic dislocation—and what it would take for Americans to be "in this together."

Something Big Is Happening: Why Didn't We Notice?

We didn't need President Trump's victory to tell us that something was wrong with our praise of openness. Five days before the 2016 election, the auditorium in Uris Hall at Columbia Business School had been packed with multiple overflow rooms. Ray Horton and I had led a town hall–style conversation on economic disruption from technological change and globalization. While the school held these faculty-student conversations periodically, I had not seen a crowd so large since the "what's happening" town halls during the global financial crisis in 2008.

We talked about cultural and economic factors, but the conversation centered on events. Why had the British voted to leave the European Union a few months earlier? How had Donald Trump, an unconventional candidate with heterodox and populist political views, thrashed a bevy of conventional and credentialed Republican opponents to become his party's standard bearer? And, mirabile dictu, would he beat Hillary Clinton, the former First Lady, United States senator, and Secretary of State, a fixture in national politics?

Horton and I explained the relative struggles of people left behind by the United Kingdom's openness to Europe and to global finance. While tighter integration with Europe and the world had improved incomes on average, much of the gains had gone to London elites, leaving workers in Manchester and Birmingham feeling removed from economic gains from integration—and too close to regulatory "thou shalts" from unelected European bureaucrats. We also explained that candidate Donald Trump had run an effective primary campaign, in a crowded field, by sizing a base delighted with populist messages on trade, immigration, and elites (all bad in his telling).

We did less well in grasping the confluence of forces from disruption's wake that would help bring Trump to victory. I had even less excuse than many: My brother, a country-western entertainer, had tipped me off about the strength of Trump's support in the heartland, including states considered difficult for the GOP to carry.

The town hall that day, the trip to Youngstown, and this book are about that story, its underpinnings, and its implications from an economic perspective. That the election result was a surprise, that Brexit was a surprise, and that the revolt of the *Gilets Jaunes* (Yellow Vests) in France later was a surprise, should concern us.

Back in November 2008, the queen of England had gone to the London School of Economics to dedicate a new building for the economics faculty. How partial Her Majesty is to economics, I do not know. While conversing with economist worthies, she asked, referring to the searing global financial crisis, "Why did nobody see it coming?"

She asked one of the clearest and most to-the-point questions of that crisis. How could something so earth-shattering come as a surprise to so many experts? I have no schadenfreude; the queen would likewise have embarrassed my colleagues and me had she put her question to the Columbia Economics Department.

The question could well be asked about candidate Trump's victory in 2016. To the extent that we failed to see it coming, what does that say about economists, business leaders, and politicians? Three points come to mind. First, high-frequency news and events tend to dominate serious and cocktail discussions, while low-frequency but large changes get short shrift. Second, to notice something one has to look for it, and we were too busy admiring the upside of openness. Finally, we didn't have ready ideas on adjusting to these slow-moving but damaging forces.

We went to Youngstown to notice, and we heard about a lot—jobs lost and opportunities gained, failing schools and opioid addiction, and a feeling that people in power rarely respected the community's dignity. These were the results of the disruption since Black Monday 1977.

The undercurrents were there—earnings growing much faster for those with skills tied to technological change and globalization, like those of my students and me, than for average workers. Income mobility is actually declining for millions of Americans. It was the flip side of a coin that brought significant economic gains for the nation as a whole.

Openness to trade and innovation brings gains on average, riches to some, and risks to others. Those risks—akin to the prospect that one's human capital might be wiped out and skills rendered irrelevant or less valued—are undiversifiable, in economic parlance, and beyond individuals' control. Add to these forces the political response to the financial crisis of 2007–2009, where the government bailed out banks while homeowners faced foreclosure and couldn't refinance at now-lower rates. Anxiety hardly seems perplexing when the issue is put this way.

Even worse, populist calls to action, by Trump or leaders overseas, were not new. The number of people affected by economic disruption had grown. It was less a new script than a really large argument.

Meanwhile, for all the papers and think-tank conferences on education, training, social insurance, and geographical mobility, serious policymaking was limited. Public assistance remained focused on helping people in recessions, not the once-and-for-all structural hits to human capital from economic disruption.

Hence the trip to Youngstown. Horton, hailing from Sibley, Iowa, and I, from Apopka, Florida, thought we should notice, take a look. And we did so with the students—to broaden their understanding of the economic situation, yes, but more to build their social context for future business leadership.

No one had to tell the people of Youngstown about big change. The mill closures had happened quickly, with little corporate or public assistance. Any older citizen we met on the trip could tell graphic stories about those disasters. The city's population fell from 100,000 in 1950 to 65,000 at the time of that trip. Depopulation did not right the ship, as the town continued to struggle with job losses, not to mention weak public schools and opioid addiction.

Still, our trip was exciting. From a steel mill to local business leaders, to faculty and students at Youngstown State University and community leaders, we saw a portrait of a city and a region hit hard—and fighting back. Graziosi said the city had taken blow after economic blow, while the talk from politicians had not turned to action. We spoke with citizens who loved President Trump and those who despised him. The students hit the town each of our four nights; I was a party pooper by comparison.

The university offered education and training with the Youngstown Business Incubator. We heard a lot about entrepreneurship and new technology. Steelmaking was back—we saw the Vallourec Star mill, located in a historic factory site. But its floors had engineers and robots, and few workers. Automation had boosted productivity in steelmaking, especially as companies adjusted to foreign competition and new methods of steelmaking. The job growth in Youngstown now came not from manufacturing but from health care, education, retail, and the arts. Something big was changing there and in many other places in America.

The Wall and the Bridge

Four themes dominated discussions with students on that trip to Youngstown and with another group on a return trip a year later. First, they *noticed*—they made the connection between economic shifts and the lives of individuals and a community. Particularly for non-U.S. students, who thought of New York as America (!), the experience was eye-opening. Second, they wanted to know why political and business leaders—and even economists—had *not* seemed to notice. Third, they realized there was no silver bullet to "fix Youngstown," which connects to the political looking-the-other-way. Finally, they wondered whether so many people hit hard by economic forces beyond their control would support the market economy and political process that allowed such devastation to occur.

These discussions were perceptive all around, but the final theme has stayed with me the longest. Our economic system, with its openness to change, is our goose laying the golden eggs. Advances in living standards and opportunities don't happen in a static economy. Change—messy, even disruptive—drives growth. People will support that change only if they believe "we are all in this together," that we will all gain or can at least adapt. The disparities between New York City and Youngstown called that belief into question.

The simplest solution is to hold back change, to make things like they used to be, with *walls*. Can we erect barriers to trade, to automation and technological advance? Will walls keep jobs and communities safe? Tough questions, but "Build the Wall" is a simple and compelling slogan.

On a return trip to Youngstown in fall 2018, with other colleagues and students, the conversations were more hopeful. A comfortable and trendy downtown business hotel had opened, and I participated in a panel with local economic development officials and academics on "the future" and what it would take to get there. Perhaps most hopeful was a tasty (if heavy) Mexican lunch with Rick Sokolov, the chief operating officer of mall giant Simon Property Group. Simon Property had acquired Youngstown-based DeBartolo malls some years before. Sokolov enjoyed the lifestyle of the area and chose to move there; he was betting on its future.

Sokolov's optimism combined hope and strategy. His hope was that the Mahoning Valley's rich economic history could serve as a beacon for others like him who enjoyed the area. The business strategist in him saw opportunities ranging from onshoring manufacturing to technology hubs in partnership with the Youngstown Business Incubator. He saw an opening for retiree health care as a low-cost location between Cleveland and Pittsburgh.

The best alternative to building a wall is *to build bridges* to promote these possibilities. Like the one over Mill Creek Park, bridges can take cities like Youngstown to new opportunities while remaining connected to the past. A bridge has to have a foundation and a path for crossing it. Not everyone needs the same bridge, but the bridge is a common service and therefore analogous to "we are all in this together." Figuring out how to build the bridges and get people across them, not a "Build the Wall" soundbite, is our subject here.

A bridge-based approach to managing economic change and disruption is not just about a list of programs and interventions from local, state, and national governments. It requires a rethinking of economic policy for a fairer capitalism, to ensure participation and prosperity for many more people—the "mass flourishing" goal of classical economists.

This rethinking requires work by policymakers, business leaders, economists, and all of us as citizens. We must center on the idea that dynamic capitalism is a social as well as an economic construct, with mass flourishing and not just "higher GDP" as its goal. We must match the rhetoric of classical economists with policies and actions that reconnect individuals for success.

Policymakers need to take an inventory of public goods and social insurance for preparation and reconnection. That inventory will likely suggest the need for both higher taxes and a reorientation of how taxpayer funds are allocated across priorities.

For business leaders, three observations are in order. The first is to remember that social support for dynamism and innovation is not a given, and is essential in a democratic society. Second is to follow the queen's question and "notice": to be aware of dislocations affecting employees and communities in response to economic shifts— especially when those shifts boost their business profits. Third, business leaders must focus on maximizing the long-term value of their firms, which will reveal the desirability of many investments in local communities.

As for economists, I write to chide our profession here. We, too, must notice. We must go beyond laissez-faire endorsements of change (no pain, no gain!). We need to refocus on mass flourishing, on ways to include more people in dynamism instead of letting them flounder in disruption's wake. Many contemporary critics of economists, with arguments ranging from "the basis of economics since Adam Smith is wrong" to "economists are selfish, disinterested observers" (ouch!), are off-base, as we will see. In fact, many economists are exploring bridges across disruption. More should, and the question "Why did nobody notice?" is still real.

In particular, economists need to recognize that calls to build a wall carry moral weight, enough to convince people to trade off economic efficiency to help dislocated individual communities. Arguments to build a bridge, therefore, need not just efficiency analysis, but also a moral connection to individual dignity and mass flourishing.

All of us share the responsibility to deliver this mass flourishing in our economy by forcing the political choices and budget priorities to help bring it out. If we fail to build bridges, the rush to walls from demagogues and policy entrepreneurs should not surprise us.

President Trump, of course, left office in January 2021, succeeded by Joe Biden, an experienced politician. The COVID-19 pandemic has upended the economy, employment, and business. But these changes do not diminish the economic, political, and social consequences of structural shifts in technology and globalization. President Biden is facing public and political skepticism about trade as he tries to strengthen U.S. ties globally; he will not deal with walls against openness as easily as Presidents Clinton, George W. Bush, and Obama managed. The pandemic has magnified structural shifts from technological change, disrupting work arrangements and diminishing some old job prospects while amplifying new ones. It, too, brought forth calls for walls in global supply chains and protection for particular jobs and businesses.

Against this backdrop, a doubling down on neoliberal openness orthodoxy is unlikely among conservative politicians. "Change is good" can have the breezy ring of "Greed is good" in the 1987 film *Wall Street*. Meanwhile, the left's equity-based offerings of greater public assistance for many Americans run the risk of creating a wall against participation in the dynamic economy. Bridges are needed now more than ever for Americans bearing macro risks of major changes to prepare and reconnect them more to the economy.

Those bridges and their economic roots are our subject here.

2

How We Got Here:
Falling Walls and Missed Bridges

The Walls Came A-Tumbling Down

"Mr. Gorbachev, tear down this wall!" thundered President Ronald Reagan in West Berlin in 1987. The Berlin Wall, the symbol of the Iron Curtain, kept people, ideas, and goods stuck in place. It finally came down on November 11, 1989, followed by the Soviet Union itself two years later. These collapses opened a new era of openness for labor, capital, and commerce in the next few years.

Serving in the first President Bush's Treasury Department at the time, I saw the optimism in Washington for a world with fewer walls—for American democracy and American business. A fully global market led to hopes for reduced conflict, just as the 1957 removal of trade barriers in the European Economic Community had aimed to substitute trade and prosperity for war.

Ominously, policymakers paid little attention to the effect on American workers.

Four years later, Mexico, Canada, and the United States ratified the North American Free Trade Agreement (NAFTA), inspired by the European Economic Community. The pact gradually reduced tariffs, custom duties, and other trade barriers, while working to secure intellectual property rights and resolve cross-border disputes. Some critics claimed NAFTA's openness would advantage multinational companies over working people. Independent presidential candidate Ross Perot warned of "a giant sucking sound" of jobs leaving the United States for Mexico. Yet Bill Clinton, who favored the pact, won the presidential election that year, and he gained ratification with crossover support from Republican senators to replace skeptical Democrats.

Most economists have a positive view of NAFTA's benefits for the United States and the overall North American economy.[1] Even President Trump, who renegotiated it as the United States-Mexico-Canada Agreement, left alone most of NAFTA's fallen walls.

Even more significant for product and labor markets was the entry of China into the World Trade Organization (WTO) in 2001. The country had stagnated for decades under the Communist leadership of Mao Zedong, but his successor, Deng Xiaoping, experimented with economic liberalization. Manufacturing exports grew modestly in the 1980s, increased in the 1990s, and exploded after 2001. Chinese living standards, and eventually the nation's standing as a global economic and political power, rose markedly.

Likewise, India's economy had been hobbled for decades after independence by bureaucratic regulation and protectionism. With prodding from the World Bank and the International Monetary Fund, the country began liberalizing in the 1990s. The government worked to make the economy more market-oriented and service-oriented, and to increase domestic and foreign private investment. It also joined the WTO's predecessor in 1994. Walls came down, the Indian economy integrated with the rest of the world, and living standards rose.

Simultaneous with these falling walls in the 1990s and 2000s were the disruptions of technological change. The costs of communication, computing, and automation all fell dramatically, precipitating a "death of distance" in business. Indeed, those changes trace back to the 1970s, enabling, for example, nimbler factories to compete with

Youngstown's integrated steel mills. Far-flung supply chains became easier to manage. The new technologies tended to boost overall productivity, further enriching the world economy.[2]

Unfortunately, these macro-level gains came with losses for less-skilled workers in old industrial areas. Many of these workers lost their jobs or saw their wages fall. A number of them dropped out of the workforce entirely. What had happened in Youngstown in 1977, due to Japanese imports and technological obsolescence, now happened on a much larger scale in the United States.

By 2019, before the COVID-19 pandemic, 74 percent of college graduates were participating in the labor force, and only 2 percent were unemployed—signs of economic health. But for high school graduates, those figures were 58 percent and 4 percent, and for those with only some high school education, 46 percent and 5 percent.[3] The coronavirus pandemic of 2020–2021 only intensified this disparity and prompted significant distributional questions about otherwise beneficial forces.

Those twin advances, globalized trade and technological disruption, have been harsher for employment and earnings than many commentators had predicted. Most alarming has been declining employment and participation for men between the ages of 25 and 54 ("prime-age males" in economics vernacular), with those same regional disparities.[4] Benjamin Austin, Edward Glaeser, and Lawrence Summers found that these disparities mirror differences in long-term GDP growth rates, particularly in the region they refer to as the "eastern heartland" (including Youngstown).[5]

Besides declining employment and labor market participation, less-skilled workers have suffered from lower wages when they do work and lower reported levels of happiness. Even worse, Princeton economists Anne Case and Angus Deaton (a Nobel laureate) found higher midlife mortality among whites since the late 1990s, bucking earlier trends of improvement. While tying the increase directly to higher levels of alcohol and drug addiction and suicide, they linked these "deaths of despair" to areas with weakening local labor markets, falling labor force participation rates, and declining marriage rates.[6]

Economists and policymakers took impressive steps to unleash trade and technological advances. But they were slow to recognize the downsides of these steps, and they have not applied the same creativity to help the losers from this regime of openness.

Challenges in the Wake of Falling Walls

Let's delve into how these tectonic forces of dynamism and disruption have shaped both opportunities and challenges for economies and for individuals. The *opportunities* are the familiar market-based gains from trade and higher productivity. We benefit from concentrating on producing goods and services where we excel, and buying those items where we don't. We're also generally better off when machines do more of our tasks, freeing us for more rewarding activities.

The *challenges* involve the costs of adapting to different ways of doing something (due to technological change) and to greater competition for customers (due to globalized trade, as well as some changes in technology). These challenges are more complex in today's economy than in the simpler economies for which classical economists advocated openness.

Three factors make adaptation difficult and costly for many individuals in industrial economies like the United States. The first is the *long-lasting character of the change,* which continues beyond business cycles. Most technological change nowadays is what economists clinically, if accurately, call "skill-biased"—the rewards go mainly to highly skilled workers. Improvements in machine and computer design, robotics, and artificial intelligence raise the demand for people who design, program, or operate these technologies, while reducing demand for lower-skilled individuals' labor in largely repetitive tasks. Remember the steel mill in Youngstown run by Vallourec Star, a subsidiary of a French firm, mentioned in Chapter 1. It opened in a former steel factory, but it emphasized robots, not the sturdy steelworkers in the rhetoric of many politicians. It demonstrated that *the jobs and skill mix of yesteryear would not come back.*

As a result, treating the problem with short-term fixes such as temporary unemployment benefits won't help. Our main labor market policy, unemployment insurance, aims to support workers in only *temporary* layoffs, not structural changes. Attempts to go further, such as Trade Adjustment Assistance, have been anemic (see Chapter 6).[7]

Likewise, most manufacturing activity is *geographically concentrated,* particularly in the Midwest, causing regional shocks. When agriculture became more efficient in the nineteenth and early twentieth centuries, we had a massive migration to cities and industrial areas. But fewer Americans are moving across regions now than in decades past. Impediments to geographical mobility include occupational licensing laws, which force mobile workers to go through lengthy processes to gain entry into a variety of occupations. Another is the high cost of housing in high-growth areas, due to stringent land-use regulations. These barriers hurt less-skilled workers the most.

Too often, workers just try to obtain a new job in the same familiar industry. Exhortations by politicians to "bring the jobs back"— echoed in Youngstown campaign speeches by presidential candidates from both parties for decades—encourage this improbable approach. Workers lack connections to new, growing industries, as well as the skills for available jobs, hence the need for training and skill development.

With an overreliance on stagnant industries, and an overabundance of less-skilled workers, these regions are hit particularly hard.

Their tax receipts are falling, which means less funding for training and income support. How can they, or we, *improve* local opportunity and mobility where the outcomes are poor?

The third factor is the heightened *speed of change*. American manufacturing employment and earnings prospects in the United States dropped immediately after China's entry into the WTO. That meant a faster increase in the earnings potential of *Chinese* workers, as it lifted tens of millions of Chinese out of poverty. It also led to a faster increase in global labor supply for many low- and mid-skill tasks, particularly in manufacturing, lowering the costs for employers. India's entry into the modern world economy, a decade after Chinese modernization began, likewise quickly altered global markets for labor in business services via outsourcing of work. But this rapid change, combined with the first two factors of the long-lasting feature of labor market shifts and the geographic concentration of many of their impacts, only made adjustment more difficult and costly, as it caught many policymakers, particularly at the national level, by surprise.

All three factors of this disruptive change—its long-lasting quality, regional concentration, and speed—explain why it damaged many workers' prospects while benefiting the economy as a whole. Those workers suffered from domestic and global economic forces beyond their individual control. They bore risks they couldn't overcome through individual agency or working harder; they simply were unprepared to compete in the suddenly altered economy. Without policies to address long-term job loss, the falling walls left many workers vulnerable to the market economy's dynamism. The United States, like other industrial economies, has emphasized social insurance programs to deal with workers' job and earnings risks over business cycles beyond their control. Unemployment insurance, for example, provides short-term income support during a period of temporary job loss for an individual.

These workers, who bear the risk of declining prospects from overall-positive-for-the-economy shifts in technological change and globalization, need help with *preparation* (training in new skills) and *reconnection* (support during a transition back to economic participation during that training). The failure of U.S. economic policy to address—or, at times, even notice—this need has fueled the fires of populism.

These factors associated with major observed adverse shifts in labor demand have consequences for variables such as labor force participation, hours worked, unemployment, and average weekly wages, not to mention how involuntary unemployment reduces happiness itself.[8]

The China Shock

Chinese imports loom large in these discussions, so they deserve focused attention. First, let's set them in the context of trends in U.S. manufacturing jobs over time.

U.S. manufacturing employment had periods of decline during cyclical downturns and waves of imports before China joined the WTO. Most notably, it fell from 13.7 million in 1977 to 11.8 million in 1986 due to competition from other Asian countries (recall the Youngstown steel mill closures) and the dollar's high foreign exchange value. But each time, the jobs had largely bounced back over the next decade, at least on the national level if not in Youngstown.[9] By 1999, manufacturing employment was up to 17.3 million.

The China shock was different. By 2019, even as the national economy was strong, manufacturing employment had fallen steadily to 12.8 million, a net loss of 4.5 million jobs.[10] Employment in construction and other areas of the booming housing industry offset those losses for a while after 2000. But the housing bust after 2007 made the manufacturing losses plain to everyone.[11] With both geographic concentration and lower mobility, those lost manufacturing jobs translated into large labor market effects for the U.S. economy as a whole.[12]

While the flood of Chinese imports was far from the only cause (automation was also important), some economists have emphasized its outsized role. David Autor, David Dorn, and Gordon Hanson describe a "China shock," through which rising imports starting as early as 1990 directly reduced employment, wages, and labor force participation in some local markets reliant on import-competing industries.[13] Those effects were long-lasting, particularly for workers new to the labor force or with low initial wages.[14] Labor market effects from the China shock also may have hurt the economy as a whole as the manufacturing decline reduced the demand for intermediate inputs made in the United States and as geographic concentration limited the substitution of nonmanufacturing for manufacturing jobs.[15]

By focusing on this shock, we can show not only the gains and losses from trade, but also how economic policy affects their size and distribution. As China opened to the modern world economy, it sextupled its share of world value added in manufacturing products and its demand for the raw materials to make them.[16] Government policymakers promoted manufacturing as a path to competing in the higher-value-added portions of world trade.

The mirror of this boom is the shock to China's trading partners, including the United States. It raises questions about where the shock hits the U.S. labor market (Who is affected?), knock-on effects elsewhere (How do market forces adjust to the shock?), and what governments can do to offset these effects (Which public policies work?). I served on the U.S.-China Economic and Security Commission from 2017 to 2019, and that shock consumed much of our time. But it was underappreciated in the administrations of Presidents Clinton and

Bush that ushered China into the WTO, including the latter's Council of Economic Advisers when I headed it.

To begin, the China shock—through lower-priced manufactured goods—offered *gains* to U.S. consumers and to some U.S. producers using Chinese suppliers. Such gains are real and broadly shared; they figure prominently in economists' explanation of "gains from trade." Your Econ 101 professor taught you that.

As for the losses by other producers and many domestic workers, your Econ 101 professor *did* tell you that, too. How much they and the overall economy lost depended on how easy it was to move from manufacturing work into other productive activities and jobs. It also depended on the ease of moving from hard-hit to more promising areas.

Autor and his coauthors indeed emphasize the regional concentrations of job losses along with declining wages, particularly for low-skilled workers.[17] Those effects are persistent, more often leading to disability benefits and early retirement than to adjustment to different jobs.[18] And on the whole, social insurance has been weak.

Autor compared benefit payments for areas at the 75th versus the 25th percentile of trade exposure over the period from 1991 to 2007. He concludes that for an incremental $100 in local exposure to import competition, public support in income assistance, Medicaid health care payments, and disability and Social Security retirement benefits increased by only $45. As for Trade Adjustment Assistance (TAA), that offset was just 23 *cents* in the more- versus less-exposed areas.[19] As we will see in Chapter 6, TAA came up as a policy topic only when new trade expansions were sought—it received little sustained attention or interest in its augmentation.

Why don't more workers switch to new industries? Sudden job displacement within a job category and region can leave some workers worse off for an extended period. One explanation, as mentioned in Chapter 1, is that workers prefer to obtain a new job in the industry where they already have the needed skills. This preference is embedded in politicians' cry to "bring the jobs back." Of course, to the extent that labor-market shifts are long-lasting, a wait-and-see strategy is unlikely to bear fruit.

Another possibility is a skills mismatch to available job opportunities, highlighting a role for training and skill development. And as noted earlier, real and perceived barriers to mobility to jobs in a new area both lengthen and make more costly the work adjustment process. Low levels of schooling and skills are likely the main issue. Katherine Abraham and Melissa Kearney studied the decline in the U.S. employment-to-population ratio from 1999 to 2018, and found most of this decline was among people with a high-school degree, or at best some college attainment. They connected both trade patterns (especially the China shock) and technological change (especially robots) to the falling employment rates. A third, smaller contributing factor was the growth in Social Security Disability Insurance caseloads.[20]

Economists have also connected the China shock to political outcomes. Autor's group found a strong correlation between votes for Donald Trump in 2016 and economic damage from Chinese imports.[21] The greater the job loss in a community due to Chinese imports, the greater the support for Trump, to the point of winning him the presidency. Had the 2002–2014 period seen import penetration at half the actual level, Hillary Clinton would have won Michigan, Pennsylvania, and Wisconsin—and the election. Other researchers have found similar links between Chinese imports and support for Brexit in the United Kingdom and nationalist parties in Europe.

Neoliberalism's Rise and Falling Walls

Walls fell from the 1980s to the 2000s due to the rise of neoliberalism. Governments embraced openness and dynamism, while ignoring the disruptive forces that accompanied this openness. This preference for openness, long ascendant in the economics profession, had moved into the zeitgeist. Like the classical liberalism of Adam Smith and then nineteenth-century free-market capitalism, twentieth-century neoliberalism emerged in reaction to state meddling in private industry and trade.

For our purposes, neoliberalism is essentially a hands-off view of government in the economy. Neoliberals were leading critics of the "Keynesian consensus," whose macroeconomic policy failed to overcome the stagflation of the 1970s. While neoliberals focused on regulations and other domestic policies, they also promoted openness in trade.

The work of economists such as Friedrich Hayek and Milton Friedman—as academics, Nobel laureates, and public intellectuals—shifted the field toward markets and a skepticism of government intervention. Center-right political leaders such as President Ronald Reagan and U.K. prime minister Margaret Thatcher channeled those scholars' influence by name. President Bill Clinton, a center-left leader less enthralled publicly to Hayek or Friedman, nonetheless was a champion of neoliberal openness to technological change and globalization.

Hayek, a prominent member of the Austrian School of economics, scholar of investment, and the business and intellectual sparring partner of John Maynard Keynes, effectively launched neoliberalism with *The Road to Serfdom* in 1944.[22] Serialized in *Reader's Digest,* the book presented a blistering critique of socialism. It argued that government tinkering and planning diminished not just economic efficiency, but also individual liberty and freedom. The additional moral dimension arose because a state that could gather the information needed for a planned economy would necessarily usurp liberty.

Hayek's views came out powerfully in the article for which he is best known in economics, "The Use of Knowledge in Society."[23] He

HOW WE GOT HERE

argued that because information is spread throughout workers and consumers and businesses in the economy, we need the price mechanism to share and synchronize local individual knowledge. People can use prices to discover information they do not possess. The complex economy's prices, if left alone by governments, enabled people to rapidly adapt to changing markets. The only alternatives were to assume that all individuals had complete and correct information—implausible—or to have state planners forcibly collect the information, at a loss of individual liberty and "the road to serfdom." A neoliberal argument's game, set, match.

Likewise, Milton Friedman, with wide-ranging research on consumption, monetary policy, and unemployment, matched scholarly success with an outgoing public-intellectual presence in magazines and on television. He became a popularizer of neoliberal limits on state intervention; one quoted, if not always followed, by conservative politicians such as President Reagan. His nontechnical 1962 book *Capitalism and Freedom* argued for light-touch government and for eliminating barriers to opportunity, with little attention to the inequality that might result.[24]

Hayek and Friedman did not call for the state to keep its hands entirely off the economy. Both argued for a state role in creating public goods, securing property rights, and policing competition. But they said very little about the state helping to prepare individuals to compete in a dynamic market economy, or offering social insurance to workers when structural changes disrupted their participation. This lack of attention to outcomes, and economists' skepticism of any limits to openness, cemented their position as defenders of change, whatever its wake.

In turn, conservative politicians embraced these ideas as benefiting the economy as a whole or entrepreneurial opportunity or innovation—true, actually—but with little thought to near-term economic losers from global markets and technological change. With their lack of attention, they jeopardized broad social support for capitalism's golden goose. Aggressive state intervention might well drain the economy's efficiency and individual liberty. But did it follow that markets by themselves would guarantee opportunities for participation in—and broad social support for—the capitalist market economy? As we will see in the next two chapters, this important question was much on the mind of classical economists like Adam Smith.

A History of Walls

While neoliberals confidently celebrated openness, dislocated workers wanted a return to the past. My students and I heard that firsthand in Youngstown in 2017 and 2018. The anemic public policy response to struggles there and elsewhere led to a simmering distrust of elites in the heartland. Why support economic trends with collective benefits if so many people suffer in their wake?

That mistrust started playing out well before the 2016 election. It picked up steam in Republican Patrick Buchanan's insurgent campaign against incumbent George H. W. Bush in the 1992 presidential election. Railing against disruptive forces of globalization and technological change (along with immigration) and labeling President Bush a "globalist" (sound familiar?), Buchanan's "Make America First Again" campaign stirred the hearts and minds of many dislocated workers. Buchanan ultimately fell short, as did Ross Perot's independent challenge later that year. The constituency that Donald Trump would eventually ride to victory was simply not yet large enough.

"Build the Wall" is quite an old story. In 117 CE, Hadrian took over the open and expanding Roman Empire. Hadrian, preferring to protect what had been gained, turned the empire inward and famously built a wall to separate Roman Britain from what is now Scotland. Designed to control trade, the wall sealed off the territory—but precipitated decline.

Fast-forward—really fast—to the end of the Middle Ages. Most European countries embraced mercantilism, which maximized exports and minimized imports. Mercantilist thinkers and leaders counted wealth in gold, silver, and population; all increased by running a surplus through high tariff and nontariff barriers. The mercantilist Navigation Acts, which Britain imposed on its American colonists, helped provoke them to fight for independence against the crown. Economists such as Adam Smith began objecting (see Chapter 3), but to little avail as long as economies were still largely agrarian.

In 1815, for example, Britain restricted imports of inexpensive grain (corn) and other food items. The Corn Laws helped landowners and farmers keep prices high, but raised the cost of living for households and hampered the growth of the emerging manufacturing sector. Nonagricultural capitalists and the country's general turn to openness did lead to the Corn Laws' repeal, but not until 1846. Indeed, economic historians point to Prime Minister Robert Peel's conversion to economic ideas in support of openness, a shift which still cost his government an election. The shift paid off over time through greater openness elsewhere to British manufactured goods, putting the country on a path to prosperity.

"Wall" arguments long held sway on the American side of the Atlantic Ocean, too. The new federal government in 1789 established a tariff both to protect newly starting domestic industries and to generate revenue for itself.[25] After the Civil War, the government relied heavily on tariffs to protect domestic industries, ranging from iron and steel to wool. At that time, these were industries of the present and future that were nascent in the United States compared to the United Kingdom, the world's nineteenth-century industrial behemoth. So the tariffs were not protecting fading industries. Such protection was politically popular in the industrial Northeast, but much less popular in the South and West. William McKinley campaigned for and won the U.S. presidency in 1896 on a platform of protectionism and prosperity; he won reelection four years later on a promise of reciprocal trade agreements, in which we would reduce trade barriers to match reductions by other nations.

By the late 1920s, most of the industrial economies had substantially reduced their import barriers. But in the beginning of what became the Great Depression, Congress passed the Smoot-Hawley Tariff of 1930. Today's wisdom says economists can't collectively agree on anything. Not true: 1,028 economists signed a petition asking President Herbert Hoover to veto the bill; business executives like Henry Ford and Thomas Lamont chimed in, too. To no avail: Hoover signed the bill, and international retaliation led to a steep decline in global trading volume. While the tariff was not the only culprit in the decade's economic collapse, it amounted to a negative supply shock on a weak economy. It also frayed international economic linkages at a time of heightened economic and political tensions. Tariff walls are costly.

After World War II, many leaders blamed the economic collapse and social disarray at least partly on tariffs. To boost trade and counteract international political tensions, the United States led the way in promoting the 1947 General Agreement on Tariffs and Trade (GATT). With the fall of the Berlin Wall, this push for openness gained global momentum, and tariffs gradually fell here and elsewhere. The World Trade Organization (WTO) superseded the GATT in 1995.

Yet those early decades of openness required little political attention to the downside for workers. In the twenty-five years after World War II, with foreign rivals rebuilding from the devastation, both industry and labor in the United States prospered. It helped that the federal government in 1944 had built a bridge with the Servicemen's

Readjustment Act. Fearing a renewed depression at war's end, Congress had passed this "G.I. Bill" to send returning troops to college.[26]

That "good old days" period was a rare and halcyon one. Global competition took off after 1970, and many communities (like Youngstown) felt the pain from steel to television sets to shoes and clothing. America's unassailable "Big Three" auto manufacturers felt new pressure from Japan's Toyota and Nissan and called for a wall in the form of quotas on Japanese cars. Those calls intensified even during the ostensibly laissez-faire administration of President Reagan.

Yet thanks to neoliberal ideas, even as these industries struggled, the United States maintained and even increased openness, and then encouraged it for the rest of the world. The trouble is that neoliberalism discouraged not just tariffs, but any substantial intervention to help dislocated workers. Neoliberals were so skeptical of government that the few programs that Congress did pass, such as Trade Adjustment Assistance, never got enough funding or support to make a difference.

Looking Back on Technology's Walls

Over time, a similar response developed about technological advances. In the early 1800s, Ned Ludd purportedly inspired English protests against the stocking frame, a knitting machine developed much earlier, in the reign of Queen Elizabeth I. Movement followers, or "Luddites," worried (not without reason) about risks they now found difficult to manage—about being displaced by machines that were increasingly efficient in making textiles. Ned Ludd proved elusive, likely because he did not really exist. The fictional Ludd was made up from details of an incident in Leicester two decades prior, wherein an apprentice named Ludham destroyed a knitting machine.[27]

In the first century CE, the Roman emperor Vespasian blocked the use of machines to transport columns to the Capitoline Hill in Rome, fearing the displacement of labor. Then in the fifteenth century, Johannes Gutenberg's printing press worried stationers and card makers. Queen Elizabeth I blocked a 1589 patent for William Lee's knitting machine, fearing the collapse of employment and an increase in vagrancy. The "Luddite" protests began soon afterward, with workers vainly trying to prevent new technology by destroying another model of knitting machine.

In the United Kingdom, workers smashed wheat-threshing machines in 1830 to protest job losses. A century later in the United States, President Roosevelt's short-lived National Recovery Administration limited the installation of new machines to protect jobs.

Nevertheless, most people have held a positive view of new technologies. These advances transformed their lives as consumers with better communications and time saved. Improved machines boosted productivity and increased wages for many workers. Sometimes they played out only gradually, as businesses had to adapt in order to use them—as with electrification in the 1920s or computing, the internet, artificial intelligence, and robotics in recent decades.

Openness to new technology and trade also feed off each other. Innovations in markets open to trade and technology have brought massive improvements in living standards—the great dividend of competitive capitalism. Beginning in the late eighteenth century, people learned to accept what economist Joseph Schumpeter termed "creative destruction."

The economic miracle of the Industrial Revolution in the West, beginning in Britain, was repeated in Southeast Asia after World War II. And China's opening to the modern world economy since the late 1970s and India's opening beginning in the early 1990s have bettered the economic fortunes of hundreds of millions of people.

That wonderful track record, however, blinded elites to the damage to particular workers and communities. Trade and technological change have brought large aggregate risks impossible for an individual to manage on his or her own, and the U.S. economy is more mature and less flexible in responding to shocks.

Perhaps as a result of elites' myopia and negligence, Luddite techno-pessimism is still alive and well. Even some prominent economists, such as my former Northwestern University colleague Robert Gordon, worry about future employment prospects. While Gordon's concerns relate to macroeconomic headwinds to growth, other employment concerns arise from adjustment over time to general purpose technologies that automate many existing jobs. People are recalling John Maynard Keynes's fret in 1930 that technology would drastically reduce employment. Going further back still, the classical economist David Ricardo, for all he got right on the virtues of openness, enunciated similar fears.

Fears of Inequality

There's also a larger worry at play in the rising appeal of walls. Media coverage of populist woes in the heartland is more widespread today than in the 1970s and 1980s because critics are tying these trends to deep social changes.

Before we had globalization and advanced technologies, U.S. employment was evenly divided among low-, middle-, and high-wage occupations. David Autor found that in 1970, the split was about 31 percent, 38 percent, and 30 percent, respectively.[28] The United States proudly presented itself as a middle-class society. But by 2019, the share of workers in middle-wage occupations fell by 15 percentage points (40 percent) to 23 percent. Shares of jobs created requiring higher skill levels rose.

In a macro sense that's actually good news, because many of those workers moved up into the high-wage category. But the shift makes the economy less equal, with a rising class divide. With skilled occupations delivering higher incomes, and everyone else stuck with stagnant wages, income inequality has grown to heights not seen since the 1920s. These anxieties have intensified with the large and unexpected dislocations from the 2020–2021 coronavirus pandemic—disproportionately affecting less-skilled workers. The stage is set for loud and sustained calls for walls of various kinds.

Missed Bridges

Falling walls have boosted economic opportunity around the globe—and for many Americans, producers as well as consumers. Technological advance and globalization are often intertwined. Apple's superb iPhone reflects the company's design talent and knowhow but also links to the Chinese company Foxconn for low-cost assembly of the labor-intensive device. Millions of Americans have boosted their careers, incomes, and leisure opportunities by taking advantage of digital and global changes.

But those gains blinded political leaders and economists to the economic dislocation of millions of Americans. Their shock at the 2016 election of Donald Trump as president demonstrates their—our—failure to notice and acknowledge the problem. It's no wonder that a broad cross section of the public distrusts economic and policy elites. Ignoring the suffering of workers left out of the open economy is no longer tenable—it will lead inevitably to a new series of walls. Economists, policymakers, and business leaders have to change course to preserve broad public support for the market economy.

Fortunately, we can reconnect those workers to the dynamic world economy. We can build bridges, not walls, to prepare and reconnect them to compete in the altered competitive landscape. Those bridges need to address the structural aspects of the dislocation, its geographical concentration, and the speed at which it happened. That means building bridges that persist across the business cycle, are customized to the hardest-hit areas, and are ready as the dislocation is happening, rather than cobbled together over many years when the situation's severity is fully understood. Both in our trip to Youngstown and in Amy Goldstein's account of economic decline in Janesville, Wisconsin, local business and community leaders treated a short-term problem when a much larger, long-lasting, and fast-moving one lay before them.[29]

By improving the distribution of gains from disruption, bridges may also offer hope for an end to "us versus them" economic populism. Otherwise, we'll fall into another cycle of building walls, tearing them down with great fanfare, facing a populist outcry, and then building them back up. Bridges aren't just about economic efficiency—they can also remedy the moral failings of markets, as even economists have recognized.

3

Mass Flourishing: The Unknown Adam Smith

Nowadays, we all know Adam Smith as a founder of economics and the great proponent of the "invisible hand," not the visible hand of government. But he actually thought of himself first as a moral philosopher. He wrote *The Theory of Moral Sentiments* in 1759 partly to counter David Hume's emphasis on individual "utility."[1] Smith stressed the moral links between the individual and society, focusing on "mutual sympathy," or what we call empathy.

Smith got interested in economics mainly in reaction to another powerful idea—mercantilism.

What Is the "Wealth of a Nation"?

When I teach modern political economy at Columbia, I begin with Smith, whose *Wealth of Nations* is foundational for modern economics and capitalism, neither of which existed in their current form in 1776.[2] I show students a first edition of this book, but also a first edition of a 1698 book, *England's Treasure by Foreign Trade, Or, The Balance of Our Foreign Trade Is the Rule of Our Treasure.* The latter book, by Thomas Mun, set Smith off.

Mercantilism was the economic orthodoxy of the day, and Mun's short book was one of its cleverest statements. It pushed for building up trade surpluses so the nation could increase its stocks of gold and silver, wealth in the mercantilist view. Governments could thus build wealth by restricting imports of foreign goods. This zero-sumism of mercantilism has hardly disappeared today, as recent U.S. protectionism suggests.

Smith rejected this approach, and not just because it was economically inefficient. He observed that for mercantilists, "nation" meant the sovereign. Princes used gold and silver mostly to acquire luxuries or mercenary armies, not to promote the prosperity of their subjects. He had a different view of the wealth of a nation, focused on individual subjects. For him, in effect, individuals as consumers were kings. He wanted to promote the happiness of everyone in the nation, not just the elites. This insight is crucial to our analysis here and to modern economics. Yet Smith's analysis is incomplete—we need to add some elements to cement its relevance to today's more complex economy and to the challenges seized upon by today's mercantilist tinkerers.

The Moral Philosopher

Who was Adam Smith?

Born in Fife, Scotland, in 1723, to a lawyer father and a mother from landed gentry, Smith pursued his scholarly bent early. He began his study of moral philosophy at the University of Glasgow at 14 years of age and pursued postgraduate studies at Oxford. He enjoyed teaching and was disappointed in the prowess of Oxford faculty relative to his days at Glasgow. (In *The Wealth of Nations* he attributed a lack of faculty concern with teaching to the substantial endowments of Oxford's colleges, which therefore did not need to attract students, a familiar lament today.) So Smith taught at Glasgow and became acquainted with the philosopher David Hume, an intellectual fellow traveler in the Scottish Enlightenment.

His *Theory of Moral Sentiments* was a hit and drew many students to this shy professor. But his growing discomfort with mercantilism led him toward economics. He took a leave from his academic position to pursue a well-paid post as tutor to a young aristocrat. In his travels to Paris in that post, he met not only Benjamin Franklin but also the French physiocrats, a school of thought founded by François Quesnay that opposed mercantilist micromanagement of trade and the economy. The physiocrats' motto—*Laissez faire et laissez passer, le monde va de lui-même!* (Let do and let pass, the world goes on by itself!)—gives us the familiar phrase *laissez faire.* Those words became an expression for—argued for, if not actual—government disengagement from the economy. The expression was to provide both guidance and confusion in the evolution of economic policy.

With his tutoring assignment complete and himself more financially secure, Smith returned to Scotland to work on *The Wealth of Nations.* His magnum opus hit its mark and was a blockbuster out of the gate. Oddly, and always a cautionary tale, the supposedly laissez-faire Smith was then appointed to a commissioner of customs post in 1778. The philosopher now thought of as the father of capitalism died in Edinburgh twelve years later.[3]

Now to Smith's attack on mercantilist elites.

From Gold to the Golden Goose

To the mercantilists, a nation's wealth (and the sovereign's status!) could be measured by the stocks of gold and silver it acquired—which in turn came from a "favorable balance of trade." To mercantilists, "favorable" meant that a nation that exported more than it imported. (But simple arithmetic of the global balance of trade shows that not all nations can generate a surplus of gold and silver at the same time, so conflict in the mercantilist trading system was inevitable.)

In practice, governments intervened by steering commerce and trade through subsidies, licensed monopolies, and various privileges for some types of businesses or specific merchants or manufacturers. This tinkering came with costs in reduced trade and higher prices to consumers—not to mention antagonizing colonists. (Another big event in 1776 suggests that Smith was on to something in opposing the mercantilist restrictions applied to America!)

Smith advanced a new view of national prosperity—its consumption of goods by its people—in other words, their living standards. The goal of the economy in *The Wealth of Nations* was to make the economic pie as large as possible. It was only to boost that consumption that he argued for free markets and competition. *The Wealth of Nations* might seem a departure from *The Theory of Moral Sentiments* in stressing the invisible hand rather than mutual sympathy. But he saw individuals acting in their own self-interest producing a superior outcome for everyone in society, a greater "wealth of the nation." As he famously observed in Book I, Chapter 2 of *The Wealth of Nations*:

> It is not from the benevolence of the butcher, the brewer, or the baker, that we expect our dinner, but from their regard to *their own interest*. We address ourselves, not to their humanity but to their self-love, and never talk to them of our own necessities but of *their advantages* [emphasis added].

In describing the "invisible hand," Smith stressed *competition*. A manufacturer or merchant cannot overcharge consumers for fear of being outmaneuvered and overtaken by a nimble competitor. Firms with higher productivity and efficiency would displace weaker firms, with more goods going to everyone as a result. Workers would be paid fairer wages because of competition for their services. Consumers would benefit from lower prices free from privileged sellers or government fiat. The *market system* of competition became the economy's golden goose.

With vigorous competition among businesses, an individual pursuing his or her own self-interest promotes the broader good—and thus higher living standards—through low prices and a wide variety of goods and services. Smith didn't want complete laissez faire. He worried about price-fixing conspiracies, monopolies, and businesses joining to influence politics and legislation. A market free of these contrivances and interventions helped generate prosperity; overly powerful businesses and interest groups would not. Because of the importance of competition to the smooth and efficient functioning of Smith's market economy, he argued for rigorous legal disciplining of anticompetitive behavior, including what we would call rules against price fixing and vigorous antitrust policy.

Competition can be hard to accept. Today's celebrants are often dominated by tenured academic economists and rich winners from competition. It is also decidedly not the historical norm. Governments have restricted competition for centuries, from the guilds of the Middle Ages to state-sanctioned monopolies such as the Dutch and British East India Companies.[4] Mercantilists celebrated state tinkering for monopolies as the best way to harness market forces for national wealth.

Against this conventional wisdom, Smith saw competition as a *positive* force, the central element of a successful market system. Just as the American Declaration of Independence signaled a competition in governing systems, *The Wealth of Nations* sought it for the economic system. Smith's intuitive "invisible hand" argued that profit-guided firms would produce the goods and services individuals desire at the lowest possible price. Consumer sovereignty—antithetical to the mercantilists—became the punch line.

Two centuries later, Nobel laureates in economics Kenneth Arrow and Gerard Debreu added the jargon and mathematics of contemporary economics to formalize Smith's intuition:[5] When agents in the economy act independently and are sufficiently small in market size, competitive markets lead to an efficient allocation of resources. Ever concerned about social good, Smith hailed this intuition as promarket, but not necessarily probusiness.

Smith also encouraged specialization and the division of labor. *The Wealth of Nations* includes a now-classic reference to a pin factory in which workers divided the work by specializing in a specific task. Compared with 100 or so pins producible each day by workers doing all tasks themselves, the factory that Smith chronicled had ten workers doing specialized tasks producing 48,000 pins each day. This spectacular improvement in productivity provides lower prices to consumers and higher wages to workers. And it is an essential metaphor for Smith's economy. As the market gets larger, continued reorganization of tasks and openness to new ways of producing stimulates still greater production, lower prices, and improved standards of living.

In its Introduction, *The Wealth of Nations* thus stood the mercantilist concept of wealth on its head:

> The annual labour of every nation is the fund which originally supplies it with all the necessities and conveniences of life which it annually consumes.... [T]his produce ... bears a greater or smaller proportion to the number of those who are to consume it. ... [B]ut this proportion must in every nation be regulated by two different circumstances: First, by the skill, dexterity, and judgement with which its labour is generally applied; and, Secondly, by the proportion between the number of those who are employed in useful labour and that of those who are not so employed.

Smith's insights guided Britain's subsequent economic approach to the Industrial Revolution, with laissez faire eventually applied to both domestic and international trade. Later economists cited the power of competition to assume that workers, landowners, and capital owners would use their resources in the most profitable way, resulting in equal rates of return in equilibrium across uses. In conjunction with the invisible hand, competition also enabled a general equilibrium in which prices and quantities were determined by market forces.

Smith extended specialization and the division of labor in his further criticism of tariffs. While it is David Ricardo, in his later analysis of the costs of Britain's Corn Laws, who developed the concept of "comparative advantage" important in contemporary economics, Smith took his own effective swipe at the costliness and inefficiency of tariffs.[6] He saw that Scots could make wine from grapes grown in hothouses, but heating costs would render their tipple an order of magnitude more expensive than French wine. Better to trade good Scottish wool for a French claret—why protect producers and disadvantage consumers? After all, consumers' well-being is at the core of the wealth of a nation.

Government, the Market Economy, and Mass Flourishing

Much of this analysis is familiar, but Smith gave the government important responsibilities beyond protecting competition. Smith was *not* a champion of a laissez-faire absence of intervention. Indeed, government should play significant roles in Smith's view, roles that foreshadow our discussion of government's role in today's economy. We can map Smith's philosophy onto our more complex economy's opportunities and challenges.

While Smith is sometimes caricatured as "antigovernment," he mainly opposed mercantilist privileges for specific businesses. He also opposed a large public debt taken on to fund overseas adventure. Instead, Smith wanted government to provide what economists today call public goods, such as the national defense, the criminal justice system, and enforcement of property rights and contracts—the institutional underpinnings of commerce and trade. He also favored public works to provide infrastructure to keep commerce flowing freely.

But then he went further, in a way that is often unacknowledged. To prepare workers and enrich their lives, he called for government to provide universal education. He drew this connection between education and liberty as well as work in a free society. We will return to this theme of preparation.

While Smith believed in keeping taxes low, enough to pay for the government, he advocated a broad tax base of various sources of income—from wages, profits, property, and business transactions. He also argued for progressive taxation, in which higher-income individuals, with greater ability to pay and a larger pecuniary benefit from governmental action, would pay higher rates.

Smith's concept of national wealth thereby centered on "mass flourishing." This notion from the Enlightenment emphasized not just higher living standards but also full *participation* in the economy.

Here Smith gives clear guidance for policy. Its magisterial tomeness notwithstanding, *The Wealth of Nations* offers wonkery. The overarching "invisible hand" gathers but one mention, against references to 266 individual Scottish parliamentary acts and English statutes! The philosophy and policy purposes of the book come together: the competitive invisible-hand economy, supported and enforced by government, generates prosperity and higher living standards than mercantilism, and that prosperity promotes human flourishing. Indeed, capitalism and economic liberty are not ends in themselves; they are means to the important end of mass flourishing of individuals and societies.

While Smith refers to flourishing in its economic sense at several points in the book, he mentions it in the broad social sense early on. He calls for higher wages to stress the importance of "improvement in the circumstances of the lower ranks of the people."

Most mercantilists in Smith's day opposed higher wages for workers for elitist reasons—they believed that putting more money into workers' hands would just diminish their industriousness and advance a dangerous taste for luxuries. Smith opposed this elitism: The "improvement in circumstances" was an essential element of mass flourishing, the end of the capitalist economic engine (that engine itself being the means).

> Is this improvement in the circumstances of the lower ranks of the people to be regarded as an advantage or as an inconveniency to the society? . . . Servants, laborers and workmen of different kinds make up the far greater part of every great political society. . . . [W]hat improves the circumstances of the greater part can never be regarded as an inconveniency to the whole. No society can truly be flourishing and happy of which the far greater part of its members are poor and miserable. It is but equity, besides, that they who feed, clothe, and lodge the whole body of the people, should have such a share of the produce of their own labor as to be themselves tolerably well fed, clothed, and lodged. (Book I, Chapter 7)

This powerful passage is important for our story because it shows Smith's concern for *inclusion,* for *mass* flourishing. He justifies market competition, the golden goose, not on individual self-interest, but on how it promotes mass flourishing. The primary benefit of "the market" (or modern capitalism) is not a larger economic pie than mercantilists could deliver, but how it raises the conditions of those who struggle at that successful market's margins.[7] The opening chapter of *The Wealth of Nations* aims for "that universal opulence which extends itself to the lowest ranks of the people," so that "a general plenty diffuses itself through all the different ranks of the society."

Smith's second book thus came back around to his first. He effectively linked mass flourishing to mutual sympathy; individuals in a society are bound together in mutual affection and support. We will return to this thought in the modern concept of social insurance. Both economic and political flourishing come from inclusion, mutual ties, and mutual support.

Bringing Smith's Market Economy Forward: Growth, Dynamism, Innovism, and Flow

Smith lacked a theory of per capita growth in the economy over time, and he wrote before the massive increase in living standards through the Industrial Revolution. After 1800, per capita income in the United Kingdom (and the United States) exploded, a thirtyfold increase. People are even better off than such fantastical numbers suggest because of great improvements in the quality of goods and services that we buy which are not well measured by national income statisticians. And, of course, many of today's offerings—from smartphones to computers to air-conditioning—were not available even in 1900, let alone 1800.

Smith's omission partly reflects technical difficulties in modeling growth. Higher output can come from growth in inputs like labor and capital, but what determines their growth? Today's economists highlight population growth and society's willingness to work, save, and invest. Still more important is growth in productivity, or the efficiency with which inputs are used to produce goods and services. Smith's pin factory example links how things are done with the level of productivity. But what factors determine productivity *growth* over time, not just a onetime step improvement? Today's economic analysis focuses on technology and the process of generating ideas. Since continuing economic growth is still crucial for people marginalized by capitalism, it's worth asking whether the economic foundations expressed in *The Wealth of Nations* are still relevant for today. Where does growth come from now, and do those sources still require openness?

The short answer is yes, but to answer these questions, we need to understand the two kinds of forces promoting growth: exogenous and endogenous. *Exogenous* forces are those operating on an economy, largely out of the hands of economic actors. The usual example is technological change—both better machines and better techniques. The better our ways of doing things, the faster we can grow—but we can't dictate the pace of innovation. *Endogenous* forces are those within the economy that we can control.[8]

In recent years, economists have developed endogenous growth theories to explain technological change within the economy. Their models suggest that, unlike physical capital (machines and factories), some kinds of human capital and knowledge may experience a virtuous cycle of higher returns. For example, as a country like the United States becomes richer, it invests more resources in education and on-the-job training. This added human capital improves productivity and enables further investments in this area.

By the same token, firms have an incentive to increase on-the-job training as they install new physical capital. For example, as personal computers became widespread, firms invested in teaching office workers to use them. Similarly, when computer-aided robots spread through manufacturing, automobile firms invested heavily in training their workers. Growth has also enabled economies to invest in creating knowledge, and with more knowledge, the economy produces better capital goods. Wealthier firms have both the resources and the incentive to raise their spending on research and development.[9]

So growth is a wonderful thing, but what really drives it? Inputs, but more important, ideas. And bridges. To see why, we focus on the ideas of two prominent economists studying the explosion of individual incomes in industrial economies after 1800—Edmund Phelps and Deirdre McCloskey. Phelps, my Columbia economics colleague (and Nobel laureate), has done much to connect this growth to Smith's foundational ideas.[10] He starts with Smith's emphasis on a great many individuals (not the state or privileged firms) searching for new and better ways of doing things. This relentless search produces innovative ideas, processes, and goods that drive growth—but only if the political economy allows openness. This argument contrasts with simpler models of growth in which scientific discoveries exogenously expand the frontier of technological possibilities. Smith's messy "bottom-up" version of the market therefore puts mass innovation at the heart of economic growth. Phelps's second argument reflects how Smithian societies committed to openness are best able to prosper and promote growth. He even titled one of his books *Mass Flourishing,* an idea championed by classical economists like Smith.

Phelps's argument has two important implications. The first is to debunk the sometimes fashionable view of secular productivity decline—that we have run short of new things to discover and exploit.[11] The second is to give an answer to economies struggling with growth in a period of structural changes from technology and globalization; slowdowns in innovation are likely due not to scientific barrenness but to walls against openness.

Phelps's concern with economic dynamism draws him to Smith's arguments against mercantilist tinkering in the economy. He sees policies to stymie changes as a major enemy of innovation. Like Smith, he worries about the hidden costs of tinkering with competition by blocking change from the outside and by enabling rent seeking on the inside. These "corporatist" policies inevitably embolden vested interests and cronyism, slowing change and growth. Even seemingly small interventions can subtly diminish dynamic innovation, as we will see.

Phelps's analysis of dynamism foreshadows an argument advanced throughout this book: Accepting walls against change, even modest ones, is self-defeating. It both hampers innovation and favors well-connected elites over ordinary individuals. Just as Smith saw the mercantilists' tinkering as limiting economic possibility and flourishing, Phelps sees similar outcomes from corporatist tinkering. This critique, like the classical economists' assault on mercantilism, displays the costs of walls, but with little attention to alternatives for dealing with political concerns arising from disruption. Phelps's dynamism is necessarily messy, creating growth in the aggregate with many individual gainers, but also many individual losers.

Economic historian Deirdre McCloskey has similarly latched onto the continuous, large-scale, voluntary, and unforced search for betterment as driving new ideas with commercially tested possibilities for growth. She elevates this "innovism" to a cultural force, preferring the term to the more familiar "capitalism" (the former emphasizing new ideas over the Mr. or Ms. Moneybags of the latter), and connects it to economic liberalism.[12] Echoing Smith, she emphasizes how an open economy allows individuals, from the moderately to spectacularly talented, to "have a go." This economic liberalism requires competition to enshrine liberty and mass flourishing.

In McCloskey's telling, growth depends on a liberal tolerance and openness to change, which encourages many people to be alert to opportunity. Sustaining that tolerance, though, in the presence of structural shifts with many losers, requires more than paeans to Smith.

The Wealth of *Today's* Nation

We are now ready to close the loop on Adam Smith's advice for today's economy and economic policy in sorting out gainers and losers from disruption. We have seen that Smith stressed openness to new ways of organizing tasks and businesses (specialization and division of labor) and new markets (at home and abroad) as keys to prosperity—and, with the right stewardship, mass flourishing. His opposition to the "walls" of mercantilism was not just, or even primarily, for their restrictions on trade but because such walls inevitably encouraged government tinkering for favorite and special interests. This tinkering limited not only the size of the economic pie, but also individual liberty and flourishing.

Again, Smith and other classical economists lacked a formal theory of growth in the economy and living standards. But Smith's intuition about the value of competition and openness was spot-on for modern models of economic growth—including rising productivity from technological change, new business processes, and the availability of new markets. Growth itself is critically influenced by innovation and ways of organizing and doing business, which, in turn, are disruptive. The necessary disruption creates large gains for the economy as a whole, and for many individuals and businesses in particular. It also creates losses for some individuals and businesses in the economy, at least in the short run. This process—with the "dynamism" of searching for new ideas, business methods, and markets, in Phelps's term, and the "innovism" of a cultural openness to such newness, in McCloskey's term—is essential for prosperity and mass flourishing.

Both dynamism and innovism rely on a tolerance of change. They were critical in the Industrial Revolution unfolding after Smith's writing, during which technological change and openness replaced the earlier capitalist "buy low, sell high" search for commercial opportunity. For Smith, walls interfered with competition, inefficiently tinkered with markets, and favored specific groups rather than promoting mass flourishing. Adding growth's dynamism-and-disruption dynamic makes it clear that walls are costlier still in the modern economy. These interventions misdirect or limit innovation and the spread of its gains.

As we will see, erecting even a small wall in the interest of social protection is short-sighted. The gains expected by builders of protectionism are not really there. They trade off prosperity and mass flourishing for illusions of betterment.

Psychologists have echoed this appreciation for mass flourishing by emphasizing the value of striving. They've argued that happiness depends not just on (passive) material and social abundance, but also on active engagement. People seek feelings of economic independence and earned success, agency and "having a go," and the prospect of advancing during the course of one's career. In that sense, flourishing is like being "in the groove" of the dynamic economy.

Psychologists call this kind of engagement "flow," to use Mihaly Csikszentmihalyi's formulation.[13] The flow state, apropos of our purpose here, is not just about continuous engagement, but also about adjusting to the skill and complexity required for the activity— balancing the challenge of the task and the skill of its performer. As the task becomes more complex—with structural changes in the economy and work—individuals need new skills in order to return to flow. The market economy delivers the basis for engagement, but flourishing in these times of disruption requires greater attention to preparation and reconnection.

The Economic Basis for Preparation and Reconnection

Political thinkers are often suspicious of proposals for greater preparation and reconnection, on the grounds that these inevitably interfere with market-based competition. But Smith saw an important role for government in facilitating this competition. His thinking encompassed four steps. First, drawing directly from that intuition, the wealth of a nation centers on living standards and consumption possibilities. Second, those living standards at a point in time are made greater by the invisible hand of competition, promoting mass flourishing. Third, part of competition is preparing individuals to compete. So, being free to "have a go" depends on being *prepared* to compete. Finally, if many people are dropping out of participation in the economy, we need public (and private) efforts to *reconnect* as well as prepare them. Failing to do so makes it impossible to reach the inclusion that Smith set as the ultimate goal of his economic system.

Seen through the lens of today's more complex economy, Smith was not concerned about government-provided education undermining competition, and neither should we be concerned about modern preparation and reconnection doing so. Expanded roles for government and business need not repeat the mercantilist misadventures. And fortunately, we have many tools to promote both training (investments in skills for jobs today and in the future) and reattachment to work.[14] We explore these tools in Chapters 6 to 8. Economic thinking about mass flourishing did not conclude in 1776!

Yet we must not forget that Smith helped to found modern economics mostly as an extension of his work on moral philosophy. Cries for walls have outlived Smith's intellectual destruction of mercantilism for a simple reason: Significant structural forces in modern capitalism are forcing difficult adjustments for individuals, businesses, and communities. Economics is inevitably conditioned by social conditions. It is little wonder that calls for walls against disruption come forth from these big changes.

Hence the importance of bridges, which Smith articulated only in a general way, but which clearly emerges from his moral concerns with mass flourishing. One important update to Smith makes a "bridge"-policy orientation clear. He urged governments to provide universal education, to prepare people to participate fully in the economy. Today's twist stresses *preparation* more broadly. Just as Smith noted the value of public goods and education for the economy, today's bridges must prepare individuals to compete in a dynamic, changing economy, not the economy that was.

A second bridge-policy twist to Smith's recommendations is more complex. "Preparation" depends on bridges of connection. But structural changes can sever some job categories or businesses from the economy, while creating new jobs and business opportunities. Governments must therefore offer a bridge of *reconnection*—support during a long period of change while one prepares for the economy that is and will be.

We will return to preparation and reconnection in an analysis of social insurance later in the book. Both are about participation—about active engagement in the economy by everyone, mass flourishing. While Phelps and McCloskey help connect Smith's ideas to economic growth, they are less clear about the place of individuals in society. As a result, they and other economists have left the field vulnerable to cries of fostering inequality and elitism—and to walls of protection.

Enter here a thinker less well known than Smith, but whose writings help shape the building of bridges: Karl Polanyi, who connected bridges to markets and society. Born in Vienna in 1886, he is variously described as an economic sociologist or political economist. In his 1944 opus *The Great Transformation,* Polanyi linked the market not just to economics but also to history and to social support.[15] Polanyi said modern society depended on webs of ties through communities and associations, not just transactions between individuals. The impersonal workings of the invisible hand needed those ties to achieve the mass flourishing Smith desired.

If Phelps and McCloskey bring forward the market of *The Wealth of Nations*, Polanyi's "embedded" economic order depends on the mutual sympathy of *The Theory of Moral Sentiments*. In Polanyi's view, the disembedded laissez-faire nineteenth-century model dislocated society and undermined support for markets. He cited embedded models with more reciprocity, from medieval feudalism to emerging socialism, yet neither of these promotes Smith's markets and mass flourishing, mutual sympathy notwithstanding. He therefore called for looser, nonstructural ways to generate empathy in society.

While Polanyi's text lacks the policy ideas of Smith, or of Phelps or McCloskey, it does explain that bridges offer foundations for social support of markets. A limited degree of social insurance can reconnect individuals to work without undermining change and dynamism. We do not need to resort to walls that undermine mass striving and economic participation. As we will see, accompanying dynamism in the lineage of Smith's market is social insurance in the lineage of Smith's mutual sympathy.

Who's Elitist Anyway?

Chapter 2 described how economists celebrated the falling of walls from the 1970s to the 2000s but were slow to recognize the downsides to the resulting disruption. They made only half-hearted attempts to compensate the losers. This chapter describes the deeper intellectual failure at the heart of this poor response. In helping to found modern economics, Adam Smith emphasized its benefits to the full society. He was not a simple-minded maximizer of macroeconomic success via the free market. He attacked mercantilism precisely for its elitist privileging of the few over the masses. Yet too many economists have ignored Smith's moral concerns and focused on the wonders of the invisible hand. How ironic, then, that many observers of capitalism have made the same charge against Smith's intellectual descendants that he made against mercantilists.[16]

Smith emphasized inclusion in order to produce not just a richer economy, but also mass flourishing. Since Smith, capitalism's dynamism and economic growth—with its growth in living standards—have been driven by innovation and openness. But to maintain that openness in the face of structural change, we need bridges of preparation and reconnection. We also need to clarify how these bridges differ from the reasonable-sounding walls increasingly offered by well-intentioned observers, the subject of the next chapter.

4

Adam Smith Schools Today's Commentators

From the 1920s to the 1960s, long before Youngstown's Black Monday, Massachusetts faced its own slow-moving crisis. Its once-dominant textile mills were steadily losing ground to lower-cost rivals in southern states. Business and government leaders initially pursued a wall-based strategy. The state's congressional delegation tried to persuade other federal lawmakers to require southern mills to pay wages commensurate with New England's. But Congress balked, leaving the people of Massachusetts to choose between retrenchment—accepting lower wage levels to retain industry—and economic development—building bridges to new opportunities. Massachusetts chose the latter.

The state had a tiny but promising electronics sector, and leaders worked to funnel capital into existing and new firms. Some of that capital came from modest state and federal government assistance, but most of it came from creative venture financing. The plan of action was less government-directed industrial policy than business financing to help small electronic firms get off the ground. The lead players were local business leaders, through the New England Council, and the First National Bank of Boston.

Over time, public–private partnerships and stewardship by business leaders elevated the electronics industry to a critical mass, enabling it both to offer high-skilled jobs and to compete for large federal defense contracts. Without walls or retrenchment, Massachusetts revived its industry and has regained its place as the richest state per capita.[1]

While Massachusetts had some inherent advantages, such as a solid financial services industry and a tradition of strong education, its bridge-based approach can work elsewhere. Adam Smith's insights can point the way—but only if we resist the temptation to erect walls.

With both economic and moral arguments, Adam Smith made a splash with the publication of *The Wealth of Nations*. As explained in the previous chapter, he focused on the living standards of ordinary people. That wealth—the nation's economic pie—could be expanded by competition and openness to new ways of doing things, new markets, and new ideas. His ideas as both an economist and a moral philosopher offer fresh insights on capitalism's path forward and can help us assess recent appeals to erect walls. The market capitalism of *The Wealth of Nations* has surged in recent decades with liberalism's celebration of dynamism and innovism, while still facing challenges of connection and reconnection to the economy for more people.

Smith's goal was mass flourishing—mass engagement with the productive economy and the fruits of its output. Attaining that mass flourishing required ensuring that the least well off were connected to the economy over time, a reflection of the bonds of mutual sympathy articulated by Smith in his earlier book, *The Theory of Moral Sentiments*. Those bonds from Smith the moral philosopher (we will see) require bridges, ideas only sketched lightly by Smith, but very important today.

Smith attacked walls, of monopoly privilege and of limits on efficiency. Those walls are still all too real in today's discourse. Here we explore three kinds of walls—to protect workers, to limit imports, and to strengthen society. In each case, proponents claim their proposed wall shaves off just a bit of efficiency to achieve a greater good.

Yet in doing so, these walls risk throwing out, not slimming down, the wealth-of-the-nation baby with the disruption bath water. And the walls distract us from creatively building bridges to connect to the work of the future.

There is abundant mischief by politicians in each area, with well-meaning and well-articulated explanations. But with Mun's mercantilism, Smithian refutation is clear, with some contemporary twists.

What's the Wealth of the Nation?

Oren Cass is an earnest and smart contributor to the discourse on offering opportunity for workers in depressed industries and places. A former editor of the *Harvard Law Review,* he has been a management consultant, an advisor to Republican presidential candidate Mitt Romney (as I was), and a scholar at the Manhattan Institute, and is now a policy entrepreneur with a think tank called American Compass. "True north" for that think tank is "a vision for the renewal of work in America," also the subtitle of his 2018 book *The Once and Future Worker.*[2]

Cass carries none of the bombastic demagoguery of some political opponents of openness. Indeed, his book offers an interesting diagnosis of the larger social and economic problems driving structural change and populist protests. He also offers policy ideas for training and reskilling workers, while supporting low-wage work, which are noteworthy and similar to policies discussed in Chapters 6 and 8 here.

But—and it's a big "but"—Cass's argument is built on an intuitive, but fatally damaging, notion. He argues that from Adam Smith onward, economists have gotten the big picture wrong—the "wealth of a nation" lies not in consumption or living standards but in jobs, good jobs, even *particular* jobs, using manufacturing jobs as the symbol of "good jobs." If this is true, economists' big-picture claims about gains from a market economy and the "dynamism" and "innovism" it brings—our focus in the last chapter—are misplaced. We would need to start over. The tinkering with the market economy that drew Smith's ire may actually be part of a solution to making the economy right by recentering policy on jobs and the dignity of work. And, if some policies resemble recommendations from mainstream economists, why bother splitting hairs about policy foundations anyway?

Adam Smith attacked mercantilism because its tinkering in the economy for special business reasons made citizens worse off by shrinking incomes and living standards. Openness to new ideas and ways of doing business was critical for prosperity and necessary, though not sufficient, for mass flourishing. Later thinkers saw that openness led to a continuous process of disruption and greater opportunity and "wealth of a nation" over time. Yes, paeans to openness have often skipped over disruption's wake, where some businesses and workers are left behind by change. But can we just make a course correction, or do we need a new economic framework and system?

Cass suggests the latter. He starts with a simple idea, which he terms his "Working Hypothesis," that a labor market in which workers can support families and communities is the central determinant of long-term prosperity and should be the focus of public policy.

This goal as a hypothesis makes descriptive sense on an intuitive level, as opportunities for work and the dignity it can bring are surely important. Cass is making a moral as well as economic argument, insisting that society works better when more people have solid and meaningful employment. A stronger society in turn yields a stronger economy in the long run.

Cass's formulation is certainly appealing, as he observes that politicians on both the right and the left claim fealty to "good jobs" and to policies that supposedly support those jobs, from tax cuts and deregulation to new public spending and fighting climate change. He is also correct that, while championing jobs, these leaders have often raised the costs of low-wage work, encouraged nonwork through well-intended social benefits, and turned a blind eye to the need for training in a churning economy.

So should we recenter policy on jobs, on work? That immediately raises several economic problems. Smith's focus on consumption and open competition led to rapid economic growth and amazingly high living standards and opportunities. The search for ideas and their commercial application, free from concerns about protecting jobs, has propelled the economy in modern times. The fluid U.S. labor force has gross flows—total numbers of jobs created or destroyed—that are vastly larger than the net flows reported by the Bureau of Labor Statistics in the highly watched *Monthly Employment Situation* released on the first Friday of each month.

If jobs are to be the center of policy concern, *which* jobs? Employment in the United States, as in other advanced economies, has evolved from agriculture to manufacturing to services. Large increases in agricultural productivity released labor to a growing manufacturing sector. Spectacular increases in factory productivity in recent decades have freed people for opportunities in the services sector, from technology to health care to tourism and entertainment to financial services to education, and so on.

Who determines this mix of jobs over time? Returning to the classical economists' telling, per Smith, consumers express their wishes through market competition. Their tastes and incomes shape opportunities for firms and dictate hiring.[3] Competition ensures efficiency in business and low prices and substantial variety for consumers. The open market allows individuals to "have a go"—as major entrepreneurs, yes, but also as small business owners or investors in skills to advance in or change one's career.

In Cass's telling, policy should focus not just on jobs, but on *manufacturing* jobs. He goes on to criticize economists like former chairs of the Council of Economic Advisers Gregory Mankiw and Christina Romer for missing this point. To back up his criticism, he notes that factories offer higher-wage jobs for less-skilled workers than, say, home health care or Walmart. Many individuals we spoke to in Youngstown would likely agree.

Winding up from there, Cass shows how high wages from manufacturing raise incomes and spending in communities, spending that supports service-sector workers and firms and their incomes. And, yes, many Americans are not satiated with what they want in goods. Why not produce more? Produce more here? With more jobs? Good jobs?

Relatively high wages in manufacturing reflect *productivity* in that sector (your Econ 101 professor told you that). Manufacturing *employment* has declined in the United States in recent decades, but not simply because companies moved jobs overseas. Factory jobs have also declined globally, now even in China, as the twin forces of productivity in manufacturing and shifts in consumer demand propel the economies. Even Cass acknowledges that today's American factories need fewer workers because of automation. The shift of employment opportunities that follows is a global story, not simply a story of the fallout from American capitalism.

One very practical way to see the folly of investing in particular jobs of the past is the significant evolution of jobs available in the economy. One hundred years ago, we would not be talking about the job market in computers, solar energy, or air travel. By 1940, the U.S. Census added as a new occupation "automatic welding machine operator," in 1990, "certified medical technician," and in 2010, "wind turbine technician." Indeed, economists David Autor, Anna Salomons, and Bryan Seegmiller estimate that fully 60 percent of jobs done in

SMITH SCHOOLS TODAY'S COMMENTATORS

2018 had not yet been designed or invented in 1940![4] New jobs include technology-related occupations in engineering, information technology, and alternative energy. But those jobs are not just technology-related, e.g., home health aides, fitness coaches, or chat room hosts. We would not have wanted to protect "1940" jobs—and we should not want to focus on "today's" jobs.

The evolution of jobs and industry happens within larger structural changes. Old work declines and may be eliminated, but new work grows and often exceeds the old.[5] Technological change is not necessarily a job killer in the aggregate. Indeed, the portion of American adults working rose throughout the twentieth century, even as many jobs were automated.[6] While many factors are at work here, automation makes workers more productive in core nonautomated tasks, from physicians using diagnostic machines to home-repair specialists using electronic tools. A more relevant question, discussed later, is whether workers are prepared for the jobs of tomorrow.

As explained in Chapter 1, while chair of the Council of Economic Advisers, I forcefully argued with President Bush over steel tariffs. When I showed him the chart with declining agricultural employment from 1900 to 1940, I asked if he wanted to put more workers back on farms. He said no, of course not. But efforts such as Cass's inevitably try to do something similar, to restrict the evolution of work in response to consumer demands. The second chart, a map of the nation by county, illustrated the loss of jobs across regions in other industries from steel protection. There would be no free lunch.

I lost that argument with the president because he believed the losses in economic efficiency from tariffs would be outweighed by the economic (and political) gains to steelmaking areas of the country. But Cass caricatures economists' views in suggesting that we have to choose between a pure laissez faire and extensive government involvement. As Smith himself noted, government has a role in providing public goods, funding industrial infrastructure, and ensuring competition. The last point implies that the government should remove barriers to competition at home. It also should counter against unfair trading practices abroad. Taking aim at intellectual property theft or illegal export subsidies is an entirely legitimate—and desirable—action by government.

What's dangerous, and ultimately costly to the nation's—our—living standards, is when governments protect a specific sector, industry, or firm. That protectionism reduces the "wealth of the nation." And domestic regulation and tax policy should not put our firms at a competitive disadvantage abroad, an observation that would surely win approval from Cass's bête noire, economists.

These arguments are not abstract. While some manufacturing jobs carry the higher earnings Cass emphasizes, how many such jobs will be available over time with technological change? Are they better jobs than those that might evolve? Surely many textile workers in Massachusetts in the 1950s thought they couldn't do better than what they had, but the state's workers are surely better off as a whole with the move into electronics. Many job categories today did not exist a generation or two ago. And again, who will decide what "good jobs" are to be promoted in moving public policy toward the economy in Cass's imagination?

Cass offers what looks like a gentle industrial policy guided by social scientists worried about work. But it results in something worse, a tinkering through the state for special interests, precisely the kind of tinkering that prompted Smith's criticism of mercantilism. Two decades ago, University of Chicago Booth School of Business economists Raghuram Rajan and Luigi Zingales wrote a compelling critique of Cass's position: While government should be an umpire to ensure the workings of competition and market forces, as Smith argued, private interests will inevitably compete behind the scenes in a self-interested manner to influence outcomes.[7] Rajan and Zingales worried in particular about an alliance between struggling incumbent firms (for whatever reason) and unemployed or disaffected workers. The steel firms and workers in the debate with President Bush brought their point home to me. Once we start making exceptions as Cass suggests, their alliance can turn the "umpire state" toward a "protectionist state," generating some winners with many more losers—the economy as a whole—from lower living standards.

Such fears are borne out by political interest in these ideas. President Donald Trump famously called on walls—both physical and metaphorical—to protect the nation's workers against disruptive structural changes brought about by trade or technology. But now a younger generation of Republican elected officials is drawing close, too. Sen. Marco Rubio of Florida, formerly a proponent of openness, suggests that markets have undervalued American workers' contribution to production. Sen. Josh Hawley of Missouri wants to tackle corporate elites and refocus on preserving jobs for working people. Sen. Tom Cotton of Arkansas has embraced economic nationalism. Advice from Milton Friedman to Ronald Reagan's party this is not—walls are on offer.

Everyone in this debate is surely committed to mass flourishing and getting more workers fully participating in the economy. What is to be done, then? We don't need to go back to mercantilist-style tinkering with markets; we can focus on helping individuals compete. That support for training, preparation, and low-wage work—also helpfully stressed by Cass—is entirely appropriate and occupies our discussion later. Marrying that support with industrial policy is self-defeating.

This avoidance of government tinkering is not just *practical*, but also *moral*. Part of Smith's intellectual assault on mercantilism was to attack the power of special interests. Taking Rajan and Zingales a step further: Once government explicitly starts tilting the playing field of commerce, various businesses or trades will band together to use government as a tool to redistribute income to themselves at the expense of the public. The return of budget earmarks in 2021, blessed by Congress and the Biden administration, heightens this concern. As described in a different way by Nobel laureates James Buchanan and George Stigler, these interest groups make economists inherently skeptical about many forms of economic regulation as benefiting special interests, not the public at large. Smith depended on the process of competition to drive the invisible hand, not on individual competitors. (Recall from our discussion in Chapter 3 that he viewed businesspeople as having a natural tendency toward anticompetitive behavior if left to their own devices.) He defended business as an organization for exploiting new opportunities, markets, and ways of doing things, but his work—as with that of economists to follow—was "promarket," not "probusiness" in the sense sometimes touted by conservative politicians.

That's why a little bit of special-interest tinkering is hard to contain. If policymakers assist the automobile industry and its workers, why not the steel industry, or textiles, or even computer chips? We've already seen how large-scale bailouts of financial institutions, as occurred during the 2007–2009 financial crisis, suggested that government "had the back" of large, connected firms. Meanwhile millions of homeowners current in their bills remained stuck with costly mortgages during the crisis—unable to refinance, even though the U.S. Treasury had already assumed mortgage credit risk when Fannie Mae and Freddie Mac were placed under federal conservatorship. Fast-forwarding to 2020, the COVID-19 pandemic revealed a much more vigorous response by the Federal Reserve to the credit dislocations experienced by large firms than to the woes of small and mid-sized businesses.

Real or perceived special-interest intervention by the state thus leads not only to economic inefficiency, but also to social distrust. The tinkering—by limiting the invisible hand of competition, a source of economic gains in Smith's market economy—yields a smaller "size of the pie." It has a corrosive effect, with many people concluding that some "slices of the pie" are unjustly received, and that ordinary people shouldn't bother trying to "have a go" at it.

This latter concern has fueled the analysis by Rajan and Zingales. Subsequent to that work, Zingales conducted further research connecting state tinkering with crony capitalism. Far from a world in which tinkering helps individuals in society writ large, Zingales's *A Capitalism for the People* describes a vicious cycle.[8] Protection confers—and is perceived to confer—benefits to some at the expense of others. If individuals perceive the economic system to be corrupt and lacking broad legitimacy, the system with its property rights and dynamism will also be under attack. While government already intervenes to provide public goods and subsidize merit goods (like education), the tinkering Cass suggests aims at specific industries, firms, and jobs—which is very much Smith's concern. A little bit of tinkering becomes a lot of tinkering and will be a dangerous thing, and anyone who can't justify special privileges is left out.

We should therefore avoid special-interest tinkering on principle, regardless of the social reasons suggested by Cass. Otherwise, all state subsidies or preferential tax or trade arrangements would be on the table, *pace* Smith. We cannot practically expect to root out special-interest tinkering while preserving the seemingly "good" interventions that Cass suggests. Should policymakers chase after all large firms, because these are more likely to lobby for their interests? No—such firms may simply be more efficient. Should we use regulation to limit political power seeking for protection? If so, how? Who watches the regulators' motives? *Quis custodiet ipsos custodes?* (That is, who watches the watchers?)

Instead of putting all this effort into building walls, let's focus on credible bridges of preparation and reconnection. We can build public support for competition and dynamism, limiting populist appeals for walls. Self-interested industries will make a Cassian argument for their special pleading, but public support for such pleading for walls, a requirement for democratic success, will be less forthcoming with strong support for bridges.

That's why Cass's otherwise reasonable argument for trade-offs falls flat. He asks, shouldn't we be willing to give up a few cents on the dollar of efficiency to ensure broad social solidarity? Isn't that the price of "mass flourishing"? Well, no: Such small trade-offs are *not* really what is on offer in the anti–wealth of nations logic.

Once tinkering is used to protect one job class or industry, why not another, and then another? Smith's competitive economy still requires government as an umpire. Government as a coach instead raises very different issues of accountability. And by reducing efficiency, we generate fewer resources for Cass's other policies, including supporting work through wage subsidies. It is the success of the market economy itself that provides the wherewithal to finance bridges of support. The walls shrink, not expand, the resources that can be applied toward that or any other worthy end.

By contrast, Cass's arguments about the dignity of work *should* catch our attention. To be able to participate broadly in society is a core element of mass flourishing, which in turn is a prerequisite for sustained political and social support for the market economy. Bridges, supported partly by government, promote this engagement. As we will see later, connecting and reconnecting people and places is the outlet for a sensible supplemental government role, creating a virtuous circle of prosperity and mass flourishing.

It is true that here, Smith's call for mass flourishing requires some tuning up. The economy Smith outlined and described was a simpler one than today's, before industrial and financial capitalism gained momentum. Structural shifts happened slowly, giving people time to adjust. With our rapid and long-lasting technological change and globalization, "having a go" requires skills and support for acquiring new skills when needed. While not an explicit feature of Smith's description of the economy or a role of government, such support is essential now for sustaining the invisible hand and mass flourishing.

We need to allow big job changes today, while fostering connection to those jobs. A key example is how data analytics and artificial intelligence are creating many new commercial opportunities and transforming jobs. Ginni Rometty, the former CEO of technology behemoth IBM, has highlighted "new collar" jobs as a twenty-first-century destination for people without four-year college degrees. As digital technologies transform manufacturing and other sectors, we will need a great many people with technical skills in these areas. Beginning in 2019, IBM worked with the Consumer Technology Association's Apprenticeship Coalition in twenty states. Focusing on states from Kansas to Minnesota to Louisiana—not just coastal tech hubs—the initiative opens up these new employment pathways. Walls to preserve existing manufacturing jobs would only get in the way of this promising future. As we will see later, both governments and businesses have a role to play in preparing workers and would-be workers for jobs, not in protecting firms and industries.

What's Wrong with Trade Walls of Protection?

Peter Navarro, a wiry and energetic Harvard-trained economist, emerged in President Donald Trump's administration as a forceful skeptic of free trade's benefits for the United States and a harsh critic of China's economic policy.[9] Hailing from an academic perch at the University of California at Irvine, Navarro became the inaugural occupant of the post of Assistant to the President and Director of Trade and Manufacturing Policy. From there he sparred with economists and "globalists," arguing for tinkering that would warm the heart of Thomas Mun. The passing of Trump's presidential tenure has not ended this neomercantilist posturing for walls in Washington.

Reflecting President Trump's argument that trade is a zero-sum game, Navarro saw winners (China or Mexico in his telling) and losers (sadly, the United States). He took on a tough crowd early in his tenure at the Trump administration, speaking to the National Association for Business Economics at Washington, D.C.'s Capital Hilton Hotel in 2017. (I was there, speaking just after him.) He launched into an attack on trade deficits and economists who defended them. While Navarro's slamming of economists was overstated—many economists have for years discussed costs of dislocation from globalization, while celebrating trade as an aggregate win—he channeled many members of the public and the newly elected president in questioning the wisdom of these deficits.

Navarro's zero-sum logic is unsettling to economists and many businesspeople, as it implies that one party can gain only if another loses. It contrasts with the centuries-old finding that trade generally makes nations better off on average. In Navarro's logic, a large tariff on Chinese imports just moves production from China back to Youngstown (an example he used)—bad for China but good for us, the zero sum.[10]

But this zero-sum logic is blind to the long-standing experience of gains from trade in boosting economies worldwide, including ours. It also sidesteps the reality of retaliatory policies against American exporters—think General Motors or Boeing, or even Hollywood. As argued above, it searches for a past that cannot be brought back, nor is it desirable to do so. And it ignores the fact that international supply chains now are common for U.S. manufacturing. As companies shifted away from low-cost goods to complex and costlier products such as airplanes and medical devices, they sourced lower-cost commodity components from China (or Mexico or Vietnam). Thus the profitability of health care equipment in Wisconsin depends, in part, on acquiring inexpensive components from the global supply chain.

American firms thus have little reason to "bring home" all manufacturing, even with large tariffs on Chinese imports in place. Far better to help workers buffeted by globalization and technological change through education and training investment infrastructure, and place-based aid.

Still, why are Navarro's ideas politically appealing? Did economics get it wrong?

No. Navarro, like many protectionists, argues that producing more goods and services at home at the expense of imports makes the nation better off. Consistent with mercantilist logic, he adds macroeconomic accounting for GDP, the value of all final goods and services produced over a period:

$$\text{GDP} = \text{Consumption} + \text{Investment} + \text{Government}$$
$$\text{Purchases} + (\text{Exports} - \text{Imports})$$

Consumption represents the value of household spending on goods and services; investment represents the sum of residential (housing) investment and business spending on the future (investment in equipment, structures, and software); government purchases are spending on goods and services (not transfer payments); and exports and imports are, respectively, sales to and purchases from other countries by domestic firms and organizations. Arithmetically, holding all else constant, an increase in exports or a decrease in imports raises GDP. Eureka!

But this mercantilist logic doesn't advance past arithmetic for two reasons. First, household or investment spending is best satisfied with goods and services produced most efficiently, wherever that production occurs. That simple observation reflects the value of open markets. Protectionism will lower consumer spending because people will have fewer goods and services to choose from. Second, GDP arithmetic, or "national income accounting," exposes the folly of focusing on the trade surplus or deficit as the principal measure of economic well-being. Like all commercial transactions, a transfer of goods and services from sellers to buyers across national boundaries requires financing—that is, paying for those goods and services. If we rearrange the terms in the above accounting identity to focus on the "current account" balance of exports and imports of goods and services, we get:[11]

Exports – Imports = (GDP – Consumption – Government Purchases) – Investment = Saving – Investment

That is, the current account balance—the focus of Navarro and trade hawks, Republican and Democrat alike—is the mirror of the difference between spending and saving by the nation (by households, businesses, and governments). If we want to end our trade deficit in physical (merchandise) goods and services, we have to save more and invest less.

This simple rearrangement, so far still just arithmetic and national income accounting, is picked up by economists, most of whom focus on the gap between saving and investment. Consider Germany, which saves more than it invests at home. That excess saving goes abroad to finance spending elsewhere. Germany's buildup of debt from other countries as financial claims means it has no choice but to run a surplus of exports over imports. Meanwhile in the United States, national investment exceeds national saving, the opposite of

Germany. Financing that higher investment requires borrowing funds from abroad (from Germans and others). Those financial transactions, reflected in a financial account surplus, will just be the mirror of commercial transactions, reflected in the current account deficit. For the United States, the value of imports of goods and services must therefore exceed the value of its exports.

Economists generally move from this arithmetic and accounting to focus on an economic interpretation, emphasizing slower-moving shifts in national saving and investment. A country can change its financial account balance through policies like stimulating investment (lowering the balance) or running government budget surpluses (raising the balance). The saving and investment decisions underlying the financial account are thus the by-product of a web of spending decisions by households, businesses, and government. If the United States runs a financial account surplus from higher investment relative to saving, it *must* run a current account deficit, with the value of imports exceeding the value of exports.

All this makes neomercantilist trade policies difficult. First, we cannot think about addressing the "trade deficit" without considering the determinants of and consequences for saving and investment decisions. Second, focusing on a bilateral surplus or deficit in trade with a single country does not affect the overall trade balance—which stems from a certain level of national saving and investment. Put concretely, holding constant an excess of U.S. national investment over national saving, running a lower trade deficit with China just means a higher U.S. trade deficit elsewhere, say with Vietnam. So we shouldn't reduce concerns over trade generally to a set of stories about trade issues with individual countries.

In focusing on trade in general, we miss dislocations from markets for individuals in particular. Economists aren't wrong about the long-term determinants of growth, but absent participation and reconnection for individuals in the open-market economy, it is easy to see Karl Polanyi's concerns about undermining support for this openness leading to social and political consequences.[12]

Indeed, anti-trade diatribes carry both an obvious and an equally important *sotto voce* point that economists and policymakers must confront. Some nations, China in particular, certainly *have* employed unfair trading practices against both the spirit and letter of commitments to the World Trade Organization. The Chinese government has heavily subsidized state-owned enterprises, manipulated currency in some periods, and encouraged theft of intellectual property from foreign investors and joint venture partners. Regardless of any trade deficit, China's behavior merits a response, and Navarro was right to call it out.

Economists' condemnation of "China tariffs" and U.S. unilateral intervention is fair, particularly when they advocate a multilateral confrontation of China's unwillingness to abide by WTO rules. But so, too, is a question back to economists about their earlier relative lack of interest in the subject beyond Econ 101 nostrums about trade. More powerful are the *sotto voce* effects of trade and globalization on the structure of the U.S. labor market. Trade and, even more, technological change have disrupted manufacturing employment for decades. From steel in Youngstown to autos in nearby Lordstown, Ohio, and throughout the industrial heartland, many towns have suffered heavy job losses with industrial employment experiencing structural declines. As we will see, policy responses to help prepare and reconnect these workers were tepid, and pursued with much less enthusiasm than were liberalizing trade agreements. Couple that with the China shock described in Chapter 2, and it is little wonder that gatherings in Youngstown and elsewhere were receptive to invectives against trade deficits and calls for walls of protection.

The departure of the Trump administration and Peter Navarro as a White House mercantilist does not imply a return to Clinton-era or even Obama-style globalization in economic policy. Simply put, too much political and economic reality makes that snapback unlikely. Yet there are economic lessons we can draw from recent experience that can guide a policy rethinking. These lessons illustrate the value of the Econ 101 descriptions of trade and its consequences.

First, President Trump's much-ballyhooed tariffs on steel, aluminum, and other products did not reduce the U.S. trade deficit. The merchandise trade deficit in 2019 (before the pandemic) was actually higher than it was in 2016. The Trump administration's tax cuts boosted excess spending over saving, raising national investment over saving and ensuring a rising trade deficit. Special tariffs on Chinese imports, to the extent they altered trade, just diverted buyers to Vietnam or other overseas producers.

Second, where these tariffs did not alter trade, they resulted in higher prices for American consumers and workers. Recent evidence bolsters the simple economic idea that the China tariffs were passed on to U.S. consumers, reducing their purchasing power. Product tariffs on steel may have protected some jobs in the U.S. steel industry, but they caused many more jobs lost at car and farm equipment firms now less competitive because of costlier supplies.

Third, trade agreements, while imperfect, maintain global economic linkages that are good for many reasons. Navarro and the Trump administration initially opposed NAFTA, which has knitted together the North American economies to their mutual benefit. But the rebranded United States-Mexico-Canada agreement actually changed little, preserving a no-tariff regime.

Finally, while the Trump administration correctly called out some Chinese trade practices as contrary to the World Trade Organization's rules, it largely ignored multilateral engagement with China. China could therefore retaliate against American imports it was buying, especially in agriculture, so taxpayers had to spend tens of billions of dollars to assist farmers. Meanwhile China seems to have committed even more strongly to state-owned enterprise.

A better economic engagement going forward involves working with our allies (principally, the European Union, Japan, Australia, and Canada) to confront China within the World Trade Organization, and devising a successor to the Trans-Pacific Partnership to strengthen American economic relationships in Asia. Our awkward divorce from the Trans-Pacific Partnership allowed China to push ahead as a regional leader by considering joining the successor Comprehensive and Progressive Agreement for Trans-Pacific Partnership.

As with Cass's misunderstanding of the wealth of a nation, Navarro's extended séance with Thomas Mun missed a critical point. One cannot build just a small wall in the mercantilist game. Mercantilist tinkering limits competition and the ability to "have a go." The bias against imports limits gains from specialization and comparative advantage, harms consumers through higher prices and more limited choices, and reduces the productivity of domestic firms. Not only does it bake a smaller pie, but it restricts the possibilities to prepare for mass flourishing in the dynamic economy.

What's Wrong with Business Walls of Protection?

Colin Mayer, a well-regarded Oxford academic scholar of finance and its role in society, has written about information problems in corporate finance for decades. He and I have crossed paths pleasantly many times on both sides of the Atlantic, sharing scholarly interests in corporate finance and corporate governance.

In 2018, Mayer completed a study as the academic lead of the British Academy's program on the future of the corporation. Such studies are important because of the significance of major corporations in economic activity, employment, and generating wealth. Mayer's findings, presented in his book *Prosperity,* argue for corporations to move away from simply maximizing value for investors.[13] Instead, he wants them to address wider challenges, not just economic but also political and social. If Cass and Navarro take aim at the core of industrial capitalism, Mayer's target is financial capitalism and how corporations apportion their surplus. Mayer's efforts are not unique: In the United States, prominent corporate lawyer Martin Lipton has led a similar charge with his "New Paradigm."[14]

Adam Smith saw firms as engines of prosperity, but he paid little attention to their organization. Chartered "corporations" did exist at the time of the publication of *The Wealth of Nations,* but most firms were much smaller and simpler than in the industrial capitalism soon to follow. What mattered in Smith's telling was competition and openness to new markets, ideas, and ways of doing things. Using government to provide public goods and set the rules of the game—and, today, preparing all individuals for competitive engagement—completed the circuit, allowing mass flourishing.

Views of the role of the corporation in society have evolved with capitalism. Many observers have focused on the distribution of power between owners of the firm (shareholders) and those who control corporate strategy or the deployment of corporate assets (managers). As companies evolved from smaller owner-managed firms (with, by construction, no conflict over the distribution of power) to larger corporations led by hired executives with many individual shareholders, governance conflicts arose. Both legal and finance scholars have studied extensively this evolution as a contest between "principals" (shareholders) and their "agents" (managers).

Prosperity goes beyond this focus on principals and agents. It calls for including other stakeholders, such as employees and local communities, at the corporate decision-making table. It goes on to suggest that corporations help to cushion blows from globalization and technological change.

Mayer, who describes the rich history of the corporation as a business organization, argues for a purpose-driven corporation, as befitting the origins of corporations as government charters for specific, socially important activities. It is true that "joint stock companies" were created by governmental charter for specific activities, such as opening up foreign trade—as with the Dutch and British East India Companies. In contrast to family-owned entrepreneurial businesses or partnerships among individuals, corporations could raise permanent capital from shareholders with limited liability, so that investors could lose only the funds they had personally contributed. Society granted these benefits in exchange for the corporation pursuing its chartered purpose.

Corporations certainly *do* need a purpose, as does any successful organization. In today's corporate life, such concerns are raised even by prominent investors. Laurence Fink, the CEO of BlackRock, the world's largest asset manager, has famously sent CEOs annual letters inquiring about their corporate purpose. CEOs themselves have weighed in through the Business Roundtable with the 2019 publication of the *Statement on the Purpose of the Corporation*. In that statement, 181 CEOs whose companies are members of the Roundtable pointed out both the need for purpose and for corporations to consider the well-being of all stakeholders, including workers, suppliers, and local communities, as well as investors.

But care is in order here, starting with Adam Smith's own antipathy toward corporations. He feared that the privileges bestowed on the British East India Company, the leading corporation of his day, prevented all-important competition. Smith wanted to free people to pursue many kinds of opportunities, and he distrusted special privileges for any business.

Instead, he wanted all companies, including corporations, to serve as a competitive force in the pursuit of opportunity. That pursuit of opportunity via the invisible hand, supported by openness without special privileges, would generate prosperity for the firm and for the economy as a whole. Such competition requires, as well, competitive rewards for suppliers of labor (workers) and suppliers of capital (lenders and shareholders).[15] The mass flourishing he sought required not just competition but, implicitly, the idea that everyone could compete, without special corporate privileges getting in the way.

Still, why not ask firms to look out for stakeholders besides investors? Mayer notes that the word "company" comes from the Latin words meaning "[breaking] bread together." Words for "company" in non-Romance languages share the same idea of a collective activity. Given the structural changes we've discussed, shouldn't firms lean against disruption for their workers and local communities? Why not have firms provide greater support?

Former Delaware Supreme Court Chief Justice Leo Strine, Jr., takes the question and Mayer's inquiry further.[16] He argues that competitive corporations have reduced worker pay, raised profits, and boosted executive compensation. In his view, companies could do more for workers and wages.

Such arguments raise a counterquestion: If dynamism and disruption are two sides of the same coin, can firms hold workers or communities harmless from change and still generate the economic and social benefits from that change? That is, can we hold constant, or nearly so, the size of the market economy's pie from dynamism while pushing firms to insure their stakeholders?

In Smith's world of competitive markets, they could not. A firm that raised wages above the competitive level would find it difficult to compete against other firms. Even when a firm has rents—think U.S. automobile manufacturers or steel firms in the 1950s and 1960s—

trying to protect workers from global competition and technological change can ultimately put both firms and workers in a vulnerable position. And the large firms with rents today, technology firms like Amazon or Alphabet, are exactly the ones least likely to have workers and communities buffeted by structural change.

Where might American policymakers and business leaders look for guidance in evaluating the desirability of protecting jobs, particularly "good" jobs, from disruption in today's complex economy? The experience of Airbus in Europe offers a sobering and revealing example.

Airbus was born of European industrial policy in 1967, when several governments came together to produce commercial jets to compete with U.S. aviation behemoths Boeing, Lockheed, and McDonnell Douglas. Their consortium finally gained traction in the late 1980s, when it launched the successful A300 jet series (with the British firm BAE Systems as its "wingman," designing and constructing aircraft wings). By the late 1980s, Airbus was winning big globally, with its A320 plane a potent competitor to Boeing's best-selling 737 jet.

Nevertheless, Airbus struggled with low profitability. With its strong sense of social responsibility, reinforced by government representatives on its board, its leaders tried to protect jobs in individual European countries. In 2012, a new CEO, a German named Thomas Enders, forced the issue by seeking a merger with a major defense firm, while grappling with the inflated costs of running a jobs scheme inside the firm. With "jobs" on their mind, the governments of the United Kingdom, France, and Spain, by then the majority owners of Airbus's shares, killed the merger.

Enders pushed back, arguing that the firm could no longer survive the job guarantees, as it duplicated jobs across multiple European economies. With Airbus's viability as a competitor to America's Boeing at stake, Enders persuaded the government shareholders to reduce their collective ownership to a minority stake and grant management authority to rescue the business. Enders's systemwide cost cutting put Airbus on a sustainable path, eliminating duplicative operations and employment. It fell to those governments to prepare affected workers for more sustainable jobs.[17]

Airbus is first a cautionary tale for proponents of social responsibility such as Mayer. Calls for firms to change corporate governance to protect jobs, however well intentioned, are just calls for walls of another kind—walls that will neither restrain the tides nor advance prosperity or mass flourishing. Indeed, firms alone cannot provide insurance against global market forces, skill-based technological change, or the emergence or destruction of job categories. Such calls therefore risk bringing together affected businesses and workers to lobby to stop this change.[18] Such interest-group alliances will undermine the path to the richer economy that can support mass flourishing.

But Airbus also offers a lesson to economists. Public support for dynamism ultimately requires broad social and worker buy-in. And there are some actions corporations can or should take to benefit their employees. Even Milton Friedman, in his famous full-throated defense of corporations' focus on shareholder value maximization, expected profit-maximizing firms to invest in workers' skills and training to increase the value of employees' contributions to the firm.[19] Governance proposals to require that firms report on workforce investment, suggested by reformers like Mayer or Strine, are a useful step that won't weaken competition. But, again, firms cannot provide insurance against market forces.

The firm may also provide funds to communities in its own self-interest, as those contributions improve the public value around the firm and the productivity of its workers. And a firm acting in its long-term self-interest can and should invest in resilience and not push for hyperefficiency of its production and supply chains in the narrow sense of Smith's pin factory.[20] Such investment could include spending on workers or communities close to its home to secure production ability in alternative global conditions, a lesson the COVID-19 pandemic forcefully brought home. It is just that business corporations' calling for or erecting walls against competition to protect workers or communities will not succeed, either economically or morally.

Everyone has heard the old saw "If you're so smart, why aren't you rich?" If Adam Smith offered killer arguments against mercantilism's walls and tinkering over 200 years ago, why are walls and tinkering prominent in today's economic and political discourse? To economists: If you're so Smithian smart, why aren't you winning?

Smith's answers to these questions, with some subsequent contemporary tuning up, remain spot-on. The wealth of a nation lies in the consumption and living standards of its people. Mercantilist tinkering with openness and markets shrinks the size of the pie. Taking business's eye off competition and efficiency also reduces the size of the pie. The counterclaims to these points are walls, and they will fail to deliver. And their shrunken possibilities limit mass flourishing, both directly in reducing the economy, and indirectly in restricting people from "having a go." Economists have lost ground in public debate because we haven't explained what companies and governments *can* do to support dislocated workers and communities.

The next two chapters go deeper into why the lure of walls in policy remains so strong and why economics points to bridges— today's policy formulation of Smith's mutual sympathy. Those bridges are the modern tune-up of the link between the wealth of a nation and mass flourishing.

5

Why Walls Are Still Attractive

In October 1980, three years after its Black Monday, Republican presidential candidate Ronald Reagan came to Youngstown. While touring shuttered steel mills, he told former workers: "We've got to protect this industry and all industries against dumping [of below-cost foreign goods]."[1] Four years later, President Reagan imposed "restraint agreements" that limited steel imports to 19 percent of the American market—at the same time that he was removing regulations from much of the domestic economy. While his successors dropped those limits, steel protection rose again under the second President Bush (see Chapter 1), another Republican seemingly committed to open markets, as well as recently under President Trump.[2]

The falling walls we discussed in Chapter 2 created enormous opportunities for businesses, workers, and whole economies. I and most of my students benefited handsomely. But those falling walls also carried large risks to the economic futures of many. It is unsurprising that dislocations in their wake led to calls for new walls.

In Youngstown, the Columbia students and I heard continuing demands for steel protection. President Trump certainly echoed that clarion call. But even the leader who told the Soviet Union to "tear down this wall" found walls appealing at times. Like President George W. Bush later, Reagan knew the political appeal of protectionism. As years passed without an economic revival, people in many devastated American manufacturing communities grew to distrust government elites and capitalism generally. They asked, "Why should we support economic trends that are supposed to improve our collective lot, if so many of us are suffering in their wake?"

Mentioned in Chapter 2, these questions drove Patrick Buchanan's campaign against President George H. W. Bush in the 1992 election. Jump ahead to 2016, when President Trump ("I'm a Tariff Man") rewarded his "America First" supporters with protectionist measures on steel and other goods.

Before we delve into bridges, we need to better understand walls against trade and technology. Economists have long denounced both kinds, with good reason, but the continued popularity of walls tells us something important about politics and economics. Misunderstanding them can wreak havoc with both our living standards and our social fabric.

Trade Walls Past and Present

After all, Britain embraced mercantilist protections for its growing empire until the mid-nineteenth century (see Chapter 3). Even with Adam Smith, David Ricardo, and other economists pointing out the damage, the kingdom switched course only after it became a global manufacturing powerhouse. A lack of openness to trade, decried by these classical economists, erects walls of protection for some—and increases costs for many. Mercantilism, a policy to maximize national exports and minimize imports, held sway in European economies from the fifteenth to the eighteenth centuries. Mercantilist policy prized a current account surplus, abetted by high tariff and nontariff barriers to imports.

Mercantilist thinkers and leaders counted wealth in gold, silver, and population. Walls of protection would secure those stocks, and prosperity would follow. Even British political elites sidestepped the implications of Smith's ideas, as the mercantilist Navigation Acts imposed on the American colonies helped foment the American Revolution against the crown.

Surprisingly at the time—and to some extent today—openness to new activities, markets, and ways of consuming is good! Early critics of mercantilism measured wealth in the generation of resources to fund consumption and emphasized gains from openness to trade and technology—again, arguments familiar in today's debates. To Smith, a capitalist economic system enhances consumption and prosperity if it is open to competition and efficient production by specialization, both contradicting mercantilist advice.

Following Smith, fellow classical economist David Ricardo stressed that specialization according to comparative advantage would lead to gains from trade—casting trade as a positive-sum activity, not the zero-sum activity of mercantilist lore. In Ricardo's telling, two nations trading could both be better off by doing so: Suppose England could produce cloth more efficiently than Portugal and Portugal could produce wine more efficiently than England. Specialization in Portugal in wine and in England in cloth, then trading, could improve the lot of both because of differences in either absolute efficiency ("absolute advantage") or relative efficiency ("comparative advantage").

Other classical economists threw stones at the mercantilist cathedral window. John Locke's *Second Treatise* emphasized the link between labor and the true wealth of a nation. David Hume went at the heart of the mercantilist goal of an enduring positive balance of trade, noting that the mechanical operation of a gold or silver standard would imply bullion inflows to a mercantilist economy, raising prices and lowering the value of bullion—mercantilists' wealth—in terms of other goods.

The British Empire embraced free trade only after it gained dominance in much of the world in the late nineteenth century. Likewise, the United States liberalized trade after World War II devastated most of its economic rivals. Until the 1970s, both industry and labor in the United States prospered, with little foreign competition. This success made it easier for the United States to play a leading global role in championing openness to globalization and trade. But, as we noted earlier, the federal government also passed the Servicemen's Readjustment Act of 1944 (the G.I. Bill), advancing education and skills for returning troops.

Funding for the G.I. Bill eventually tapered off, along with those halcyon postwar economic years when the United States was the only undamaged major economy. Global industrial competition intensified in the 1970s, with U.S. workers and many communities (such as Youngstown) feeling the pain from steel to automobiles to television sets to shoes and clothing.

For much of the difficult post-1970 period for many industries, the United States maintained and increased openness, per the advice of economists. The administration of President George H. W. Bush advocated the GATT philosophy of openness and low barriers to trade. Free trade with Canada, begun under President Reagan in 1987, blossomed eventually into the North American Free Trade Agreement, ratified in 1993 in the presidency of Bill Clinton, over strong opposition from U.S. labor unions. Presidents Clinton and George W. Bush shepherded China into the WTO, offering it the same low tariffs promised by the United States to any other WTO member (so-called most-favored-nation status).

Elites' Opposition to Walls

In an important sense, the turn of the twenty-first century represented a high-water mark among U.S. economic and political elites about the optimistic outcomes of openness and a future economy. That high-water mark saw much more emphasis on industries and jobs of tomorrow, and on lower prices and greater choices for consumers, than on hard-to-bear risks for many from openness to technological changes and globalization. But even then, President George W. Bush imposed tariffs on steel (despite my efforts as his economic advisor), and President Barack Obama imposed tariffs on Chinese tires (likewise against the advice of his economic advisors). They gradually succumbed to the mounting pressure for walls that candidate Reagan saw in 1980, coming from people whose livelihoods and prospects were upended by risks beyond what they could manage.

In the absence of effective bridges like the G.I. Bill, people grasped for any solution at hand. Bridges like Trade Adjustment Assistance, which we introduced in Chapter 2 and will evaluate in the next chapter, were more like a rickety catwalk. That a renewed call for walls simmered under the surface now, in retrospect, seems like something we should have expected.

As Adam Smith knew, walls are costly. Trade restrictions raise prices and slow productivity growth, wages, and profits. To avoid walls, we need preparation and reconnections to opportunity that are more complex today than Smith imagined.

The failure is obvious. From the 2001 steel tariffs to the 2017 restrictions on imports of Mexican sugar, protection has yielded far greater losses to nonprotected downstream firms and consumers than the temporary benefits to the government-chosen favored few. In the case of the 1980s restrictions on Japanese car imports, economist Robert Crandall estimated the cost per U.S. job saved to be ten times the wage of a worker protected.[3]

Protecting jobs brings the unintended consequence of blocking new entrants to the labor market, especially young people and those from minority groups. Policies to make firing costly, common in some European economies and proposed for the United States by some politicians, raise unemployment. They also create insiders protected by the policy and outsiders unable to find work. Protection heeds the cry of "build the wall," yet invariably, more people over time are left outside than behind the wall.

Paraphrasing President Trump, if tariffs are a wall, who's going to pay for it? According to several recent studies, we all do. The president's economic team insisted that tariffs have no impact on domestic prices—foreigners pay them through lower prices they receive or a weaker currency. That American free lunch did not come to pass.

Economists estimate substantial costs to Americans from the recent tariff war with China and other countries. Kimberly Clausing concludes that it imposed costs of $400 per year for the average household.[4] Mary Amiti, Stephen Redding, and David Weinstein found the tariffs causing significant welfare losses to consumers in prices, reduced variety of goods, and higher markups on many goods. These also hurt American firms through more costly and complex supply chains.[5] Political claims notwithstanding, Amiti, Redding, and Weinstein, as well as economists Pablo Fajgelbaum, Pinelopi Goldberg, Patrick Kennedy, and Amit Khandelwal, find that *Americans,* not the Chinese, are paying the cost of the China tariffs.[6] Nor does the pain end there. Economists Aaron Flaanen and Justin Pierce at the Federal Reserve Board conclude that higher prices as a result of the tariffs have reduced manufacturing employment (the jobs tariffs were supposed to protect) by 1.4 percent.[7] Ouch.

Elites—economists, business leaders, and politicians—are right about the costs of protectionist walls. Still, those arguments don't seem to make the political "sale," because of the absence of bridges. The same is true for walls against technological change.

Looking Back on Technology's Walls

In the 1810s, Ned Ludd inspired English protests against the automated knitting and weaving frames. We saw that his followers, "Luddites," worried about being displaced by machines ever more efficient in making textiles.

From Luddites back and forward, many have sought to build a wall against technological change. But most people, not to mention economists, look positively on technological progress. It transforms our lives as consumers with faster and better communication. Robots boost productivity—and increase wages. Technological advances work their way gradually through productivity and wages as businesses adapt their organizations to use them, as with electrification in the 1920s or computing, the internet, and artificial intelligence in recent decades.

Openness to new technology and trade also feed off each other. The complementarity of technology and certain skills is more valuable in global markets. Think of a global market for a recording artist or movie star or key software developer—or even an Econ 101 textbook author!

Disruptive changes brought about by innovations in markets for trade and technology have generated massive improvements in living standards—a huge dividend from competitive capitalism. But the willingness to accept Schumpeter's "creative destruction" is only recent in history, and it is still tenuous. The economic miracle of the Industrial Revolution in the West, beginning in Britain, was repeated in Southeast Asia after World War II. China's opening to the modern world economy since the late 1970s, and India's opening beginning in the early 1990s, have bettered the economic fortunes of hundreds of millions of people.

Again, this mass economic betterment toward mass prosperity is not principally the by-product of saving and capital accumulation, as virtuous as that process can be. It is not hard work and accumulation alone that deliver sustained improvements in living standards. That improvement requires productivity, innovation, and innovism (to return to McCloskey's felicitous phrase)—and the change that comes with them. As we've now realized all too well, new technologies have also brought fear. They generate risks impossible for an individual to manage on his or her own. While protectionism draws more political attention, job churn due to technological advance looms much larger—and was a far greater factor in Youngstown's Black Monday than steel imports.

That concern extends even to economists, from David Ricardo to John Maynard Keynes to Robert Gordon. Should this fear concern us today with populism's rise? We can confidently say no: HAL, the rogue computer in *2001: A Space Odyssey,* is not coming for all of our jobs. Waves of technological change in the past, from steam power to automobiles to electrification, have generated whole new categories of jobs even as they removed others. But whether many Americans are *prepared* for those jobs, prepared to be *reconnected* to work if they lose their job—and to support the economic system delivering those jobs—is very much at stake.

A dynamic economy, past and present, both creates and destroys jobs at a high rate. Prior to the labor market calamity of COVID-19, the U.S. economy lost an average of 1.7 million jobs per month (out of roughly 160 million jobs). But it also added 1.85 million new jobs, for a net increase of 150,000 jobs. These gross flows of job creation and destruction are the real story. And their size shows the sheer folly of erecting walls to protect existing jobs.

Still, we need to address who bears which risks in society. Technological change does inflict long-lasting aggregate structural shocks on vulnerable workers. We can reduce this risk without dampening technological dynamism.

Dynamism Does Deliver

It's important to remember just how bountiful open economies have been—so we can apply some of that bounty to helping people who lose out. The disruptive capitalist system delivers—big time (not a phrase in *The Wealth of Nations!*)—as Adam Smith saw early on. Disruptive changes brought about by innovations in markets open to trade and technology are responsible for massive improvements in living standards. The only recent willingness to accept Schumpeter's creative destruction focuses attention on the Industrial Revolution. That revolution made possible Edmund Phelps's "indigenous innovation," in which innovations build on each other in an open economy. Present at the creation, Adam Smith correctly observed that the enrichment this process brought depended less on state wealth than on innovative potential to generate resources for higher living standards. And that innovation requires change, disruptive change.

Despite some heated rhetoric, that bounty has not gone solely to elites. As American Enterprise Institute economist Michael Strain has observed, real wages for typical workers (not managers or supervisors) have risen by one-third since the 1990 business cycle peak.[8] The highest earners have gained far more, but the increases for average workers are substantial. After adjusting for taxes and government transfers, most workers have done even better. They are not living through the mordant stagnation implied by today's political discourse, from President Trump's "American carnage" to U.S. senator Elizabeth Warren's "hollowed-out" middle class.

Indeed, much of the appeal of walls stems from fears of a declining middle class, with shrunken employment opportunities and declining upward mobility. The middle class is shrinking, "squeezed," or even "dead."[9] The rhetoric has shaped the zeitgeist, with 61 percent of survey respondents in a 2018 Pew Research Center poll saying that the federal government offers too little assistance to the struggling middle class.[10]

The data are more positive than this rhetoric suggests. The "hollowing out" of the middle actually comes more from individuals moving *up* in income than moving down. Economists David Autor of MIT, Lawrence Katz of Harvard, and Melissa Kearney of the University of Maryland observed that technological change compressed routine administrative and production tasks, while generating high-skilled, nonroutine jobs in computer programming or management and low-skilled jobs in food and retail service.[11] Autor later added that growth in higher-skill jobs has recently exceeded that in lower-skilled jobs, potentially adding more opportunities to move up than down.[12]

Economists Adam Looney of the University of Utah, Jeff Larrimore of the Board of Governors of the Federal Reserve System, and David Splinter of the Joint Committee on Taxation estimate that middle-income households have benefited significantly from a progressive federal tax and transfer system.[13] Between 1979 and 2016, market incomes for households in the middle three quintiles of the U.S. income distribution (the "middle class") saw their market incomes (before taxes and transfers) rise by 39 percent. Adjusting for taxes and transfers, the corresponding growth is 57 percent, with all of the relative gain occurring since 2000, the period in which concerns over structural economic changes have been heightened.

This more nuanced picture still leaves us with challenges that help drive middle-income anxiety over structural change. If income gains are possible by shifting to more complex new jobs, how will people develop the skills to move up? And if middle-income gains depend partly on net fiscal transfers, are such transfers sustainable? We will return to these important challenges and questions later in this chapter and in Chapters 6, 7, and 8.

Why Don't Arguments Against Walls "Make the Sale"?

Squaring economic reasoning with populist fervor implies that either the fervor is overwrought or something subtle is happening. The answer is a bit of both.

Politicians' commentary and even the opinions of business elites (such as hedge fund billionaire Ray Dalio and JPMorgan Chase CEO Jamie Dimon) have fanned the sense that "something is broken." Media coverage of populist woes in the heartland and the struggles of many low- and mid-skilled workers is more widespread today than in the 1970s and 1980s, when the shocks of technological change and globalization began in earnest.

With new higher-wage occupations arising in health care, computer services, and personal services, more workers are rising above middling pay categories. That move up is good news—*if* everyone is prepared to compete and manage the risks from change. But people aren't.

This wake is a result of structural change and creative destruction, in which jobs are destroyed and others are created. But those words sound like technical and disembodied econ-speak to many individuals whose long-term, future economic prospects are at risk from new technologies or trade. There is a distinction between these job changes and what we often hear about rising or falling unemployment rates over busts and booms in a business cycle. Familiar business cycle movements in employment usually bring temporary layoffs or separation from work, with reattachment when times get better.

That's why disruptions from technological change and globalization feed the present anxiety—feelings amplified by dislocations from the COVID-19 pandemic. Policymakers have fallen short in two ways. They have underemphasized both preparation for emerging skills and jobs, and reconnection to productive employment when structural forces knock people out of the workforce. Most labor market policy dates to the 1930s' concern with cyclical disruptions, so it fails to address structural disruptions from technology and trade.

These policy holes make walls appealing in two ways. Without preparation, people fear lost opportunity for themselves and their neighbors. Without reconnection, people fear social inequality as affluent households better weather income fluctuations. In policy terms, the first fear calls for *opportunity policy;* the second calls for a rethinking of *social insurance.* Both are mechanisms through which society as a whole mitigates the risks of structural shocks on individuals. Without them, twenty-first-century capitalism can't achieve Adam Smith's mass flourishing.

We Once Did a Better Job

In *The Communist Manifesto* of 1848, Karl Marx and Friedrich Engels noted: "The bourgeoisie, during its rule of scarce one hundred years, has created more massive and more colossal productive forces than all preceding generations together." They were not praising capitalism so much as expressing their anxiety about it—fears that we still grapple with today.

An economic system has to fulfill several roles. Two of them are familiar: mobilizing resources for productive activity and allocating output and income. That much capitalism has accomplished stunningly well, as even Marx and Engels observed. (Those authors accepted many of Smith's foundations of how a capitalist system works, though they disagreed on its evolution.) Yet two other roles define a successful, long-lasting economic system: improving living standards over time and delivering this prosperity widely—mass prosperity.

Here, questions can be raised about whether today's capitalism delivers a broad and growing base of prosperity, not just high average prosperity enjoyed individually by a few. In a time of rapid technological change and global trade, solutions to these shortcomings are urgent. Popular support for capitalism—especially the willingness to accept the disruptions that drive its progress—depends on preparing people to participate and helping them reconnect after dislocation.

America in the late 1800s and 1930s faced severe economic pressures, which did make people question capitalism itself. Those periods brought forth policy responses to soften capitalism's rough edges, by expanding economic opportunity in the first period and embracing social insurance in the second.

In the 1860s, Congress and President Abraham Lincoln created land-grant colleges to break down barriers to individual opportunity. Then in the 1930s, in the midst of the Great Depression, President Franklin Roosevelt pushed through sweeping social-insurance policies. These reforms strengthened unemployment insurance and introduced Social Security. Government policy aimed to embrace workers buffeted by cyclical forces beyond their control amid capitalism's chilly winds.

Together, these policies—perhaps call them "Lincolnvelt"—have been vital for capitalism's adaptation and survival. Technological change and globalization have disrupted mass prosperity in developed countries, while generously rewarding highly skilled professionals and entrepreneurs. Meanwhile, a hollowing-out of many middle-class jobs by these macro forces has left many voters worried. These twin "Lincolnvelt" reforms, echoed in measures such as the G.I. Bill of 1944, can guide us today. In the next chapter, we return to these economic ideas for better ways forward.

What's important about these measures is that they don't undermine economic dynamism. People are still free to start up new firms or imagine entirely new products—the breakpoint separating traditional economies (characterized by feudalism or mercantilism) from the modern industrial economies. This openness replaces stasis with advancing living standards. Nor do the measures free people from the labor market itself, as direct transfer payments would do. The Biden administration's initiatives are not Lincolnvelt.

When considering economic progress, most people think about higher productivity from new technologies. But technology, like manna from science's heaven, is not enough. While some economists, at least since Schumpeter, have focused on innovation from shifts in technology and science, there is a still greater economic story to tell. After all, the former Soviet Union had plenty of new technology, yet it still collapsed from economic stagnation. Public funding for science and technology, not bad things to be sure, will not by itself right the innovation ship. Nor is prosperity principally the result of savings and capital accumulation, or hard work.

Innovation requires an open, free-moving ecosystem of entrepreneurs, producers, consumers, and financiers, with broad public support to sustain it. It is this support for openness to trade and new technologies that makes a virtuous cycle of innovation and growth possible, not just exogenous technology as manna from science's heaven. Support for business and market institutions is very much part of the story of growth, advancing living standards, and mass prosperity. And, as Phelps has observed, it is a decline in innovation's virtuous cycle and support for new ideas and innovation that drive regress in productivity growth. Gains from innovation are not inevitable. They can, though, be nurtured by public policy.

This focus on newness and innovation goes beyond engineering breakthroughs or adapting existing technologies to different users. Gains come from new ideas and product explorations among businesspeople—in software, communications, games, and transportation, for example. That such ideas and products emerge only from an economy open to them is a core element of Phelps's indigenous innovation. In an actual economy, of course, openness to new markets and new ways of doing things requires an openness to disruption—and disruption's wake. Once we start thinking that disruption is too costly for many people, we undermine support for openness and hold back the virtuous cycle of innovation and growth in living standards.

Many game changers in economic life stemmed more from a new way of addressing opportunity than from a scientific advance. Think the printing press, interchangeable parts, the lightbulb, frozen foods, radio and television, or hydraulic fracturing ("fracking"). Each depended on entrepreneurial insight and practical ingenuity at least as much as new science or engineering. And each led to disruption with benefits for many, achieving broad enough support to overcome a costly disruption's wake for others.

Now we can go beyond the simplistic framing of this problem, between laissez-faire public neglect and walls. Walls too often reduce openness on trade or technology, or indirectly protect incumbent firms, the technologies they employ, or the workers they hire. Even requiring an innovative firm or entrepreneur to share with its own stakeholders is a wall-like tax on dynamism. Indeed, Phelps, in work with Raicho Bojilov, concluded that job satisfaction is higher in countries in which the overall direction of a firm and its innovation are decided upon by the firm's owners.[14]

Instead of laissez faire or walls, we can build bridges. Public policy can help dislocated workers and communities reconnect and participate anew in the dynamic economy. In more recent decades, vibrant sectors in technology and communications have experienced disruption and growth. Some more traditional "heartland" industries have tried to build walls against change, garnering sclerosis instead.

What Exactly Does "Compensation" Mean Here?

Most economists' sanguine reading of technological change's bounty, of course, is not universally shared. Along with openness to trade, openness to new technology improves our lives in ways seen, unseen, and possibly not acknowledged. Yet for some individuals, this openness is a significant macro risk beyond their control. Loss of a job or earnings is concentrated—as in the old saying: "When you lose your job, the unemployment rate is 100 percent"—and most certainly noticed. Simply put, as with trade and globalization, technological changes create "gainers" and "losers." Also in common with gains from trade, technological change generates large *aggregate* gains. Economists, when they do worry about dislocated workers, have an idea about how to maintain policies with large aggregate gains: The gainers compensate the losers, who will then acquiesce to the greater good.

OK, but for both globalization and technological change, what do we mean by "gainers can compensate the losers"? That gainers *can* do so reflects the positive-sum payoffs to an economy and society from openness to trade and technological change. But what is this compensation? It should not and must not, for the sake of economic growth and living standards, be walls of protection—of particular jobs, firms, industries, or means of production. Future Henry Fords shouldn't need to write checks to buggy whip makers, nor future Bill Gateses to makers of typewriters. Such walls are the beginning of statism, of killing the golden goose of dynamism. Dynamism and its wake of change are *required* for the steady march of growth and improvements in living standards.

But who are the "gainers"? It's natural to think of the entrepreneurs who seize opportunities to trade or implement technologies and become rich in the process. Images of Jeff Bezos, Bill Gates, or the late Sam Walton evoke images of mountains of money made. Yet they capture only a tiny share of the value of their ingenuity to society. Economics Nobel laureate William Nordhaus estimates that today's entrepreneurs and innovators capture only 2 percent of that social value.[15] Building a wall to protect us from that innovation may make a few people much less wealthy, but the rest of us lose 98 percent of the bounty the first group created. Less dramatic but equally important are the moral gains in free participation that come from openness.

And who are the "losers"? Compensation cannot literally mean a payment from an individual gainer to an individual loser from change. That would be another wall. The owner of a successful new restaurant need not reimburse losses of the nearby eatery that closes its doors.

Likewise, directing gains from trade's or technology's winners to pay the losers is not what economists have in mind. Gains from openness in markets arise in no small part from signals that some activities are now worth more—and others are now worth less. Direct payments would confuse those signals.

As we saw in Chapter 4, much of the policy debate about compensation is really about walls of protection—of particular jobs, of particular industries, of workers and communities at the expense of suppliers of business capital. The accompanying box summarizes those walls.

Instead of direct payments or walls of protection, we can provide access to opportunity through preparation (developing skills) and reconnection (reimagining social insurance to cushion blows while preparation occurs).

While we lean heavily on economics for ideas and solutions, this approach is about more than economics (which may be why economists have been slow to offer ideas here). Beyond economic concepts like "income" and "consumption," bridges can promote social connection and individual dignity. More important still, they preserve freedom of opportunity and respect personal responsibility, while taking on much of the risks beyond one's own control. In order to

Walls

Industry and job protection	Safeguards particular industries or firms with "good jobs" to slow down structural changes in employment patterns.
Trade barriers	Protect particular industries or products to promote domestic production and employment.
Stakeholder corporate governance	Weakens corporate commitment to shareholders in order to increase resources directed toward employees and communities.

Responding to structural changes affecting industries and jobs, these walls protect the status quo at the expense of future gains from dynamism.

generate alternatives to walls, we need economists to make this intellectual and practical pivot.

The reforms outlined here align with a traditional vision of America and American capitalism. They are also essential. Failing to confront the problem of dislocated communities, or go beyond stale distinctions between laissez faire and walls, risks a withering of public support for capitalist dynamism. In the absence of bridges, people will always choose walls. At stake is nothing less than our economic future.

Social Insurance as a Bridge

In talking to colleagues about bridges, I find they readily understand the value of training or retraining workers. After all, a number of retraining programs even have the title of "Bridge to Work." President Obama, for example, unsuccessfully proposed a "Bridge to Work" program that would cover the wages of unemployed people working as trainees at companies.

Those colleagues are less responsive to using social insurance as a bridge. I tend to explain it as an extension of the economic concepts of household spending and saving focused on theories of smoothing consumption over one's lifetime[16] and precautionary saving.[17] The intuition is simple—going back to "diminishing marginal utility of consumption" from your beloved Econ 101 course. When consumption is high, an individual obtains less value from spending a bit more, so it's good to save. Conversely, when consumption is low, the value of additional spending (drawing from savings) is greater. "Consumption smoothing" means just that—an individual prefers to have steady consumption, rather than fluctuating highs and lows. Household saving and dissaving provide the safety valve.[18] With volatile incomes, it makes sense to boost this precautionary saving.[19]

For our purposes here, a key element is earnings fluctuations year to year for middle-income individuals. Putting aside government programs for now, such fluctuations are an "uninsurable idiosyncratic risk" in econ-speak, requiring individuals to save more to cushion the blow, take on debt in tough times, or reduce consumption when earnings fall. Household data do not paint a picture of steady middle-class earnings. Indeed, since 1979, for male individual workers, about a third of the population experiences an increase in annual income greater than 50 percent or a decline of more than 40 percent.[20] Generalizing to a household does not reduce this volatility very much, with only modest reductions in volatility implied by studies of household tax return data.[21]

While individuals and households use savings as a buffer for shock, having each individual self-insure can be a costly solution, as it ignores gains from risk pooling.[22] Just as private fire insurance or health insurance or life insurance generates benefits from risk pooling, so, too, can government-provided social insurance. Designed to smooth consumption in response to cyclical, temporary layoffs, unemployment insurance is a clear example. The nation's costliest social insurance schemes are for older Americans—Social Security to provide compulsory pooling for annuity income in retirement and Medicare for old-age health insurance.[23] Both unemployment insurance and Social Security—unlike the open-ended transfer payments now under discussion in Washington—enable workers to better take on the risks of participating in the dynamic economy.

We need additional social insurance for dislocated workers, as their income declines are potentially long-lasting instead of cyclical. This extra insurance would support them as they develop new skills. A broader concept of social insurance in this setting would provide funds for reconnection (as with subsidies to raise demand for low-skilled workers and/or their wages). This rethinking of social insurance is a core element of a "mass flourishing" policy agenda, and we will tackle it in the next chapter. It is thus an antidote to calls for walls against change, which threaten average prosperity. The rest of the book explores the possibilities for both kinds of bridges.

Walls, Bridges, and the Wealth of Nations

Center-right economic elites in the United States have for decades championed laissez-faire policies for openness and a smaller government, all in the name of economic growth and wealth creation. Center-left elites have focused on distributional concerns and greater social spending. Debates are caricatured as a battle between "neoliberalism" and "democratic socialism." Neither "side" focuses on the core element of mass flourishing—maintaining average gains from openness and disruption by providing individuals with a bridge to new opportunities and recovering lost potential. It's hardly surprising that the failing relevance of the traditional right-left debate and the absence of bridges have given the inside political track to walls.

When economists today talk of reigniting prospects for growth in the United States or other advanced economies, they have in mind structural reforms of, say, the tax system or regulation or corporate governance. But this agenda just extends their traditional neoliberal laissez-faire approach. If, however, we recognize that dynamism is a virtuous cycle that requires broad public buy-in, we will develop structural reforms to prepare people for success in the innovative economy and reconnect individuals who slip away in disruption's wake.

Economic history is replete with examples of walls to protect against losses from openness to trade and technological change. At the same time, the history of economic thought stresses gains from openness. Walls are costly. How to blunt or avoid the "wall" impulse is a key task for public policy.

6

Bridges

He had argued for bridges all his life, and now he was finally in a position to make them happen on a large scale. Abraham Lincoln, the son of an illiterate dirt farmer, devoted his political career to enabling ambitious strivers like himself to achieve economic respectability and comfort. He had little to show for his relentless campaigns for internal improvements, however, until becoming president in 1861. His election led to the disastrous splitting of the federal union and the Civil War, where he showed his greatest leadership in restoring the union while abolishing slavery. But the crisis had the silver lining of freeing Congress from the southern representatives who had always voted down major federal initiatives.

Lincoln worked with Congress to pass a series of bridges: the Morrill Land Grant Act, the Homestead Act, and the transcontinental railroad. The Morrill Act was especially important because it enabled states throughout the country to extend higher education to citizens of modest means. The skills developed were crucial to economic development and mass flourishing in the nineteenth century.[1]

Lincoln elevated himself through extraordinary natural talent and ambition, but he left a legacy that has elevated many other people with lesser endowments. We need similar bridges now.

The first chapter of this book mentioned a bridge in Youngstown, Ohio, a city that once symbolized American industrial progress and opportunities for businesses and workers. Local business leaders, Youngstown State University staff, and the Youngstown Business Incubator are trying to restore those opportunities after decades of decline.

Bridges have three key elements. The first is that they help people overcome a specific challenge on their way to economic flourishing—they don't provide for flourishing directly. The second is that the wider society builds the bridge, either through private organizations, governments, or public–private partnerships. Just as globalization and technological change have introduced risks beyond what individuals can handle, society must build bridges that individuals by themselves could never assemble. The third element is avoiding restraints on competition.

Land-grant colleges, free western land for new settlers, and a transcontinental railroad had all three of these elements, but there are many other potential bridges. Economic development in the United States from its earliest days focused on bridges—ways of getting to new places—to open the frontier and create new markets and businesses. Literal bridges over waterways, yes, but also canals and railroads, and later highways and airports. Bridges also connected us through falling costs of transportation and communications, making many new commercial activities possible.[2] Major advances in public education, primary and secondary as well as higher, have elevated people to commercial skills and broader social participation.

A bridge offers a path across a tough-to-traverse stretch. As we have seen, key features in our present economy create difficult stretches for many of us, while creating immediate gains for many others. To maintain broad support for openness, we need a broad social commitment to bridge building for aspirations, rather than wall building for fears.

It *Does* Matter

If bridges are so obviously better than walls, why are walls getting all the attention? This question turns out to be central to our economic future. As we have seen, the economic gains from capitalism are the flip side of disruptions in technology, in markets, and in the value of skills and activities. No disruption, no gain, full stop. Disruption creates gainers and losers and can force individuals to bear large aggregate risks beyond their control. Support for it and, as a consequence, capitalism's benefits, is not inevitable. Classical economists understood this point with an emphasis on mass prosperity. And successful adaptations to economic change have grasped this point—and point the way forward.

Popular econo-bashing notwithstanding, economics is *not* the problem. Both the language and practice of economics offer an answer. More important still, Smith's foundational ideas for capitalism offer the way out. The problem traces ultimately to economists who have failed to engage seriously with widespread social anxiety during periods of change. It's not a rhetorical accident that "blame the economists" has become a fashionable theme, from politicians like President Trump to writers like the *New York Times*'s Binyamin Appelbaum and Columbia University's Nicholas Lemann. These authors cast a jaundiced eye toward the dismal science and its high priests—as obfuscating, poorly focused, or even captured by business interests.

A fundamental problem is the disconnection of too many economists from the world that surrounds them. In a revealing scene in the movie *Back to School,* Rodney Dangerfield, as an older college student, asks an economics professor in the midst of a boring lecture for a real example of his point. Surprised by the temerity of the question, the professor answers over and over: "It doesn't matter."

It certainly *does* matter. Globalization and technological change boost living standards in the long run, but only through a great deal of structural change. What happens along the path from here to there? Who wins? Who loses? By how much? Economists' tendency to address these concerns as mere "transition costs" is cause for alarm. Our sometimes breezy admonitions have translated into policymakers' inaction. Aggregate risks to earnings from new technologies or shifts in global markets are not burdens that individuals can easily bear. We need more than laissez faire, or even Adam Smith's competitive leveling of the playing field. We need economists' creativity in devising bridges to future opportunity in disruption's wake. The structural changes call for a rethinking of training and social insurance programs. The need front and center is a richer discussion of training and social insurance as an economic response to individuals' absorbing costs of large risks from disruption beyond their control, not just to booms and busts in the economy.

We economists certainly start from a strong position. Disruptions from technological change and globalization have brought immense gains to Americans and to the world. Improvements in technology have brought wide-ranging new consumer goods (like smartphones and smart appliances), transformed work (through advances in computing and artificial intelligence), and increased current and future productivity (using automation, robotics, and artificial intelligence, for example). And openness has brought great benefits to American consumers, mostly through cheaper and more varied goods. In a widely cited study, economists Gary Clyde Hufbauer and Lucy Lu concluded that the combination of trade liberalization and cheaper transportation and communication owing to technological change increased per capita GDP by about $18,000 from 1950 to 2016.[3] In many emerging markets, notably China and India, openness has been transformational, lifting tens of millions of people out of poverty.

Economists have been too quick to celebrate these advances, making us lose sight of the downside of openness. Change has significantly reduced the prospects of workers in job categories left less valuable with new advances—in much of manufacturing, for example. Economists have recognized that these workers bear a kind of uninsurable macroeconomic risk—yet we've done little to reduce that risk. No wonder workers are frustrated, and putting that frustration into politics.

Gainers Can Compensate the Losers

Too many economists simply wave their hands and say that the gainers will compensate the losers. After all, "disruption" arguments are familiar in Econ 101. Disruptions—whether from competition (domestic or foreign) or innovation (both creative destruction of old things and nondestructive creation of new things)—have always generated "gainers" and "losers." If you think back to the exciting days of your college economics class, I am reasonably sure the professor intoned in your large lecture hall or small seminar room that such disruption makes us collectively better off, *and the gainers can compensate the losers.* Hopefully, we're ahead of the instructor in Rodney Dangerfield's class on this point: Introductory textbooks prod the professor and the students to remember it.

But have we remembered it? In the absence of real, effective programs to achieve that goal, it's no wonder the public is skeptical. Most people support free trade in general; a February 2017 NBC News/*Wall Street Journal* poll found a plurality agreeing that free trade has helped the United States. A CBS poll conducted a year earlier found that almost half of respondents said that trade restrictions destroyed jobs. Yet a 2016 Bloomberg poll asked people to choose between the costs of restricting imports and the gains of protecting jobs; protecting jobs won overwhelmingly.[4] If people favor the concept but not the reality of openness, then it's on a shaky foundation.

Let's go back to Econ 101. Why is trade good? Your professor or textbook almost surely championed classical economist David Ricardo's idea of "comparative advantage." With two countries, if each specializes in the good or goods they produce more efficiently, there are gains from trade. Incomes and consumption possibilities improve in both countries. Students and most people grasp this idea pretty quickly.

But that result is "on average," and no worker or business is exactly average. If openness to trade increases and competitiveness changes, some industries and employees within the economy will prosper; others will see their fortunes fall. That's where students and many people get nervous. As with any economic change, greater openness to trade produces both gainers and losers: Returning to Youngstown, Ohio, eliminating steel tariffs in years gone by would have reduced domestic steel company profits and employment. Of course, U.S. consumers generally and workers at the nearby automobile manufacturing plant in Lordstown would have been better off if tariffs had been eliminated. (The Lordstown plant closed partly as a consequence of the tariffs.)

If practice, like theory, shows greater *total* benefits from openness and trade, why is there a political or social problem? Not everyone wins, and they know they've lost, sometimes significantly. At least as far back as Nicholas Kaldor in 1939, economists have pointed to policy changes so the gainers can compensate the losers, but we haven't been clear about how such compensation might occur. The individual gainers, of course, are not lining up to compensate losers, whether from trade or technological change.

This lack of paying is easy to understand. Gains from openness are spread as small wins for each individual—modestly lower prices for some goods and a wider variety of goods. Losses are concentrated and significant—stagnant wages at best, falling wages or outright job loss at worse—a long-lasting bad deal for many who experience it. Losers notice costs to themselves from big risks and get frustrated, while gainers barely recognize their improvements and move on.[5]

An overarching lesson for economic policy is the greater the benefits of disruption from openness, the more gainers should compensate losers. For all the laissez-faire praise from Democratic and Republican leaders, rapid globalization since the 1990s has exposed many workers to disruption—just as globalization under the nineteenth-century gold standard failed to accommodate populist concerns for people exposed to aggregate risks. So today's globalization and technological change need a safety valve to prepare and cushion those left behind. Only with these bridges can we get the flourishing and dignity that productive engagement with the economy makes possible.

More important than individual contributions are the actions of *institutions,* public or private. Risks beyond what individuals can bear should be addressed by markets or government, and preferably by bridges. Yet the public policy debates have been muddied by two secondary arguments for walls. The first argument is that economic elites have appropriated gains from workers by not paying them for enhanced productivity. Inequality has taken off, the argument goes, because improved productivity after the 1970s went almost entirely to the owners of capital and their hired executives, not to the majority of workers. As a result, we need stronger unions and labor regulation to redress the balance.

The second argument, hearkening back to Oren Cass, is that economists' longtime focus on levels of consumption, which Adam Smith first argued for, weakens our productive capacity in the long run. Instead of maximizing consumption with openness, we should build walls to protect and maximize our levels of production—which in turn will strengthen families, communities, and corporate capabilities for long-term innovation.

Both these arguments work from real problems (rising inequality and weakening communities), are intuitive and even politically seductive. But they are wrong on the economics, and dangerously wrong because they distract us from the hard work necessary to build bridges to the future.

Start with inequality: The argument is that corporations have used openness to gain leverage over workers (now part of a global labor supply) and capture most of the gains from higher productivity. In this telling, an overreliance on openness and market forces has constrained jobs and reduced incomes. This abuse of power has deprived workers of wage gains they should have obtained from the productivity boost.

If true, such a change is worrisome, as it would violate Econ 101 precepts; if the value of a worker's contribution rises, he or she should be paid more. But it is not: Researchers from Robert Lawrence to Edward Lazear to Michael Strain to Anna Stansbury and Lawrence Summers to Scott Winship find that, properly specified, compensation and productivity have risen (and fallen) together. But while *average* compensation moves together with productivity, *median* compensation—the compensation at the 50th percentile in the middle of the earnings distribution—does not.

From the end of World War II through the mid-1970s, the U.S. economy produced strong earnings growth for workers broadly, across all skill levels, as measured by educational attainment.[6] Over that period, median compensation per hour closely tracked productivity per hour.[7]

After the 1970s, average compensation still generally tracked productivity per hour, but large differences across groups emerged, with median compensation growing much less.[8] People with high levels of education (college or post-college degrees) saw much higher gains than their counterparts with only high-school education, as they benefited from structural changes in the economy.[9]

Structural change is not the enemy of low wage growth for some

Americans. The United States has held a leadership position in innovation both before and after this period of a slow-down, arguably because this innovation requires ever higher skills.[10] We don't need to resort to claiming that college-educated workers were in cahoots with capitalists to exploit their less-skilled colleagues. Productivity gains in fact have been lower for low- and mid-skilled workers, such as factory workers, than for the highly skilled, as more highly skilled workers— software engineers or many business executives—gain more from advances in trade and technological change. So the highly skilled workers earned higher wages because their work benefited from openness to trade and technological change.[11]

As a consequence, productivity—and earnings—differences across firms and individuals are getting larger. This distinction is not just academic clarity—it's a light on potential bridges. What we most need to do is improve workers' skills to be more productive now and in the future.

As for the focus on consumption leading to a hollowing out of companies, families, and communities, this claim arises from a well-meaning focus on protecting work and jobs. In the opening chapter of *The Once and Future Worker,* Cass describes a consensus between the American center-left and center-right policy community on the "economic piety" that policy should be concerned with economic growth.[12] (So far, so good—I can say from experience that economic policy advisors on both sides intone this piety.) Provocatively, Cass poses the question: "What if people's ability to produce matters more than how much they consume?" Such a question may seem intuitive given political discourse about "jobs" and "wages." But it is very far from Econ 101's emphasis—Smith's emphasis—on consumption and consumers. Are "economists" from Mars and "real people" from Venus?

In a word, *no:* As we saw in Chapter 4, such an approach casts "jobs," not "consumption," as the star of the economic and policy show. Why not pay more for domestically produced goods or maintain extra workers even in the presence of technological advance? It might protect your neighbors' well-being, or even your own. If the public judges the economic system by its ability to supply well-paying jobs with little labor market disruption, economists since Adam Smith and David Ricardo have gotten it wrong for centuries. Hmmm . . . and you liked your economics professor!

Arguments for "productive pluralism" over economic growth are just a call for a wall of protection. They don't address Smith's view of what it takes to flourish. Rather than help prepare workers for and reconnect them to productive activity, they consign them to a dreamy world of a walled-in past. We don't need a new economics of "productive pluralism." The old economics of growth and gainers compensating losers will do nicely, and we can support low-skilled workers who bear the brunt of dislocation costs from globalization and technological change. A key point from Cass's work blames men's reduced labor force participation on the decline in manufacturing jobs in the United States. It's not entirely clear that this claim is true; some economists, including Scott Winship of the American Enterprise Institute, argue otherwise.[13] But even if it were true, the solution is not to preserve or resurrect manufacturing jobs that the economy has left behind.

Protecting manufacturing jobs in the current state of the economy means building a wall against forces so large as to overwhelm the wall over time. Service jobs are growing in importance at all levels of skill in the United States and in other industrial economies. Better to equip workers through bridges to participate in where the economy is going—that's a far better long-run solution for economic engagement and connection.

Bridges for Preparation

Bridges are great in theory, but how do they leap from textbook thoughts to policy actions? Let's start with preparation, where bridges involve the infrastructure of helping workers gain the readiness and skills for the jobs of the future. Both globalization and technological change are gradually eliminating many categories of less-skilled work in the United States, so workers need to upgrade their capabilities to compete.

Technology is the key driver, so much so that economists focus on what we obliquely, if accurately, term "skill-biased technological change." As Harvard's Claudia Goldin and Lawrence Katz have observed, wage gains and their dispersion across groups over the course of the twentieth century can be described as a "race between education and technology."[14]

Think of a contest between demand and supply. In the nineteenth century, the growth of large-scale business enterprises increased demand for more-educated workers—in those days, workers who had completed high school. This was the demand horse in the race. Because many young Americans lacked access to a full high school education—the supply horse in the race—the wage premium for a high school education rose, similar to the college wage premium now.[15]

The twentieth-century push for universal high school eventually increased the supply, driving down the high school wage premium through 1960 as well as reducing the gap between earnings of clerical and factory workers. That might have driven up the wage premium for college graduates, except more individuals were attending college as well.

However, the college wage premium has risen substantially since 1980. As Goldin, Katz, and David Autor have found, the great increase in college enrollment started slowing down after 1980. Technological change, of course, has exploded in this period (the demand side), but the economists argue convincingly that the rising wage premium has come more from the supply side, due to this slowing growth in educational attainment.[16] The supply-and-demand race is therefore an important metaphor for emphasizing gains from preparation for changing jobs, though it doesn't fully explain rising wage inequality, which has largely been a story *within* the college-educated group.

Education is clearly essential to building bridges for dislocated workers and communities. The gap between earnings growth for workers with and without college degrees has grown in most industrial economies, albeit less so than in the United States.[17] Because these changes are driven by basic economic forces of supply and demand, the United States must keep investing in skill levels and education if it wants to boost productivity—and earnings.[18]

Besides classroom-based education, we need greater training, especially on-the-job training. Much of what makes us productive and effective at work is the know-how gained from working at a job. Employees benefit from this training through greater skills and higher wages. Employers benefit from training their employees to boost productivity and efficiency. This virtuous circle of gains from training is not perfect; an employer can invest in an employee, only to see the employee go elsewhere for higher wages or some nonwage benefit. Such a concern is especially real in today's fluid labor market, in which long-term or even lifetime employment at a particular firm or organization has been replaced by much more frequent job changes.

With trade and technological change continuing as dynamic forces, we need bridges to boost skills over individuals' working lives. That means we need infrastructure fully accessible to workers, in their communities. This preparation is all the more important as the economy reallocates jobs across economic activities in the aftermath of the COVID-19 pandemic. How? The best delivery mechanisms are community colleges, public training programs, and the companies themselves. We need public policy changes to advance all three, in a flexible skills training system to meet the diverse situations of adults. Most of these mechanisms are already in place, just underfunded and underused. A recent survey estimated that about half of workers received training from their employers, and about a fifth pursued training on their own.[19] More than seven million students are enrolled in community colleges for credit courses annually, nearly half of whom are over age 22.[20] Community colleges also work with local employers to develop certificate programs for training. Federal and state job training programs supplement these efforts, though they are often poorly targeted to the needs of local employers.

Community colleges are the logical workhorses of skill development, and their local presence in regional economies makes them attractive partners for employers. Economists have found that two-year associate degrees or high-quality certification programs are enough to generate a large premium over the wages of workers who have never gone beyond high school.

Yet community colleges have seen their state-level public support wither. Many states are now experimenting with eliminating tuition charges, which does boost the demand for higher learning. But numerous studies show that institutional funding on the supply side is essential to students gaining skills and completing degree programs. Free tuition means little if your institution lacks the services to support your education toward better performance and completion. This observation is especially true for the many community colleges that serve economically vulnerable students.

Accordingly, Amy Ganz, Austan Goolsbee, Melissa Kearney, and I recently proposed a *supply-side* program of federal grants to strengthen community colleges—contingent on improved degree completion rates and labor market outcomes.[21] In contrast to calls for *demand-side* support (i.e., "free tuition"), the proposal centers on *supply-side* resources—funding—for community colleges in their skill-development mission. Inspired by Lincoln's Morrill Land Grant program, it sets the ambitious goal by 2030 of raising community college completion rates (or transfer to four-year colleges) to 60 percent—the current graduation rate for students seeking bachelor's degrees. It also aims to increase the share of Americans aged 25–64 with postsecondary credentials from 47 percent to 65 percent, the level projected to meet the economy's skill needs by 2030.

This effort isn't wishful thinking: Economists Rajashri Chakrabarti, Nicole Gorton, and Michael Lovenheim found that increased state funding of community colleges leads to increases in educational attainment and completion, along with increases in credit scores and car and homeownership.[22] We just need the federal grants to have the flexibility to work like state funding.

We estimate these grants would cost $20 billion annually. That's substantial, but still small relative to other public outlays, such as the spending to stabilize the economy in the coronavirus pandemic. And these grants are an investment for our future, so they will pay off in a more productive economy (as well as stronger society) for many years to come.

As we build up workers' skills, we need to make sure that American companies are staying competitive as the global frontier of possibilities continues to advance. Federally funded research and development through universities supports basic science and technology through which innovations in manufacturing, services, and consumer and business applications occur. Firms conduct R&D as well, but with the emphasis on the "D." A strong public commitment to research strengthens preparation of the economy for new possibilities and change; the United States needs to sustain global research preeminence to ensure mass flourishing.

Total U.S. R&D expenditure as a share of GDP has been approximately steady over the past three decades. But the public investment share—used to support basic, frontier research—has fallen sharply.[23] This pattern is important and worrisome. Companies can be quite successful in "D"—bringing new applications and technologies to market—but "R" requires greater public support.[24]

Community colleges aren't enough; companies must also help prepare their workforce for changes in work brought about by technological change and globalization. They have real-time insights into skills needed in these structural changes, and they benefit from re-skilled or up-skilled employees who continue working there. At least before the 2020 pandemic, tight labor markets gave them the additional motivation for training to retain skilled workers.

Yet changes in the employer-employee relationship over the past few decades have reduced firms' incentives to invest in workers. With people changing employers frequently, taking their skills with them, investments in training have lower returns. As a result, studies by the Council of Economic Advisers, Association for Talent Development, and Society for Human Resource Management show flat to declining workforce-training expenditures in recent years. We need to reverse that trend, especially after pandemic-induced structural change, as millions of Americans seek training for new employment.

Local public–private partnerships can help convince employers to invest. Toyota's engagement with community colleges in Kentucky has been studied and praised by many workforce specialists. Nucor Steel's efforts in northern Alabama also come to mind. The company spends up to $200,000 *per trainee* in tuition, housing assistance, and wages, an investment to increase the supply of workers with mechanical and technical skills. Local economic development authorities can even engage employers and community colleges to design ways to boost workers' ties to specific firms, to raise the likelihood that firms will benefit from their training investments. We return to this point in Chapter 8.

To further encourage training, the federal government can offer a tax credit to compensate firms for the risk of losing trained workers. This policy could work like the familiar R&D tax credit, which applies to expenditures above a base level. To focus support on low- and mid-skilled workers, the credit could cover training only for non–highly compensated workers, using the standard definition in the Internal Revenue Code.

Some states, including Connecticut, Georgia, Kentucky, Mississippi, Rhode Island, and Virginia, already provide tax incentives to firms for training investments. In Congress, Rep. Raja Krishnamoorthi introduced a training tax credit bill in the House, and Sens. Mark Warner, Bob Casey, and Debbie Stabenow did so for their chamber.

This call for firms to commit to workforce development might sound like the stakeholder capitalism of Colin Mayer, Martin Lipton, and Leo Strine described in Chapter 4.[25] Corporate governance proposals that firms report to investors and society about their workforce investment are certainly helpful.

But proposals for stakeholder capitalism usually go a step further and make firms responsible for insuring employees' skill-based technological change. Calls for firms to protect employment, however well intentioned, are just appeals for walls, walls that will harm workers as well as investors. Those walls won't restrain the tides of change, and they'll distract companies from preparing workers for the economy that is and will be.

Bridges for Reconnection

It's not enough to offer workers ways to boost their skills; they also need to support themselves while gaining those skills. If Lincoln was the embodiment of Smith's level-the-playing-field version of bridge building, another adaptation to change in American capitalism emphasizes social insurance. This is public support for individuals at risk of dropping out of the workforce due to external forces. President Franklin D. Roosevelt exemplified this approach in the Great Depression of the 1930s. He championed wage supports and unemployment insurance, bridges to weather that terrible economic storm. Without those effects, public support for capitalism might well have collapsed.[26]

Reconnection therefore depends on social insurance, the public policy tool to assist individuals bearing substantial privately uninsurable macro risks of change. Otherwise, people won't be able to commit themselves to education or retraining. As we noted earlier, at one level, the economic concept of social insurance is a familiar one in American policy. How can I insure against lost wages if I become unemployed in a recession? How can I ensure that I will have an income and health care in old age when I am no longer working? Social Security, providing social insurance for old-age incomes, and Medicare, offering social insurance for old-age health care expenditures, readily come to mind. But these programs are focused on older Americans.

Roosevelt's measures, unfortunately, no longer serve as twenty-first-century social insurance. The challenge then was the business cycle, so unemployment compensation replaced earnings lost to temporary downturns over a business cycle. FDR created the federal-state unemployment insurance program, which collects taxes from employers to pay into the system on behalf of working people who lose their job for a period of time. The program is run by states, though with supervision by and administrative costs covered by the federal Department of Labor. Benefits vary by state, but they replace about one-half of wages on average (up to a cap) for up to twenty-six weeks of unemployment. Extended benefits are available in states in which the unemployment rate has risen significantly. Benefits were raised for job losses in the immediate onset of the COVID-19 pandemic, and many economists (including me) suggested program reforms to improve worker support in sharp business cycle downturns.

During an economic downturn, whether mild as in 2001 or severe as in 2008 or 2020, unemployment insurance thus covers some of lost earnings, supporting household spending during the period of a worker's job loss. This support is good—with proper design, unemployment insurance is an effective tool of countercyclical policy, smoothing household spending over economic ups and downs.

But that is *not* the labor market insurance problem faced by many Americans from globalization and technological change. In contrast to temporary layoffs, these shifts reflect big aggregate risks—they are structural, and they lead to potentially downward shifts in employment and earnings for a long period of time, even permanently. Many people in Youngstown are unemployed across the business cycle. For this problem, unemployment insurance is a short-term palliative at best. Those workers, missing a bridge back to opportunity and work, are ripe for the calls to "build a wall."

Policymakers have long understood this problem, but with limited follow-through. President John F. Kennedy helped to pass Trade Adjustment Assistance as part of his tariff-reducing Trade Expansion Act of 1962. On paper, the TAA was a clear attempt to have gainers (taxpayers generally) compensate losers. It provided 65 percent of the wages of an affected worker (whose job loss could be tied to foreign competition) for up to a year, along with education and training support.

Unfortunately, implementation under the Johnson administration fell behind other domestic priorities. Not a single TAA request was even approved until 1969! It continues to have a few recipients, but the funding is too low and reaches too few displaced workers to make

a difference. It is also unnecessarily limited to foreign competition—
we need it to address all kinds of structural change, whatever the
cause. And if the need for skills shifts dramatically, why should one
care whether the culprit is domestic competition, a foreign competi-
tor, or technological change? TAA gathers little ongoing support from either Democrats or
Republicans. Indeed, it is not an overstatement that TAA gets atten-
tion in Washington only when policymakers consider new trade deals.
I saw this myself in both Bush administrations and in presidential
campaigns thereafter. Workers could be forgiven for seeing the measure as crumbs from Marie Antoinette's laissez-faire trade cake, merely
"transition costs," to use economists' unfortunate wording.

Public policy can and must do better here, to maintain broad
public support for openness. Otherwise we risk losing the dynamism
that comes from openness, and the mass flourishing it enables. Workers won't benefit from rising productivity if we wall them off from
the structural changes that drive most of these productivity gains.
Indeed, growth itself—expanding the economic pie—remains an
essential and primary step toward advancing incomes. If workers are,
in fact, paid for their productivity and contribution to value, economic growth is key. In the 2015 *Economic Report of the President*,
President Barack Obama's Council of Economic Advisers emphasized
that if productivity had grown from 1973 to 2013 as rapidly as it had
from 1948 to 1973, "incomes would have been 58 percent higher . . .
[and] if those gains were distributed proportionately, in 2013, the median household would have had an additional $30,000 in income."

To address continued slowing productivity growth, since 2009
economists have focused on raising business investment, boosting
competition, and supporting and disseminating basic research. Reforms here center on tax reform to increase investment, antitrust enforcement to ensure competition's vigor, and a budgetary commitment

for research. Of course, growth is not sufficient by itself for mass flourishing. A policy emphasis on preparation for and reconnection to the economy for more workers remains essential.

If growth is the necessary step, but not enough, policy should build bridges to manage risks too large for an individual to manage—we must focus on a more modern social insurance addressing today's risks to earnings and work. Five policy ideas for reconnection have emerged. The first is simply direct individual support for those whose job loss is likely long-lasting. We've developed strong social insurance programs for the elderly; why not do the same to mitigate the risks of job loss during one's working years?

"Personal Reemployment Accounts," for example, would support dislocated workers and offer them a reemployment bonus if they found a new job within a given period (such as three months). President George W. Bush proposed the accounts in 2003, but the idea never became law. As originally proposed, the Personal Reemployment Account would offer up to $3,000 for training services and support and a reemployment bonus (if a recipient gets a full-time job during the first thirteen weeks of collecting unemployment insurance benefits). The "personal" characteristic comes from individuals choosing to purchase from a range of training and support services.

Republican presidential candidate Mitt Romney proposed a similar plan in the 2012 campaign. Such ideas recognize that the current emphasis on unemployment insurance and temporary layoffs is out of step with an economy in which far greater transitions and re-skilling are needed. Recent proposals have bolstered training support more than the reemployment bonus.[27] Other ideas include onetime job training tax credits available to each worker at a time of his or her choosing. These proposals are all the more valuable with workers anxious over preparing for new jobs in the wake of the 2020–2021 pandemic.

The second idea for older workers is to consider partial *wage insurance* to offset part of the difference between wages at an old job and wages at a best-available new job. This approach addresses the problem of diminished income after structural change renders old skills less valuable, as opposed to replacing lost income during unemployment. It also confronts the fact that many laid-off workers do not reach their previous level of earnings for a period of time, if ever, which converts a spell of unemployment into long-term financial distress. A small version of this insurance operates under Trade Adjustment Assistance, but that use is narrow and has many restrictions.

Such an approach reduces the risks from dynamism for older workers who lack a long horizon to benefit from returns to different skills in the new economy. Studies of wage insurance suggest that it can prevent a near-term fall in income from becoming long-term financial distress and joblessness. By itself, though, wage insurance has limited success in reducing the length of a spell of unemployment.[28] It also requires careful design to avoid lessening the incentives for retraining and searching for newer opportunities for work.

Together with Personal Reemployment Accounts, this wage insurance would reorient U.S. labor market policy toward a bridge of broad support for return to work despite structural changes. Indeed, they could be implemented in the context of a broad policy reform of unemployment insurance.

The third idea aims to keep people engaged in low-wage work, because even these occupations often provide crucial on-the-job skill improvements and the potential for advancing in the labor market. It expands the Earned Income Tax Credit (EITC), which began in 1975 as a "work bonus" plan for families. Though the initial EITC was modest, its maximum benefits were increased by subsequent Democratic and Republican presidents. Congress extended the credit in 1993 to workers without children, a key entry-level work group to prepare for work. Twenty-nine states now supplement the federal EITC with additional credits. The idea has gone global, with Canada's refundable tax credit for low-income workers and the United Kingdom's more generous Working Tax Credit.

The current EITC is still fairly small and focused on workers with children.[29] A more generous EITC for childless workers (temporarily expanded in the American Rescue Plan Act of 2021), and a broader range of income over which the credit is phased out with higher pay (to reduce the marginal tax rate on extra income from skill acquisition and work), would help keep more people in the labor market. During the pandemic, Jason Furman, Timothy Geithner, Melissa Kearney, and I proposed expanding it on both counts.[30] Alternatively, the government could boost labor demand by subsidies to employers, as Edmund Phelps has suggested. This support for work avoids the pitfalls of job protection in the worker orientation of Oren Cass and Colin Mayer, while socializing costs of the support (gainers compensating losers).

Many working-age men and women suffering from structural change are childless. Matching their EITC to what single adults with one child receive would nearly quintuple the average credit for childless workers.[31] Hilary Hoynes and Jesse Rothstein of the University of California at Berkeley have estimated that such a policy to raise the credit for single workers with no children to that of a single worker with one child, and equalizing the phaseout rate for the credit between the two groups, would cost about $20 billion per year.[32] The federal government could also bolster low-wage incomes by raising the minimum wage. The inflation-adjusted federal minimum was essentially the same in 2020 as it was in 1950, and it has fallen by 35 percent in inflation-adjusted terms since 1979.[33]

A fourth potential intervention is place-based aid, targeting assistance to areas such as Youngstown with stubbornly high rates of long-term nonemployment. Economists have traditionally been skeptical of this aid (jobs-to-people ideas), favoring encouragement to geographic mobility (people-to-jobs ideas). But declines in geographic mobility, and pronounced regional differences in employment rates and earnings mobility, have prompted a second look. Benjamin Austin, Edward Glaeser, and Lawrence Summers, for example, have called for tailoring policies such as the EITC to bolster returns to working in areas with high nonemployment.[34] Such labor market support, they argue, could be complemented by supply-side investment in local community college education, as described earlier.

This place-based aid could include incentives for revived mobility to areas with better opportunity and productivity. While many personal, family, and uncertainty considerations may limit mobility, moving was once much more common.[35] About one-fifth of the U.S. population moved every year in the 1950s, a figure about cut in half today.[36] For our purposes here, such mobility is especially valuable to lower-skill workers, who could reduce their wage gap relative to higher-skill workers by moving to more vibrant, growing areas.[37] Depending on the area, such moves can boost children's income mobility as well.[38]

The federal government has experimented with programs to offer a lump-sum payment to eligible individuals accepting a full-time job in a new area. The Moving the Opportunity program in 1994 covered five metropolitan areas—Baltimore, Boston, Chicago, Los Angeles, and New York City. Results were mixed, perhaps because the subsidies were too low.[39]

Place-based aid can also piggyback on other policy concerns. In addition to its desirability as part of a policy agenda of preparation and connection, place-based aid can ride a wave of policy action already underway. Two areas of current policy effort or discussion come to mind: the enactment of "opportunity zones," and discussions of "just transitions" for communities in the economy's decarbonization to combat global warming.[40] While the former came from center-right support and the latter from center-left, neither is particularly partisan and both could serve to expand federal place-based aid for structural economic changes generally.

Opportunity Zones were part of the Tax Cut and Jobs Act of 2017. While reducing overall tax rates and restructuring taxes on overseas operations for corporations, the law reduced taxes on economically distressed communities. Plans for zones are now in place in all fifty states, with states nominating blocks of low-income areas by census tract, which must then be certified by the U.S. Treasury Department. With a zero tax on capital gains on investments held for at least ten years, the goal is to amplify returns and draw capital to areas short of investment. To be effective in our context here, eligible zones should match areas of structural economic change where new investment can "crowd in" other investments.

To work as reconnection, this place-based aid must meet an infrastructure and workforce prepared to receive it profitably. Too often this is not the case. Older "Empowerment Zones" in the 1990s therefore supported low-wage work through wage credits and block grants for infrastructure. Today, the federal government has a patchwork quilt of regional assistance through the Department of Agriculture (Rural Development Programs, Rural Utility Service, and Rural Cooperative Service), Department of Commerce (Economic Development Administration along with TAA), Department of Defense (Industry Resilience Program in response to base closures or terminated weapons programs), and the Small Business Administration (through loan-guarantee programs). Funding for these programs is modest, and we need greater coordination across them and with local governments and development authorities to support reconnection for dislocated workers.[41]

Likewise, policies to decarbonize the U.S. economy will speed up structural change in areas focused on fossil-fuel extraction, a dislocation already apparent in coal country. The scale of this effort will require a significant expansion in place-based aid initiatives, and some affected areas match those already suffering from technological change and globalization. Researchers have found evidence for success in federal efforts in some areas (as in the Department of Agriculture and in economic and educational infrastructure programs), and the global warming and climate change debates will drive further discussion. Success is greater for federal programs when coordinated with state and local efforts.[42] For our purposes here, we could combine this support with retraining initiatives at community colleges and with R&D partnerships at universities.

Place-based aid from the federal government would be delivered via flexible block grants. For about $30 billion, estimates Timothy Bartik of the Upjohn Institute, support for local areas could bring employment rates in the bottom quartile by area to the median.[43] We return to how such an initiative might be executed in Chapter 8.

Fifth, reconnection must address access to health care, which is often tied to employment. By adjusting tax subsidies to health care, we can achieve universal catastrophic health insurance. By expanding savings arrangements for middle-income individuals, and other public programs for lower-income people, we can mobilize funds for deductibles and copayments. Broader coverage in this way reduces barriers to changing jobs, a perennial problem in the U.S. health care system that was magnified in the 2020 pandemic. It also would encourage greater employment generally, because employers would no longer have to cover rising health care costs. These higher costs reduce compensation funds available to pay wages, contributing to take-home earnings stagnation for many workers. And to the extent wages are constrained (by minimum-wage laws or competitive forces), the higher health benefit costs reduce labor demand for low- and mid-skill jobs.

These tax changes can help discourage inefficient health care spending and raise take-home pay, as economists John Cogan, Daniel Kessler, and I have argued.[44] We showed that heavy demand-side subsidies for health insurance as well as supply-side restrictions in health insurance markets have inflated firms' health care costs.

These five ideas work as bridges because they offer only temporary support, aimed at bringing people to the point where they can flourish on their own. That's quite different from another kind of social insurance: universal basic income (UBI), which would last indefinitely. Supporters—including Milton Friedman, Charles Murray, Richard Nixon, and now Andrew Yang—have touted UBI as a way to simplify transfer payments and even as a road to the self-actualization described by Abraham Maslow. UBI is now getting serious attention in the Biden administration. But UBI is focused on income, not workforce participation, and it ignores the social aspects of attachment to work. Just like calls to protect jobs, UBI is a policy wall separating dislocated individuals from new opportunities.

From an economic perspective, advancing in skills and earnings almost always builds on experience and training on the job—in work. UBI proponents say that it will enable struggling workers to better participate in dynamism. But from a social and political perspective, these transfer payments would create a dangerous insider/outsider economy. The dislocation insurance described above would be temporary and targeted, while UBI would apply to everyone on an ongoing basis, reducing incentives to engage in the workforce.

The five policy interventions outlined here represent a significant federal policy pivot toward bridges of preparation and reconnection, as summarized in the accompanying box. They also represent a substantial commitment of taxpayer resources. However, at a cost of less

Bridges

Community college block grants	Enhance skills and provide retraining; raise skill levels to those needed in the U.S. economy by 2030.
Personal Reemployment Accounts	Provide individual support for reskilling in the presence of long-term job loss.
Wage insurance	Makes up a portion of lost wages for older workers experiencing structural job loss.
Earned Income Tax Credit expansion	Increases the EITC for childless workers to offer a more potent work subsidy for entry-level workers.
Place-based aid block grants	Offer a flexible block grant to distressed communities to bolster business services to facilitate job creation.
Health care tax reform	Changes tax subsidies for health insurance to promote insurance coverage and portability across jobs, while reducing costs in forgone wages.

These bridges of preparation and reconnection enhance economic participation on top of policies to promote economic growth. They are alternatives to walls of protection.

than $100 billion per year, the expenditures are not large relative to cyclical spending increases in a recession or to the large-scale fiscal support provided during and in the aftermath of the coronavirus pandemic. For reference, federal spending in (prepandemic) 2019 was $4.4 trillion dollars. Even at spending of $1 trillion over a decade, bridge programs would be cheaper than the cost of forgiving federal student loan debt (about $1.5 trillion) or the ten-year cost of reducing the U.S. corporate tax rate from 35 percent to 21 percent in the Tax Cut and Jobs Act of 2017 (about $1.5 trillion). I return to the policy and budget framing for bridge initiatives in Chapter 8.

Back to Econ 101

Shifts in employment and earnings prospects from globalization and technological change have been unsettling millions of Americans. Many people are exposed to macro risks against which they cannot insure. Their frustration leads them to call for walls of protection from these market forces—walls that will hurt everyone in the long run. So we need creative ways to address these risks without isolating us from the manifold benefits of these structural changes.

The counterargument to calls for walls can't be just extolling by economists and politicians of laissez-faire gains. Econ 101 suggests a focus on skill development and more modern social insurance. The ideas outlined here will get more detail in the next two chapters. But it's worth mentioning that they largely apply beyond the United States.

Brexit gained appeal in Britain partly because of the unevenness in gains from openness, along with the perception that openness required an unacceptable surrender of economic sovereignty. Votes for Brexit (as for Donald Trump in the United States) occurred during a cyclical recovery with low unemployment, yet with structural forces that still left many workers behind. In France and Italy, an overweening welfare state crowds out fiscal space to connect more individuals to work of the present and the future. In the United Kingdom and the European Union, people perceive that elites—business leaders, officials and technocrats, and economists—lack ground-level experience with the economic forces they celebrate.

Political discussions outside the United States are thus stuck on walls of protection to keep challenged workers at bay. Calls for walls to protect workers, firms, and industries have only increased as political leaders struggle to cope with economic devastation from the 2020–2021 pandemic. The lack of bridges continues to fan the flames of populist calls for walls, raising concerns about business prospects and the market economic system in the process.

Populist calls for walls have been accompanied in many countries—including the United States—by pushback against contributions of expertise and experience in economic policymaking. This pushback should concern us for two reasons. First, building effective bridges requires careful reasoning and analysis.

Second, and much more important, the broad public support required for capitalism's dynamics requires both the actual bridge building and a language from economists that frames it. We don't need a new economics. But phrases like "transition cost" or "human capital" or "inevitable economic forces" must give way to bridges of connection and reconnection. More economists need to step up here, both to ground their theories in the real world of economic anxieties and to offer creative ideas for bridges.

Abraham Lincoln worked to build bridges to prepare people for opportunity; Franklin Roosevelt used bridges to reconnect many people amid disruption. Mass flourishing and the preservation of American capitalism need this full mix today.

7

Business as a Bridge Builder

Rochester, New York, is a storied American city on the Erie Canal in upstate New York. With 206,000 people today, it has many sources of renown. One visionary businessperson is at the heart of many of them, George Eastman.

Born in 1854, Eastman had a prominent career in business and philanthropy until his death in 1932. Inventor of convenient photographic film and the instamatic camera in the 1880s, he formed Eastman Kodak (along with Henry Strong) in 1892. With more than just a "Kodak moment," the company dominated the film industry for decades.

As Eastman and Kodak prospered, so too did the firm's workers and Rochester. At its peak, Kodak employed 60,400 people in Rochester, more than the other top three employers (the University of Rochester, Rochester Regional Health, and Wegmans grocery stores) combined, and had more than twice that many employees worldwide. Rochester felt Kodak's prosperity through the company's presence but also through the civic involvement of Eastman and the firm. The city houses the Eastman School of Music at the University of Rochester, which benefited as well from the entrepreneur's founding support of its dental school and as the sole beneficiary of Eastman's estate.[1]

Yet Eastman didn't rest on his technological head start. He also built bridges for his employees and the overall city of Rochester. A leading voice for what came to be called "welfare capitalism," he devised several benefit programs such as profit sharing for all employees in 1910. Three years later he set up his company's health insurance fund (to which employees also contributed) with an unusually generous $1 million donation.

His appointment of Florence McAnaney as head of Kodak's personnel department was one of the first executive roles for a woman in a major U.S. corporation.[2] These efforts helped employees (many of them from farms similar to his father's) transition to the company and develop habits of industrial and clerical life.

Eastman also focused on business's role in the knowledge frontier. Along with large gifts to the University of Rochester, Eastman was a major benefactor of the Massachusetts Institute of Technology. Over the period from 1912 to 1920, Eastman—anonymously, as "Mr. Smith"—contributed the funds to build MIT's main campus when it moved from Boston to Cambridge in 1920; he also supported its Chemistry Department.[3]

Eastman saw his business as a generator of profits and opportunity for himself, investors, and other stakeholders. A century later, businesses can do the same.

Companies have been a vital supporting player in the battle between walls and bridges. Entrepreneurs and, later, larger-scale business organizations have been engines of innovation and disruption, job creation and destruction, and opportunity and promise. Classical economists like Adam Smith valued business's openness to change and to trade and specialization. Getting the most out of business required competition for markets, customers, and workers, with government on the lookout for attempts to restrain trade. Such restraints would limit the mass prosperity and flourishing that open commerce could generate.

Welfare capitalism notwithstanding, for the most part, businesses have not built bridges themselves. They've left that to local communities and governments. But businesses can—and should—help build bridges now, to promote preparation for and reconnection to the economy. Those bridges can breathe life into the spread of prosperity and mass flourishing that Adam Smith imagined, and avoid walls that can snuff out gains from change, as with today's forces of technological change and globalization.

Shareholders or Society?
The Purpose of Corporations

Eastman Kodak and other large companies at the turn of the twentieth century invested in employees in order to develop a large and reliable workforce faster than markets or governments could do on their own. What is their equivalent responsibility now, especially as it pertains to building bridges?

In building bridges, business can expand the trust it has with the public. In prepandemic January 2020, the Edelman Trust Barometer survey found a large perception advantage for business over government in being good at what it does and solving problems. Nongovernmental organizations (NGOs) scored better than business as well as government in doing the right thing. The public sees an important role for business in preparing workers for better opportunities and wages. While business has the edge over government in accomplishing this objective, the Edelman survey also indicates the value of business partnerships with government. And then in May 2020, as the pandemic dominated the economy and the news, a subsequent Edelman survey saw improvements in trust for both business and especially government. Warning signs for large corporations and their leaders came from only a minority believing that such businesses were inadequately focused on their employees' jobs and training. Such concerns can fuel calls for greater public intervention in business to protect jobs, walls that the economy and business can ill afford.

But what is business to do here? Business leaders, like individuals generally, can and often do express social concern. That's good, and business leaders' voices are sought after and command public and political respect. There's a deeper point—business leaders should have an incentive collectively to build bridges of preparation and reconnection for workers and communities. Those bridges build businesses and business in society.

The Business Roundtable (BRT) is a forum for CEOs headquartered in a tiny space in Washington, D.C. In 2019, it put out a *Statement on the Purpose of the Corporation*. With the affable and knowledgeable Joshua Bolten, a former George W. Bush administration official, in charge and CEOs like Jamie Dimon (JPMorgan Chase), Alex Gorsky (Johnson & Johnson), and Mark Weinberger (E&Y) with the pen, the Roundtable issued a seemingly radical pronouncement.

After reminding the reader of the vital role of business in providing goods and services, innovation, and jobs, 181 of the Roundtable CEOs said corporations should commit to serving all stakeholders. Shareholders, the owners of corporations ("residual claimants" to the profits of the firm, in econ-speak), came at the end of the statement. Preceding their interests are: "Delivering value to our customers . . . Investing in our employees . . . Dealing fairly and ethically with our suppliers . . . and . . . Supporting the communities in which we work."

The statement was noteworthy because it seemed to depart from the Roundtable's 1997 pronouncement that "the principal objective of a business enterprise is to generate economic returns to its owners." The shift seemed consistent with the call for corporate "purpose" by Laurence Fink, the CEO of investment giant BlackRock, a major shareholder of most firms, and elected officials on the left and the right.

To some, this restatement struck a chord. Intoned Darren Walker, the influential president of the Ford Foundation, "It will require that corporations operate in the words of the BRT 'for the benefit of all stakeholders.' . . ."[4] Politicians from Democratic senator Elizabeth Warren to Republican senator Marco Rubio have joined the stakeholder chorus. By contrast, writing with former Secretary of State George Shultz, Stanford University economists Michael Boskin, John Cogan, and John Taylor wrote: "The statement lends credence to an incorrect view of the way American business operates in today's economy . . . and it fails to consider the practical, real-world, adverse consequences of demoting shareholders' interests."[5]

The tension between the two BRT pronouncements turns out to be straightforward to reconcile, while leaving an important loose end. But *plus ça change, plus c'est la même chose.* Let's start with reconciliation. Fifty years ago, Milton Friedman, later a Nobel laureate in economics, famously argued that corporate governance should maximize shareholder value.[6] This idea became dominant among economists and corporate governance practitioners, and it seems to take one side of the tension we highlighted.

Or does it? On the one hand, Friedman seems to say that the business of business is business. Managers and boards owe a duty to shareholders, full stop, to maximize the equity value of the firm. There is no broader corporate responsibility to achieve social objectives. Instead, shareholders could use the profits of the corporation for social purposes if they wished, less wastefully and perhaps with less self-interest than if management pursued such activities. Bill Gates, having founded a very successful company, Microsoft, didn't force his executives to launch major charitable efforts. Instead, he cashed in some of his shares and engaged in significant philanthropic activities around the globe.

Yet Friedman's guidance is less restrictive than it seems. First, in competitive markets, firms must satisfy stakeholders like workers, suppliers, and customers in order to stay in business. If not treated fairly, customers won't buy a firm's products or services; suppliers won't do business with it; and workers won't sign up or engage productively. Regulations also govern corporate behavior in these areas.

Consider, for example, the operational and human resource investments that many U.S. corporations made during the COVID-19 pandemic. Of the 100 largest U.S. corporations, sixty-nine made drastic changes to employee work schedules to safeguard employee health, and sixty-two boosted their contributions to their communities. These activities are still consistent with Friedman's investorcentric paradigm. Given that these activities were voluntary, managers can consider them in the long-term interest of their shareholders.

Further, Friedman intended that corporate leaders maximize the *long-term* value of the firm. Companies can bolster short-term shareholder returns at the expense of long-term value or viability—say, by cutting product development expenses to buy back shares today. But Friedman explicitly granted boards of directors the leeway to evaluate management on its stewardship of the firm's value *over time,* with attendant trade-offs. While excessive managerial "short-termism" in corporate finance is debatable,[7] nothing in Friedman's dictum precludes a focus on the long term for shareholder value maximization. He even noted: "It may well be in the long-run interest of a corporation that is a major employer in a small community to devote resources to providing amenities to that community or to improving its government."[8] So the Business Roundtable's restatement may serve more as a reminder of long-standing corporate concerns than as a rethinking of corporate purpose.

Focusing on long-term shareholder value maximization therefore does not imply a tolerance for poorly treating nonshareholder stakeholders or, worse, expropriating value from them. Even putting aside regulatory or legal constraints, executives and directors acting in shareholders' interest will want to preserve valuable relationships with stakeholders.

Another concern with the Business Roundtable's statement is that it is difficult for leaders of a firm to maximize more than one objective. On a practical level, operationalizing and measuring commitments to stakeholders can promote long-term shareholder value. Under the stakeholder paradigm, what management expenditure of corporate resources, short of malfeasance, couldn't be construed as addressing the priorities of *some* stakeholder?

Many corporate activities generate positive value for both a corporation's shareholders and other stakeholders. When might gains diverge? Perhaps product or labor markets are not competitive. But if true, the problem is more one for public policy action than for business decision making. Another potential divergence could arise if executives, acting on behalf of shareholders, focused on short-term corporate performance, while stakeholders focused more on the long-term impact of a company's action.

Some critics argue nevertheless that as companies have focused on shareholders, they have tended to sacrifice long-term goals for short-term results. Indeed, corporations can be encouraged to focus on the long-term value maximization that Milton Friedman intended. We can encourage long-term value maximization without overhauling corporate purpose. To align management decisions with long-run corporate interests, University of Colorado economist Sanjai Bhagat and I suggest compensating senior corporate executives and corporate directors with shares of stock (or stock options) that cannot be sold until a year or two after executives or board members leave the company.[9] Such a change would lead executives and directors to internalize costs in lost longer-term value from pursuing activities that pop value in the short-run, while diminishing it later.

More broadly, putting aside public policy and regulation, who should decide on a corporation's stand on a particular social issue? Shareholders could, of course, vote on the particular issue; though if shares are widely dispersed among many small shareholders, questions arise of whether they know their best interest and whether they would vote accordingly. Alternatively, arguing for "shareholder welfare maximization," Nobel laureate Oliver Hart and Luigi Zingales point to the greater ease of assembling shareholdings due to the prominence of concentrated shareholdings by institutional investors, and those investors' fiduciary requirement for long-run value maximization.[10] As Hart and Zingales note, a firm could set in its charter a mission of long-term value maximization, allowing a shareholder vote to change it later. But enforcing a new fiduciary duty of institutional investors—to maximize benefits to shareholders rather than investors—may be difficult in practice.

Corporate Bridges of Training

Whether companies ally with Friedman's perspective or the advocates of stakeholder capitalism, it's clear that they can legitimately invest in workforce development and reskilling for their long-term good.[11] Ideally, they would support programs open to people who are not current employees, to help dislocated and other marginalized workers who might join them in the future. And to maximize impact, they would engage with local educational institutions and governments to ensure a good supply of skilled workers for high-quality jobs.

But even programs for internal development can serve as a bridge, such as upskilling employees for digitization. Two key questions: What financial support can the firm provide in corporate training funds or tuition reimbursement to raise employee skills and wages? And what particular engagement with local educational institutions and governments can the firm pursue to guide investments in communities to ensure a good supply of skilled workers for high-quality jobs? While corporate philanthropy may certainly play a role, the questions cut to the *business* of the corporation. Friedman's emphasis on long-term shareholder value maximization puts workforce investment squarely on the table. An annual report to the board of directors, led by a designated director or board committee, would help maintain board- and CEO-level commitment and generate investor interest and questions.

Some individual businesses are already engaged in this effort, in high-profile and commercially valuable ways. That is, the actions are in the interests of the businesses that take them. AT&T, for example, uses its Workforce 2020 program to prepare current employees for emerging jobs with greater compensation. Training is mainly online, while offering credentials valued by AT&T—and other employers— in the form of virtual badges. Matching skills and jobs in local areas is key to the initiative's success.

Walmart, under CEO Doug McMillon, has invested substantially in employee skills and reskilling to attract and retain talent and improve productivity. While Wall Street initially greeted these investments with skepticism, the company pressed on with its initiatives as being in the long-run value interest of its investors. The job transformation both helped the firm add technology in its retail operations and gave employees valuable digital skills. Much of the training happened on-site, with virtual reality and gamification as tools. By 2019, the company believed its investments had raised skills, wages, and productivity, now with more support from Wall Street.[12]

Bigger bridges can occur at the industry level. Back in 2006, utility companies founded the Center for Energy Workforce Development (CEWD) to close the skills gap in mid-skill occupations such as technicians and operators. The center identified needed skills, designed curriculum and credentials, and developed best practices for individual utilities to use in working with local educational institutions. About half of U.S. jobs are mid-skill, and in 2018, there were more mid-skill job openings than workers to fill them.[13] And the jobs paid well, with good entry-level pay and pathways to even more highly paid positions.

CEWD's success led utilities to a renewed effort to identify educational partnerships to prepare and reskill workers. Evaluation centered on what has worked, emphasizing clear pathways to jobs and a focused curriculum design with community colleges.[14]

These jobs don't require four-year college degrees; people can gain skills and work experience that qualify them for many middle-wage and even some higher-wage jobs—"STARS" workers (Skilled through Alternative Routes), as defined by some researchers.[15] Those researchers identify 70 million U.S. jobs for non-college-degree holders who, based on skill and experience, could be positioned for higher-paying work. This upskilling offers a bridge for workers whose previous jobs have been adversely affected by structural changes in technology and globalization. For businesses, the focus on neighboring skills and retraining provides a richer pipeline of talent for jobs of today and tomorrow.

Business and other sources of private philanthropy can support and nurture educational interventions, like the comprehensive services model to encourage student completion in community colleges discussed in Chapter 6. For example, the Stay the Course program at Tarrant County College in Texas in collaboration with Catholic Charities, Fort Worth, has been successful at encouraging completion. Groups of local businesses could provide related funding and mentor support.[16] In Chicago, the nonprofit One Million Degrees program offers comprehensive support for community colleges. Its effectiveness can also serve as a model for business philanthropy and volunteerism.[17]

Companies can also collaborate nationally to raise the skills of low-wage workers, potentially benefiting all firms. The Rework America Alliance, formed by the Markle Foundation, draws on business partners like Google, IBM, Microsoft, McKinsey & Company, and Workday, along with public interest groups like the National Urban League and educational institutions and platforms like Arizona State University and EdX. Alliance partners support workers to identify practical training that builds on individual experience and specific job aspirations. McKinsey provides analytics to identify job paths for workers to improve their earnings based on their skills.

During the COVID-19 pandemic, for example, McKinsey constructed a data set of more than 60 million anonymized talent profiles and job histories combined with 150 million job postings. Using these data, McKinsey studied transitions of individuals who built skills and wages. Key gateway jobs out of low-wage work emerged in technology, health care, and business management. The consultancy urged employers to take a skills-centered, not just a degree-centered, view of candidates. With these bridges, companies are acting as a force for good as well as in their own long-term interest.

The Business Roundtable's CEOs have promoted workforce training and support. In particular, the CEOs urge expanding the eligibility for federal financial aid to students in nondegree, industry-recognized certification programs. They've likewise lobbied Congress to allow federal work-study funds to be used for off-campus experiences to obtain better work-related business skills. Within their own organizations, they have committed to raising starting wage scales to augment employees' economic security as they gain skills on the job.

Company commitment to supporting employee engagement is a big deal for the "mass flourishing" purpose I highlight here. Such volunteerism bolsters engagement in the community by employees and the firm, and it fosters a "we're all in it together" spirit. That spirit also redounds to the value of the business enterprise.

Such intervention by businesses is not limited to direct business concerns like workforce development or economic participation by more individuals in the economy. Broader social issues and social justice can also be on the table. For example, in 2020, the Business Roundtable threw the weight of its corporate-chieftain membership at police reform in the United States, a topic with broad criminal justice and social justice implications. The BRT advocated police engagement with communities, data collection, transparency for detentions and the use of force on suspects, and accountability of individual police officers and entire police departments. This advocacy has stimulated bipartisan congressional and state-level support for investing in programs to increase police force diversity and change.

Businesses can also come together to support new sources of talent. A key group for revived participation is incarcerated individuals. At Columbia University, where I teach, the Tamer Center for Social Enterprise works with employers to provide jobs through its Re-Entry Acceleration Program. Business school students pitch in to assist with training, and employers offer careers and mentorship. The program is scalable around the country with business support.

These business efforts are all promising. But there's a loose end, the "free rider" problem—and it's important, especially for business's role as a bridge builder. If Company A invests a lot in workers, Company B may benefit without making the investment. If Company C invests in community amenities, neighboring Company D can enjoy them without paying for them. To encourage companies to still make these investments, we need outside coordination. Governments might award tax credits for training, especially to nonemployees. Community colleges, economic development agencies, or even local business associations might partner with willing local companies to defray much of the cost.

Another solution is to train for specific skilled jobs in local areas. Amazon announced in 2019 a goal to raise skills substantially for one-third of its workforce—100,000 people—by 2025, emphasizing the critical importance of training in pushing upward mobility for employees. Its warehouses, for example, were adding technologies that required new skills from employees in emerging jobs. The company expected to invest $700 million, with a significant financial return in greater productivity. As part of the initiative, it is using evolving Bureau of Labor Statistics job data to determine new job categories and work with community colleges to give potential employees skills to match those jobs. It focuses on training local workers for local jobs. Amazon knows the free-rider problem has not gone away, but it still believes that this training pays.[18]

Likewise, in the early 2000s, the defense contractor Northrop Grumman worked with community colleges and cooperative education programs in Newport News, Virginia. It launched an internal apprenticeship program for low-skilled workers in its increasingly sophisticated ship-building program. Students who showed particular aptitude received full tuition for an associate's degree in mechanical engineering or computer-aided drafting and design. The company has retained more than 2,500 graduates from the apprenticeship program, many of whom received associate's degrees. Matching skills to particular jobs in demand has contributed to the firm's success.[19]

Besides tax credits, governments can encourage corporate collaboration through some direct policy actions. Antitrust and antimonopoly rules, for example, might be altered to enable companies to collaborate in building bridges to enhance competition for employees and raise wages. Corporate tax policy might be changed to affect levels of corporate profitability, location decisions, wages paid to workers, or incentives to invest.

Bridges to Sustain Dynamic Capitalism

These public policy interventions would still be a complement to, not a substitute for, long-term shareholder value maximization. Indeed, companies can better justify helping with bridges than with grander, tougher social problems such as climate change. Preventing global warming, for example, requires societies and businesses to reduce carbon in the atmosphere and adapt to evolving changes in surface temperatures. Investors could and should press corporations to disclose more information about the exposure of their long-term value to climate change, and corporations may act to reduce emissions and increase their adaptability toward long-term value maximization. That step is an extension of a market process and response. But that step alone will not resolve negative externalities from effects of business activities on climate change.

Significant changes to combat global warming and climate change require *public policy* changes in the United States and abroad, say, a carbon tax or alternative-energy technology subsidies. *Will* public policy play this needed role? While some of this concern reflects populist opposition to big business in response to perceived uneven gain sharing from structural changes in technology and globalization and policy responses to the 2007–2009 financial crisis, the concern's roots may deepen given the unprecedented and devastating economic impact of the ongoing COVID-19 pandemic. With political dysfunction, social challenges are going unmet, so why not turn to corporations and their leaders for progressive action on dislocated workers? But those problems involve such extensive externalities and spillovers as to require government intervention on top of business involvement.

Turning to corporations, because the political process seems broken and makes little progress, won't do.

Building bridges is enough of a social responsibility for companies—and it comes with an extra incentive, given the attacks on capitalism nowadays. Friedman takes social support for capitalism for granted, saying companies are subject only to economic production constraints (back to your Econ 101 course again) and to "law and ethical custom," in his words.

Structural changes from technology and globalization have led to skepticism about the market economy's ability to deliver goods inclusively. Businesses will find it in their own interest to invest in a skilled workforce, and perhaps in communities where they operate as well. As Adam Smith observed, the market economy and its dynamism are in part a social construct. Business and its leaders should not and cannot take public support for granted. If business does not champion bridges, it will be met with walls—of protectionism, of limits to flexibility and change, or of outright limits to profits and control.

Deep down, we are left with a complex question: What are the boundaries between what business and the market economy should do and what the state should handle? The controversy is old and traces back to Adam Smith's description of the capitalist wealth machine in *The Wealth of Nations*.

Smith argued forcefully against mercantilist tinkering by the state, as we analyzed in Chapter 3. His point was that competitive firms operating in markets open to change produced the largest potential surplus of any economic system—and hence higher living standards for citizens to spend on goods and services, the "wealth of a nation." Smith held out roles for the state as providing public goods such as national defense or institutions of justice, financed by taxation, as well as enforcement of competition. Economic historians in the Smithian tradition add to government's list the legal institutions of property rights, contract law, and an independent judiciary. While not strict laissez faire, Smith's "invisible hand" market mechanism sets out business in the "max this, subject to that" lane that Friedman traveled 200 years later.

While the state has taken on responsibility for macroeconomic fluctuations, health care, inequality in earnings or wealth, and old-age consumption, our focus here has been on the management of structural change. Seen as a problem of social insurance, these changes amount to hard-to-bear aggregate risks for individuals.

If we interpret Friedman's "subject to law and ethical custom" constraint on profit maximization as encompassing social support for the market economy, business should build bridges to opportunity in its own long-term interest. But it should also push for—and be willing to help pay for—larger public action to build bridges to broader prosperity. That push can come through business organizations' advocacy of mass-flourishing policies with elected officials.

After World War II, for example, American companies pushed hard for the Marshall Plan for Europe and then shepherded its implementation. Fearful of walls of statism, they helped Europeans reconnect to market prosperity. Today's challenges from technological change and globalization pose a similar need for bridge building championed by business.

This bridge-building role for business takes us back full circle to George Eastman, who stretched the limits of business practices in twentieth-century industrial life. He did much good for himself, for Kodak, and for his shareholders. He also nurtured progress in Rochester and the frontiers of science at MIT. Eastman and Kodak built bridges. He focused on internal employee development as well as funding higher education.

Today's business leaders need to follow suit. Removing barriers to participation and prosperity in the economy is vital for mass flourishing and support for our economic system. Businesspeople—through the Business Roundtable or the U.S. Chamber of Commerce or the Committee for Economic Development or more local organizations—must press for changes that prepare people for and reconnect them to the economy.

Those changes have broad impacts, not just for a specific firm or group of firms, but thoughtful business leaders will see those broad impacts as precisely the point. Collectively, they are pushing for more extensive sharing of gains from dynamism—and for support for dynamism. Much more than the *Statement on the Purpose of the Corporation,* that effort could be the next "Kodak moment" for companies.

8

Governments and Bridges

As described in Chapter 6, President Lincoln showed leadership in supporting the Morrill Act of 1862. This legislation funneled funds from federal land sales to new and existing state colleges across the country. But government-funded bridges such as these are inherently political and subject to forces less relevant to bridges initiated by business. The Morrill Act that provided federal support for land-grant colleges is a great example of building bridges.

Land-grant colleges evolved to provide skills for jobs in an economy undergoing structural change, from agriculture to manufacturing and from smaller to larger business organizations. They also broadened access to higher education for students of modest means and women, while offering extension services to communities.[1] The Morrill Act was both a great success and a cautionary tale. Interest groups worked to turn it into a battle between building bridges to the present and future and erecting walls to protect the past. Especially as we focus today on increased support for training and skill enhancement, the tension in the evolution of land-grant colleges is an important one.[2]

The University of Vermont, founded in 1792, was designated a land-grant college under the Morrill Act. It therefore taught "such branches of learning related to agriculture and the mechanical arts . . . in order to promote the liberal and professional education of the industrial classes." In the aftermath of the depression of the 1870s, with falling crop prices, Vermont farmers protested new industries and their symbols in railroads, banks, and the land-grant colleges that honed educational pathways beyond farming. Organizing as Patrons of Husbandry (or "the Grange"), they opposed curricula that they blamed for depopulating rural areas. In 1888, they took their protests directly to the Vermont state legislature.[3]

Matthew Buckham, the university's president, drew an ace in the hole—university trustee Justin Morrill, who as senator in Congress had led the land-grant college movement from idea to law. The 80-year-old Morrill told the legislature that the act deliberately provided education not just to those individuals pursuing farming but also for those aiming at industry. He also saw the production of scientific knowledge as a key objective.

Morrill followed up with an editorial in the *Burlington Free Press* defending an expansive view of land-grant colleges' objectives. Alpha Masser, the Vermont Grange leader, argued that land-grant colleges should be protective of rural communities in decline. But Morrill's forceful defense discouraged the legislature from putting limits on the university.[4]

Farmers protested land-grant colleges in much of the rest of the North and in Washington, but failed to remove the language on industrial education. Instead, Congress worked out an elegant compromise: It separately funded short courses and extension services in rural counties, often staffed by faculty from the land-grant colleges. Land-grant colleges persevered and prospered as bridges, smoothing America's passage to an industrial capitalist economy. Those institutions also advanced science and technology, including blazing trails in scientific agriculture. Instead of erecting an agricultural wall against wrenching structural change in the economy, the colleges prospered through imparting useful knowledge, supporting established as well as newer communities. As they balanced these competing demands, they brought together the missions of teaching, research, and service, which remain core to institutions of higher education in the United States.

We need bridges to future work because individuals can't manage the risk of disruption on their own. Social institutions must therefore provide bridges. Because of the challenges laid out in the previous chapter, we need governments to take on much of the responsibility for them—while partnering with the business and nonprofit sectors to ensure success.

From the classical economists to neoliberal champions of economic openness to change, capitalism's upsides—innovation, dynamism, and higher living standards—have acknowledged an important complication. Openness brings change—change that can disrupt businesses, individuals, and communities. But policy debates today can seem like a tired tennis match between a laissez-faire acceptance of change and questioning capitalism's economic, and even moral, foundations entirely. That change is as old as a caricature of Adam Smith versus Karl Marx. And now populists are crying out for walls, with elected officials clamoring to meet them.

For Adam Smith, government's main role in building bridges was to promote fair and open competition. Businesses would have to compete—and compete fairly—for customers, employees, profits, and markets. Openness to trade, specialization, and new ways of making things and doing business was, of course, also important. This view was not simple laissez-faire, because Smith wanted government to prevent unfair trading or commercial practices without regulatory thumbs on the scale. Likewise, two centuries later, Milton Friedman saw government as mainly an umpire.

But there's more than competition in product markets and financial markets. An emphasis on "competition" assumes we *all* can compete, that we are all prepared to compete, and that we can reenter the competition if we get knocked out. It assumes no barriers to participation in the productive economy, nor any barriers to prospering in it. Today's economy is more complex than Smith's, and many people are struggling to fit their labor into markets. We need government to build bridges to prepare them for and reconnect them to an open economy.

This need is all the more urgent with the COVID-19 pandemic. To "participate" means to have the skills and opportunity to work, and to derive reasonable earnings from that work. To "reconnect" means to face no barriers to building one's economic position and future—no barriers to starting a business, owning a home, or building one's savings. Government can design bridges to participation and prosperity.

Let's go "Smith-plus," then: *How does government build a bridge?*

Leadership and Ideas . . .

Bridge building by governments at all levels has four elements: leadership, ideas, budget priorities, and processes for support. All are important to usher in mass flourishing.

It starts with leadership. As we have seen, many political leaders or aspiring leaders have given voice to calls for walls—to "protect" against change and economic dislocation. Walls have an easy appeal to struggling workers and communities, while bridges require forceful advocates to explain the program and mobilize resources—as Presidents Lincoln and Roosevelt did with land-grant colleges and Social Security, respectively. These bridges are not afterthoughts in larger economic policy—leaders must secure broad public buy-in *before* offering ambitious policies to promote economic efficiency.[5] This appropriate policy framing sees broad participation and mass flourishing as the goal. It is this participation and flourishing that are the counterargument to walls, not laissez-faire paeans to change.

The key question is how to intervene in markets. One element of leadership lies in developing and articulating the boundaries of the market in determining economic and social outcomes, just as firms move some activities inside as opposed to relying on market transactions. Conventional approaches by economists focus on competition policy to limit market power and incentives for monopolization; regulation of product, labor, and financial markets; and taxation to address externalities (such as pollution or climate change). But I am talking about a deeper consideration, bringing together Smith's concepts of the power of the market economy's invisible hand and the philosophical underpinning of mutual sympathy.

For much of American history, governments have pursued an "outside-in" policy. They've taken structural change as given and at most pursued offsetting interventions, such as adjusting the money supply or tariffs. Individuals and communities have been left to themselves to adjust.

Just as periods of pain under the classical gold standard brought populist pressures, neoliberal celebration of technological change and globalization with little thought toward adjustment led to populist calls for walls.[6] We now need governments to pursue an "inside-out" approach, to assist people in preparing for and reconnecting to the dynamic economy. This inside-out approach would focus on individuals' ability to participate in the gains from structural changes by this preparation and reconnection. Competitive forces would continue to operate, but with temporary support for individuals.

This inside-out orientation to technological change and globalization thus elicits greater public support for the market economy—and for mass flourishing. It also presents a guide for international norms, say, between the United States and China, in which recent walls of unilateral action, as well as beggar-thy-neighbor policy through intellectual property theft or currency manipulation, are replaced by rules to advance trade. At the same time, within a country, resources could focus on affected workers and communities (through support for work with redesigned social insurance in the more market-oriented U.S. system) or on state ownership in some industries (as with tolerated inefficiency in the less market-oriented Chinese system).

Ideas also matter: We need creative policies to rethink preparation and connection. Yes, we should continue to explore education and training, especially since past efforts have yielded only mixed results. But we should also support work itself through an expanded Earned Income Tax Credit or wage subsidies. Reconnection requires a reshaping of social insurance to handle structural changes in the economy and particular industries and occupations—initiatives like Personal Reemployment Accounts or wage insurance.

We need to limit these policy ideas in three ways. First, they must not try to protect particular jobs, firms, or industries in the economy that *was*—a wall. Rather, they must bring people to opportunity in the economy as it *is* and *will be*—a bridge. Second, they must not target particular shocks, like the weakly designed Trade Adjustment Assistance. All workers should be eligible for help, regardless of what causes their dislocation. Finally, and critically, bridges are fundamentally about getting people engaged in the productive economy, not about shoring up their incomes in an open-ended way.

Toward this end, a "mass-flourishing" agenda could address barriers not just to starting a business or building one's savings for financial resiliency, but also to owning a home. Historically, credit programs to encourage homeownership steered support toward white borrowers, amplifying a future wealth gap between white and non-white households. But even today, tax subsidies for homeownership and retirement savings favor high-income over low-income homebuyers; we could adjust that.[7] We could also amend current policies encouraging business formation to redouble efforts for underrepresented groups in the economy.

. . . and Priorities and Process

Making anything actually happen depends on budgetary priorities we set through politics. The initiatives outlined here are long-lasting and significant, and their cost is modest compared to the trillions of dollars of public spending for the pandemic. Yet with COVID-related debt now at high levels, these initiatives will need to be funded.

Past inclusive bridges, such as the New Deal and the G.I. Bill, were easier to achieve politically because the federal government had no budget overhang from unsustainable social insurance spending. We need extra leadership and creativity in funding bridges for the twenty-first century. Even with some tax increases possible, large-scale bridge-building initiatives—and the participation and prosperity they bring—require a rethinking of social spending on older versus younger Americans.

Overall, leaders can make the case that bridges reflect the capitalist prescription that gainers should collectively compensate the losers from structural change. Such compensation is neither a punishment nor a handout, but a core element of a social compact for broad participation and mass flourishing from a dynamic economy. Bridges are forward-looking—offering skill acquisition and support to succeed in the evolving economy—not backward-looking attempts to prop up jobs or industries or the economy that was.

Some funds can come from existing training programs or unemployment insurance that would now be used less. Other funds could come from tax increases, say, through a carbon tax that also has strong environmental benefits. A modest increase in the corporate income tax is politically possible, as businesses will benefit from the broader social support for capitalism that bridges should achieve.

Two changes come to mind. The Tax Cut and Jobs Act of 2017 significantly reduced the corporate rate from 35 percent to 21 percent. This cut was rightly celebrated as removing a key competitive disadvantage against firms from countries with lower corporate tax rates (almost all major U.S. trading partners). It also promoted business investment, which in turn raised productivity and wages. Post-COVID, Congress is almost certain to increase the tax rate to some degree. By also reforming the corporate tax system toward *cash flow* taxation, policymakers would put most of the burden of that higher rate on firms with large profits above the competitive return on capital.[8]

Another progressive tax change to help fund bridge programs is to change estate taxation on accumulated wealth going into an estate. Under current federal law, an individual's assets upon death have their basis for tax purposes "stepped up" to the current market value at the time of death. This step-up eliminates the capital gains tax on those accumulated assets (though the estate tax is still due). If, for example, a successful business owner started with an idea (zero tax basis) and built a business worth $100 million when he or she passed away, no tax would be due on that accumulated gain. With the tax rules changed to a carryover basis, the individual's heirs would gain the zero basis as well as the assets, and would pay the capital gains tax when the assets are sold. Like the corporate tax reform, this change would generate revenue from individuals who have prospered most in the dynamic economy and improve tax fairness.

Similarly, we could reduce growth in Social Security and Medicare payments for affluent citizens. These social insurance programs would remain as designed to ensure basic income and health care support for older Americans; programs would still be universal, with all participating. But in switching to a flatter Social Security benefit, retirees with low lifetime incomes would gain a generous retirement, while people with higher lifetime incomes would receive a bit less than before. The same would be true for Medicare premiums, raising them over time for the affluent. We need to do some of this adjustment anyway in order to improve these programs' fiscal footing, and we could do a bit more to fund support for bridges to participation for younger working Americans (who will ultimately pay for these programs for their elders).

Finally, we need a process for building bridges. As Secretary of State, Henry Kissinger famously asked of the European project: Who would answer the telephone if he called "Europe"? For our purposes, who in Washington would answer calls for "bridges" or "mass flourishing"? Most of the federal policy process goes through individual agencies, such as the Departments of the Treasury and Health and Human Services. So we need to develop processes that cut across agencies.

Plenty of such examples exist. Often managed in the Domestic Policy Council, National Economic Council, or National Security Council, these processes tackle such issues as welfare or health care reform, or a complex financial crisis in, say, Argentina. The economic engagement of the bridge requires similar coordination. One model is the President's Working Group on Financial Markets, which convenes cabinet-level officials to advise the president on financial stability and regulatory issues. For bridges, a principal cabinet officer could be difficult to select: The Secretary of Labor because of the emphasis on work? The Secretary of Commerce or U.S. Trade Representative because of concerns over globalization or technological change? The Secretary of the Treasury or Director of the Office of Management and Budget because of the needed federal tax and spending commitments?

A third model involves a distinguished independent chair and members of a Taskforce on Economic Engagement, with subcabinet participants from various agencies. The taskforce would issue public annual reports on the state of economic engagement and evaluate proposed bridges and walls. It would also release scorecards of administration and congressional initiatives to advance broader economic engagement. While not carrying direct political power, such a structure can shed a light on critical initiatives and concerns. A successful example is the Swedish Fiscal Policy Council, organized under the Ministry of Finance to provide an independent evaluation and critique of the government's fiscal policy. The council's work and annual report promote vigorous public and legislative debates and could point the way for a U.S. Taskforce on Economic Engagement.

Regardless of the model followed, this government process must set ambitious "moon-shot" goals. While working with companies to address the dislocation costs of structural change, it should also acknowledge externalities that preclude firms from shouldering the burden of solutions. And third, it must explicitly embrace continued openness and push for gainers to compensate losers, while acting in a far more integrated way than the quasi-laissez-faire approach taken by American business and the U.S. government today. It must address business decisions in response to structural changes and design policies to work with business to reduce the dislocation costs of these externalities. If this approach sounds "economic," it is.

A "moon-shot" goal would center on keeping the United States at the forefront of technological change—and on benefiting from openness. The process would coordinate large federal investments in basic research and in applied research and development centers in universities around the country. A useful historical example is the Defense Advanced Research Projects Agency (DARPA), created in 1958 after the Soviet Union launched its *Sputnik* satellite. That agency supported (and continues to support) research that created the backbone of the information economy. A follow-on version, the Advanced Research Projects Agency-Energy (ARPA-E), focuses on innovation in that specific area.

From an economic perspective, a "moon shot" not only focuses public action, but also reduces the uncertainty in technological change. Following economist Frank Knight's definition, "uncertainty" refers to an unknown outcome whose probabilities of success are impossible to estimate. New technologies to solve problems fall into that category. We can set goals and interactions that generate information over time about the feasibility of specific advances, which then motivates additional investment from public and private actors.

Aggressive public action is essential to combat the many externalities with private bridges against structural change. Companies fear losing the benefits of bridgelike investments in worker training, and specific communities bear higher-than-normal risks from dislocation. When private flexibility requires shedding workers or closing facilities in areas adversely affected by structural change, an externality arises as workers, communities, and local and federal taxpayers pay the cost of remediation and support. Rising productivity and policies that support it ease job transitions, as occurred when agricultural mechanization during the late nineteenth and early twentieth centuries pushed workers into manufacturing activities and some services in which productivity was even higher.

Unlike in previous generations with automation in agriculture and industry, the shift to services has reduced wages for many low- and mid-skilled workers. In that sense, the deindustrialization of recent decades has brought a somewhat greater challenge, as rapid productivity growth in manufacturing as well as globalization have shifted work away from production. Without bridges, many of these affected workers will question the desirability of the neoliberal economic model that delivers these outcomes.[9]

Businesses are not likely to internalize higher social costs on their own to fix the problems in employment and preparation for it. Nor will we succeed with conventional taxes on competitive businesses, as these amount to walls against flexibility and economywide adaptation to change (see Chapter 4). Subsidizing work- and place-based aid, as described in Chapter 6, offers a more promising alternative.

But these interventions still need coordination with business to work effectively for workers and communities and to build broad support for the market economy. While a government process can set overall goals for skill development and good jobs, public–private partnerships around the country should be formed and encouraged to develop training initiatives.

Engaging Governments: *People* . . .

With those four elements in place, federal interventions do still need to coordinate with local governments and businesses to work effectively. A federal process can set overall goals for skill development and good jobs, but it should encourage public–private partnerships around the country to carry out the actual training and other initiatives.[10]

Federal funding is the essential driver, and it can play out in four ways. The first, as mentioned in Chapter 6, is a block grant to states to support community colleges in preparing entry-level and midcareer students for work opportunity. That support, like the federal assistance for land-grant colleges 160 years ago, will help states and regions supply local training and retraining to raise skills, productivity, and wages.

Second, our government process can also synchronize workforce skill and training programs already receiving support. The federal government, for example, funds more than forty employment and job-training agencies.[11] Within and across those programs, states blend federal and state workforce initiatives, with varying degrees of success. A systematic analysis by the federal government or the National Governors Association (which provides staff and analytical support to the nation's governors) should identify best practices and lessons from experience. Utah, for example, has an integrated Department of Workforce Services. It offers a "one worker, one plan" model, where job seekers gain a single plan with objectives and services, rather than a patchwork quilt from different well-intended programs.[12] State leadership and a clear vision for the future are critical to sustaining these bridges. And state action can proceed even when change at the federal level is slow in coming.

Utah reformed its offerings in 1997, on the heels of federal welfare reform and a year before federal workforce reform in the Workforce Investment Act. The Utah experiment offers a record of successes for other states considering ways to provide customized and comprehensive services to workers, those out of work, and employers. A key step was how Utah bypassed federal agencies to deal with the U.S. Department of Health and Human Services, which in turn dealt with the rest of the federal bureaucracy on behalf of Utah's Department of Workforce Services. While policy rightly focuses on programs on the ground, effective governmental processes at multiple levels are also important.

A third intervention, recommended by Jason Furman, Timothy Geithner, Melissa Kearney, and myself, is to redesign the match between federal and state support for unemployment insurance and Medicaid.[13] We recommend linking this federal support to state-level unemployment rates, with funding rising with higher rates of joblessness. The mechanism enables states, which must balance their budgets, to loosen budget constraints to fund more education and training in a cyclical downturn (where state tax revenue falls with the downturn) or a structural downturn even as tax revenue falls (in which incomes and state revenue fall in response to shocks from globalization or technological change).

We also recommend a general increase in federal funding for the Medicaid program. Federal and state governments jointly fund Medicaid's support for low-income residents. Because states lack financing flexibility during downturns, Congress has acted in the past two recessions to temporarily increase the share of funding for Medicaid. If the federal share of expenditures on Medicaid rises when the state's unemployment rate is high, as in a recession or in response to structural shifts, state-level budgetary constraints do not bind as tightly on critical education and training support for opportunity. States can also complement skill development by businesses. The Skillful State Network, for example, provides a forum for governors of states to share and advance workforce innovation. They can, as in Colorado and Indiana, share practices on aligning education with industry needs and providing data to job-seekers.

. . . and *Places*

As Chapter 6 observed, structural changes have left specific communities especially hard hit, even as most of the country is doing well. Economists have traditionally been skeptical of "place-based" aid, preferring a move of "people to jobs" over a move of "jobs to people." But contemporary concerns surrounding large and long-lasting differences in job availability across areas, combined with apparently limited mobility by individuals, are causing a rethink.

The variability of jobs across the country is larger than might appear. Imagine a local labor market as a commuting zone within which people can travel to work. Now consider how individuals vary across commuting zones according to the prime-age employment rate, the ratio of employed 25- to 54-year-olds to their population. The median rate for the country is 81 percent, but for zones in the 10th percentile it goes down to 77 percent, while the 90th percentile is at 86 percent. That gap of nine percentage points in employment rates is quite high, and these differences seem to have persisted for decades.[14] Most people are not uprooting themselves and moving toward opportunity as economists once thought they would.

These significant and persistent differences in availability of jobs generate real social costs for individuals in areas left behind. Various researchers have documented increases in alcohol and opioid use, single-parent families, problems for children in educational attainment and subsequent adult income, and dissatisfaction with one's life if unemployed or living in a community with high unemployment.

Fewer are moving in search of better opportunity than in the popular imagination of Horace Greeley's "Go West, young man." It's not difficult to see why individuals find comfort near home, family, and familiar acquaintances. Adam Smith observed that "a man is of all sorts of luggage the most difficult to be transported."[15] Economists have estimated that only a very large subsidy—possibly in excess of a year's income—will get most people to move. After all, local job losses from the China shock haven't led many unemployed workers to leave, and the out-migration that has taken place hasn't improved opportunities for people who stay.[16]

Governments can fund and facilitate a great deal of place-based bridges: business incubators, customized preparation for jobs by community colleges, and extension services for smaller manufacturers. Youngstown, Ohio has pursued these strategies with some success. Economists' evaluation of the benefits of these interventions indicates great promise for additional support and investment.[17]

How might a thoughtful national policy process improve the likelihood of success of place-based aid? It can focus on the most distressed areas and the programs with the highest multipliers for opportunity at lower costs per job. Three guidelines can shape a federal place-based strategy. To begin, the focus needs to be on long-term job loss from structural change. Second, funds should go mainly to reskilling people and to extension services for local businesses to support entrepreneurial activity. Third, especially given the concerns about market power we noted earlier, aid should focus on small and midsize enterprises, not large firms.

As discussed in Chapter 6, place-based aid works best when it brings concerted private and public action together. Besides Massachusetts's rebound described in Chapter 4, Pittsburgh offers a recent example.

There, private and public actors helped avoid retrenchment in the face of technological change and globalization in steelmaking. The industry declined dramatically in the 1980s as outdated technology and work practices exacerbated competitive pressures.[18] As in Massachusetts, Pittsburgh's reinvention depended on leadership by the business community, in this case through the Allegheny Conference on Community Development.

The Allegheny Conference predated steel's decline in the region. Founded in 1943 by business leader Richard King Mellon, the Conference had long worked with county government to support economic infrastructure (in the central business district) and physical infrastructure (such as Pittsburgh International Airport). Both business and public leaders benefited from cooperation.

With local governments slow to respond to steel's decline, the Conference created similar public–private partnerships and extended existing ones. The partnerships were formed to deal with regional infrastructure, but evolved to meet the challenges of business and employment restructuring. The Regional Industrial Development Corporation, created earlier to develop suburban office parks to attract light manufacturing, stepped in to redevelop shuttered USX (U.S. Steel) sites. The business-led Pittsburgh High Technology Council worked with the University of Pittsburgh and Carnegie-Mellon University.

Over time, the city switched its economic and employment base toward services (especially health care and education) and light manufacturing. The close collaboration of public officials and local business leaders was essential, along with avoiding bureaucratic decision making. So was the focus on the future.

Youngstown, the smaller industrial city chronicled elsewhere in this book, is now following a similar path of public–private coordination. The Mahoning Valley Economic Development Corporation works with the Small Business Administration to manage revolving loan funds for emerging businesses. Funds have been attracted for downtown revitalization, enough to induce the building of the Double Tree by Hilton Hotel Downtown, where my students and I stayed during our second trip to the area. The Youngstown Business Incubator offered with Youngstown State University boasts a technology campus for startups and advanced manufacturing. The low cost of living and the location between Cleveland and Pittsburgh are prompting conversations about conference locations and health care hubs. Youngstown State University actively engages with the business community for skill training and retraining.

But the city is playing catch-up. Its initial civic engagement, while ample, lost time by trying to breathe new life into steel's glorious past. While its leaders were not lacking in business engagement and local organizations, their failure to pivot early proved costly. By contrast, the similarly situated Lehigh Valley in Pennsylvania, including Allentown, moved quickly to diversify beyond steel into high-value business services.[19] Like Pittsburgh, the story in Lehigh Valley was one of bridges to the future with quicker cooperation among government, business, and universities.

Cleveland compares to Pittsburgh in its resources at the time of decline, but, like Youngstown, it has focused on current manufacturing industries. Despite the bridge-building potential of Case Western Reserve University and the Cleveland Clinic, it has looked to the past rather than the future.[20]

Finally, though not a victim of steel's decline, Grand Rapids, Michigan, offers an example of building bridges to new opportunities. The city actually *expanded* manufacturing employment by diversifying into chemicals, food, and metals.[21] With work by business leaders and the local campus of Michigan State University, the city also promoted life sciences—including having area manufacturers shift into medical supplies.[22] Bridges included the Right Place Program, which emphasized training for new jobs in manufacturing. Local philanthropy in the form of the Van Andel Institute helped significantly, too.

These examples are also a reminder that federal assistance should avoid a one-size-fits-all approach. As with the community college intervention described earlier, funds could be advanced in a flexible block grant with agreed-upon objectives and rigorous analysis of successes and lessons learned. Furthermore, these investments work best when provided along with the bridge of place-based aid. That aid works better when it comes with social insurance for individuals described earlier.

Partnering with Higher Education:
Work and Research

Public–private partnerships with universities have a long and successful track record in furthering beneficial structural change. The federal block grants for community colleges described earlier are the key move here to enable them to prepare younger and midcareer students for the skills the economy needs by 2030. The success of such initiatives will be magnified by employment partnerships with local businesses. Federal budget support can overcome funding challenges and ameliorate externality problems in private training, but businesses' active participation remains important.

The emphasis on community colleges to provide training and retraining is even more significant as the economy recovers from the pandemic's labor market damage. Lockdowns disrupted millions of jobs and tested the viability of many businesses and occupations. Community colleges stand as the best bridge between need-to-be-reskilled workers and future job needs, not just positioning them for employment but also forestalling long-term earnings losses. Block grants would keep community colleges strong, despite the likely state budget cuts in higher education.

As Chapter 7 noted, community colleges are well suited to work with business in certifying the development of needed skills. IBM, LinkedIn, and other prominent firms have worked with community colleges to offer online retraining in analytics, computer programming, and data science. Google alone has partnerships with over 100 community colleges to provide career training in information-technology support. Business organizations can also design these courses, drawing on successful partnerships with Chicago's community colleges and Broward College in Florida. These critical efforts will depend on greater federal financial support for community colleges. Public support for community colleges depends in part on completion as a factor in generating gains in earnings.[23] Successful efforts to improve completion rates incorporate a set of services beyond tuition financial aid, including broader financial assistance, academic advising, mentoring, and coaching. In a review of programs serving community college students, economists Rachel Dawson (University of Notre Dame), Melissa Kearney (University of Maryland), and James

Sullivan (University of Notre Dame) find that these initiatives are effective in raising completion rates and could be scaled with additional support, whether nationally through a block grant or locally through private philanthropy.[24]

Beyond community colleges, government entities can work with universities on skill development. The Volcker Alliance's Government-to-University initiative builds regional networks to connect local colleges to state and local government programs. The G20 network also works with nonprofit organizations and private-sector firms. Its footprint is significant—in Kansas City, Los Angeles, Pittsburgh, Chicago, and Raleigh—and offers a road map for collaboration elsewhere.

But universities offer the greatest potential in extending the frontier of knowledge through basic research. They can take those findings and partner with firms for applied research to generate new opportunities for employment. Near the end of World War II, former MIT engineering professor Vannevar Bush wrote to President Harry Truman to encourage federal investment in basic research and in the training of scientists and engineers. That entreaty led to the creation of the National Institutes of Health and the National Science Foundation (my own financial bridge to graduate school).

Government–university collaboration took off during the *Sputnik* moment of catch-up to the Soviet space program. Its success led in turn to multipliers in applied research in medicine and other areas. Today's advances in the internet, chemotherapy, computing, aviation, and smartphones are among the dividends of this collaboration. Promising developments in artificial intelligence are pushing the knowledge and opportunity frontier further.

By supporting basic research, governments can promote structural change rather than waiting passively (and therefore slowly) to build bridges toward the changes imposed by others. The federal government should renew and redouble its funding commitment to basic scientific and engineering research. Even before the pandemic, we were going in the wrong direction with *cuts* for this research in President Trump's budget for fiscal year 2020. Translating outcomes from basic research into applied research for opportunities—affecting technology, health care, manufacturing, agriculture, and commerce—requires a further step. As with the land-grant colleges, a federal block grant to states could fund applied-research initiatives in each state or major economic areas and set up institutes that could work with local businesses on commercial, employment, and skill-development possibilities.

University-based applied researchers can contribute substantially to creating jobs of the future. Ensuring these jobs of the future requires attention to both supply and demand. By "supply," I mean that good jobs require particular skills. By "demand," I mean that the jobs are created by firms (including small and midsize firms that have many entry-level workers) that are productive and thus able to expand employment. Governments can help coordinate with employers to provide skills that match needs of local firms in specific industries like information technology or health care (like Project QUEST in San Antonio). But government can also support local university–business partnerships.

Federal funding for applied-research centers around the country can extend the reach of nearby research universities into the areas around them. That is, support could build out research centers in existing universities. It could expand the community partnerships begun in 1988 with the Manufacturing Extension Partnerships.[25] The goal is for universities to jump-start local economies with local knowledge spillover.[26] Those spillovers address the good-jobs goal both by strengthening current firms and by attracting new firms to the area.[27]

As with the case of the Manufacturing Extension Partnership, the U.S. Department of Commerce could offer support for both applied university-based research and translation to business practice. The funding would center on work to boost economic activity in specific areas. Additional support for businesses operating in the targeted areas would be offered through branch offices affiliated with the universities.

Three comments about an updated version of the Manufacturing Extension Partnership are in order. First, it should be expanded beyond manufacturing into, say, an "Economic Extension Partnership." Second, it should rely heavily on the existing research universities and their local partnerships to design the programs. It should also coordinate with local businesses. Third, the partnership should complement a block grant for community colleges for training and skill development, so the emerging economic activity has a ready source of skilled labor.

Learning Lessons from the Land-Grant Colleges

I have highlighted the role of partnerships among business, government, and educational institutions in enhancing skills and building bridges to opportunity for individuals and communities. I have also emphasized the potential benefits of federal block grant support to community colleges today for that purpose. Lessons from the original land-grant colleges are important for block grants and for bridge building generally. The tension in states between walls of protection for agriculture and bridges to manufacturing are instructive for today. Structural shifts from technological change and globalization have disadvantaged some sectors and regions in the United States, while advantaging others. Asymmetry in economic fortunes raises political concerns, as does the congressional redistricting in 2022 in response to the census. In the land-grant colleges, Congress refused to drop the industrial emphasis, but did agree to fund agricultural extension programs that were an important basis of U.S. farming productivity advances. Similar compromises might be needed here, as long as these avoid walls.

To avoid the political disputes described in this chapter's opening, this federal assistance should unapologetically be about bridge building. Place-based aid, through applied-research centers, community college block grants, and encouragement of local business–government partnerships, can provide better local bridges to opportunity, while blunting the impulse—as with Vermont farmers against the Morrill Act's plans—for walls to protect the past.

More specifically, the land-grant colleges' success in preparing workers for a changing economy—while providing extension services to struggling agricultural communities—should guide today's discussions of public education's role in preparing individuals for the work of the future.[28] Renewed support for community colleges can do the same in preparing younger students, retraining dislocated workers, and working with local firms to foster skill matches to available jobs. A federal block grant to support community colleges in multiple bridging missions could build on research on land-grant colleges' links over time to economic development. For example, the Innovation and Economic Prosperity Initiative of the Association of Public and Land-Grant Universities has assessed colleges based on teaching, research, and "place development through public service, engagement and outreach." As another, the Carnegie Foundation's Elective Classification in Community Engagement program drew interest from land-grant colleges, which had to document both curricular engagement and partnerships within the community.[29]

Federal support for applied-research centers can also facilitate bridging opportunities for individuals and communities. Support for applied research and its dissemination can bolster local economies and skill development. The decentralized presence of such centers around the country can also foster partnerships between centers and local businesses for job preparation and knowledge transfer.[30]

These initiatives give workers practical skills to thrive despite structural change, and they generate support from local communities, which might otherwise see the programs as retraining individuals simply to move elsewhere. That buy-in is essential for full funding. The public–private partnerships encouraged here are more likely to succeed than training subsidies given directly to companies alone. Evaluators have found that federal initiatives such as the On-the-Job Training and Incumbent Worker Training Programs, under the Workforce Innovation and Opportunity Act, tend to lack both funding and coverage relative to workers' and firms' needs.[31]

Indeed, Congress could separately provide block grants to states to leverage state–firm programs customized to local needs and requirements. Current examples include Maryland's Business Works, which matches support for training funds going to small and midsize firms, and Connecticut's Manufacturing Innovation Fund and Ohio's Tech Cred program, which facilitate training for on-demand skills and new technologies consistent with state development goals. Federal and state policies in tandem can foster sector partnerships among firms, building on successful initiatives in Colorado (Sector Partnerships), Connecticut (Regional Sector Partnerships), Maryland (Employment Advancement Right Now), and Massachusetts (Workforce Competitiveness Trust Fund).

Bringing Individuals Together:
A Participation Economy

Another idea builds on partnerships with *individuals*. Two motivating stories stand out for me. The first, to illustrate the need for awareness, is about the social isolation of the relatively well off. When

I speak to business leaders, I often engage them informally early on by asking where and in what circumstances *they* grew up. Many, like me, grew up in decidedly noncosmopolitan places and in families with low or middle incomes. Then I ask them how their *children* are growing up. Here the answer changes to different locations in very upper-income families with limited social contact with other groups experiencing the brunt of social and economic disruption.

This lack of contact is a real problem. Returning to Queen Elizabeth II's disarming question about the 2007–2009 financial crisis— "Why did nobody notice it?"—many business (and political) leaders are doing little to branch out and see what others are experiencing in their economic connections, or disconnections. It is hard to understand or empathize or aspire to make things better if we don't "notice." Once, when frustrated about testable hypotheses for a public finance idea I had, my brilliant and thoughtful teacher, the late Martin Feldstein, observed that the answer would become clearer if I left my computer and talked with people. He was right. We need the people reaping handsome rewards from the economy's dynamism to be more intentional about exploring the participation and well-being of others.

But we likely need more. My second story traces to a dinner at Yale Law School with colleagues on a project studying causes and consequences of economic divides in America. The Gothic setting and excellent company recalled this same one-sidedness of experience, now with academics. Our dinner speaker, the smart, engaging Yale economist Robert Shiller, a Nobel laureate, observed that the last period with a "we're all in this together" ethos was World War II. That sounded familiar from stories drilled into me while growing up among adults with wartime experience at home and abroad, but it also left me unsettled. The good news is that World War II brought most of the country together with a common understanding. The bad news is that no one wants a third world war to put the band back together again. And Shiller didn't have an easy replacement—a tough after-dinner talk.

National service is a clear, and obviously less threatening, alternative. It combines public purpose toward a common good with a "we're all in this together" mixing of individuals from different social and economic groups. At its best, the volunteer military comes to mind. Or the bold adventurism of the Peace Corps. Or the social mission of the AmeriCorps program.

We should seriously consider going big here with a broad effort at national service. Such an initiative could focus on young adults, yes, but also on individuals in transition and retired Americans seeking to reengage or give back. An underlying "we're all in this together" thesis can build bridges instead of walls and push back on divisive centrifugal forces from economic change.

A voluntary, open-to-all program would likely be popular. Many young people already apply for more program slots than are available. Such national service can bridge economic experiences, provide career pathways, and strengthen struggling communities. One example would be to increase funding to states and nongovernmental organizations for positions, as in the Serve America Act of 2009.

Going further, former White House official John Bridgeland and Brookings Institution economist Isabel Sawhill have suggested an American Exchange Program, in which families would host young people during a year of service after being matched by an online program.[32] Such an idea could provide a cost-effective way of accomplishing social projects while building bridges of social connection. Voluntary national service is popular with the public, and seventy-nine senators voted for the Serve America Act. Presidential candidate Andrew Yang championed the idea in his 2020 campaign. In my worlds of universities and businesses, leaders value national service as providing the citizenship skills and social connections they look for in students and workers.

Unlike the wall's slogan appeal, the bridge has no silver bullet. But national service can provide a foundation by drawing people of different backgrounds to share perspectives and solve problems. Broad associations of individuals are also important and contributed to earlier periods of diminished polarization, as Harvard political scientist Robert Putnam has observed.[33]

Assembling the Pieces: Toward Mass Flourishing

Our emphasis on individuals' desire to participate and prosper in the economy not only harkens back to America's traditions of supporting and reconnecting to opportunity, but also bridges economic rhetoric from conservatives and progressives alike. Participation connotes work and the dignity it brings, and prosperity reflects a stake in the economy's success for more Americans. But freedom to participate also demonstrates diversity and inclusion as a core economic value. And individuals' prosperity should never be blocked by barriers that explicitly or subtly offer a privileged group a better deal than that offered to others, as walls too often do. Government has a role to play in tearing down barriers and helping people and communities participate in the work and prosperity a dynamic, disruptive economy brings. With these lessons in mind, bridges create the possibility of renewed social engagement by more Americans. We've seen their success with land-grant colleges and the G.I. Bill.[34] Walls, by contrast, claim to protect us, but end up making our divisions worse.

9

Mass Flourishing Requires Bridges

The explosion in living standards after the Industrial Revolution has brought prosperity, on average, to much of the world. As China and India opened to the global market economy in recent decades, conditions improved substantially in those countries as well. Growth in living standards is one of the hallmarks of open economies. The dynamic, open, and competitive economies championed by Adam Smith gathered wind in their sails from technological improvements and from expanding trade. Dynamism and growth go hand in hand.

Yet these benefits on the macro level have gone along with *change*, serious disruptions, and suffering for some industries, firms, and individuals. This toing-and-froing of fortunes weakens social support for dynamism and the competitive market economy. Neoliberal economists advising policymakers have noted these problems, but taken the existing economic system as given. At the same time, the lack of support for communities dislocated by technological change and globalization has shaken faith in the economic system in the body politic. Arguments for openness have given way to intuitive and populist—social and political—calls for *walls* of protection.

History teaches us that such walls fail to ensure future prosperity, or even lasting protection. But the counterpart to walls is not laissez-faire economic orthodoxy.

This book advances three principles for this counterargument to walls. First, a successful economy *requires mass flourishing,* marrying Adam Smith's ideas of the wealth of a nation and mutual sympathy. Mass flourishing requires broad engagement in a dynamic economy—preparing individuals to participate and reconnecting them when structural shifts upend occupations, firms and industries, and livelihoods. Preparation and reconnection require more than neoliberal pieties about the wonder of markets.

Second, the best way to bring about this preparation and reconnection, without undermining dynamism, is through bridges. The bridge, connecting individuals to the productive economy and building social support for that economy, is the counterpart to the wall. Bridges come from Smith's focus on having everyone able to compete. They have a long history in the United States, from compulsory schooling to land-grant colleges, Social Security, the post–World War II G.I. Bill, and local public–private partnerships for economic inclusion.

Third, building bridges requires intentional action by individuals and by institutions, private and public. Individual agency is, of course, important in preparing for and reconnecting to economic life, but the risks of economic dynamism are too great for many individuals to bear alone. Businesses must step up training and community engagement to advance productivity and to shore up support for the market economy. Governments need to rethink support for education and training and for social insurance aimed at adjusting to structural changes, not just to ups and downs over the business cycle. Achieving such fundamental policy rethinking requires a framing that builds social support, rather than taking it for granted. These intentional efforts at bridge building are the economic parry to the wall.

Mass Flourishing as a Moral
as Well as Economic Imperative

Smith, the father of economics, had a powerful answer to questions about the wealth of a nation. The prevailing mercantilist view focused on the monarch's stocks of assets like gold or silver. The sovereign aimed to increase those stocks of sovereigns, the better to fund wars and other opportunities to strengthen the nation. Governments intervened in market forces to limit competition at home and abroad for favored activities. Trade surpluses were good, trade deficits bad. Larger surpluses—and the larger stocks of specie that accompanied them—would finance wars or crown consumption. State-sanctioned monopolies generated more revenue for the crown. Elites thrived with their special connections, while everyone else made little headway.

In dismissing mercantilist logic, Smith started with a very different framing of the economy's objective. To Smith, the wealth of a nation lay in its potential for consumption by its people—living standards. He wanted to make the economic pie as large as possible. The consumer, not the crown and its ministers, was Smith's economic king.

To expand this wealth, Smith promoted free markets and competition by the invisible hand. These forces reconciled self-interest with the expanding pie for everyone. He wanted everyone to be able to compete, so he spoke well of education and other kinds of preparation. Yet today, as in Smith's day, competition and its outcomes—business success or failure, wealth or poverty, high or low wages, an expanding career or unemployment—can be hard to accept. Indeed, today's great champions of competition often are populated by tenured academic economists and rich winners of the competitive race.

Smith aimed not to celebrate business success—he was promarket rather than probusiness. At its core, the defense of an open, competitive economic system was that it generated high living standards. He therefore emphasized economic inclusion—the idea that the least well off should be recognized economic participants. Such a theme harkened back to *The Theory of Moral Sentiments'* emphasis on mutual sympathy, with preparation for and reconnection to the economy for as many people as possible. Mass flourishing was the goal, so different from that of the mercantilists, who approved of gains for a few, despite losses in liberty and living standards for many. From its opening chapter, *The Wealth of Nations* made sure that "universal opulence" and "general plenty" were associated with flourishing.

Today's economy and the structural changes it experiences are more complex than in Smith's day, with far more disruption. We now understand that growth is driven dynamically by ideas and innovation. Recall that in Edmund Phelps's and Deirdre McCloskey's telling, growth is not just about the pace of scientific discovery but also about its commercial applications. The market economy must accept those applications, with salutary impacts for many and adverse consequences for some. Societies and cultures must support these disruptions in order to gain the growth in living standards. That won't happen in the long run without broad participation in the economy. Lack of participation will lead to calls for walls against change or to protect one's own incumbent position, as with the mercantilist tinkering Smith assailed.

Think of mass flourishing as being "in the groove" of the dynamic economy, akin to psychologists' concept of flow. Like flow, flourishing requires individuals to be able to adjust to the skill and complexity required for economic participation. So a flourishing system is about keeping more individuals attached to the changing economy.

Flow and flourishing convey a sense of fully participating—of belonging—in the economy. Smith's invisible hand has deliberately impersonal workings. Social support for people, though, conveys an understanding of rich webs of ties through communities and associations, not just of impersonal transactions. We can update Smith's model with bridges that promote and build on these webs. Adding bridges of preparation and reconnection can advance reciprocity and support for openness.

Smith's reactions to walls of mercantilist limits on business's competition and efficiency are not just historical notes. Those walls figure prominently in today's discourse, too, and they will likewise undermine dynamism, however well intentioned. Oren Cass, for example, argues for promoting manufacturing jobs in particular because these paid well and offered a path to stable family life for unskilled workers. Like many observers, he calls for shaving a bit of Smithian efficiency for a broader social purpose. But these walls risk throwing out the wealth-of-the-nation baby with the disruption bathwater; mass flourishing they are not. This argument is intuitive and can be convincing to political leaders—remember my failure to dissuade President George W. Bush from imposing steel tariffs. But it is also wrong. Jobs are "created" and "destroyed" in large numbers in a dynamic economy. And good industries and jobs change over time.

Stopping this dynamic will only render those good jobs stale. This is not flourishing at all but a kind of cronyism more like mercantilism. Well-connected workers will get those good jobs, while ordinary people are stuck. Better to let consumers' tastes and incomes shape opportunities for firms and the employment patterns that follow.

Cass's defense of manufacturing jobs focuses on their relatively high pay, something the Columbia students and I heard often in Youngstown, Ohio. But not only is employment in manufacturing declining globally, any protections will keep us from the vital task of building bridges to dynamic opportunities. This concern is less an economic nicety than a worry for an alliance between struggling incumbent firms in a competitive race and unemployed workers (or workers with reduced earnings), an alliance for walls of protection.

And these walls will only beget more walls, as people lobby to get some of the privileged employment.

To be blunt, the cost of a bit of tinkering isn't a slightly smaller economic pie, a ninety-eight-cents-on-the-dollar compromise; the tinkering puts dynamism and the market system at risk. Protection produces—and is seen by the public to produce—benefits. Yes, but those benefits are for some (the protected) and come at the expense of many (the economy as a whole). The tinkering fails to connect individuals to new and promising opportunities for work and business. And if individuals perceive the economic system as bestowing special favors and lacking broad legitimacy, it and dynamism may come under attack.

One view about walls is that they came to the forefront with Donald Trump's narrow victory in the 2016 presidential election and exited with his narrow loss in 2020. But that observation is not true. Protectionist pressures had been smoldering for decades, and now the Biden administration has expressed skepticism about the benefits of trade liberalization 1990s style. Wall proponents such as Cass and, especially, Peter Navarro have expressed legitimate concerns about fair competition in global trade. But policing competition is not an excuse for outright protectionism or policy favoritism for domestic producers. We shouldn't use actions to enforce trade rules as a means to protect certain jobs or industries.

Building support for openness requires adherence to Nicholas Kaldor's maxim that gainers compensate losers. This compensation can helpfully take the form of preparing individuals to compete in the open economy (through training and skill redevelopment) and reconnecting individuals to the economy when job category or industry prospects wane. The key point is that this tinkering can easily end up limiting competition and individuals' and firms' ability to "have a go." It bakes a smaller economic pie, leaving little surplus to fund bridges toward mass flourishing.

These concerns are not simply about Navarro's rhetoric; they remain front and center in wings of both the Democratic and Republican parties. A third, softer call for walls is to force corporations to shift from competitive market machines focused on shareholders to ones focused on stakeholders generally, including employees, communities, and societies at large. Economist Colin Mayer, corporate lawyer Martin Lipton, and the Business Roundtable have sounded this call, but are such changes worth the sacrifice in business efficiency they might entail? No. If markets for inputs and goods and services are competitive, then maximizing long-term shareholder value leaves investors and the economy as a whole better off and generates competitive returns for other stakeholders. If these conditions don't apply, then we should police competition—antitrust policy in this case—not enforce a specific corporate purpose.

By the time Adam Smith wrote *The Wealth of Nations* as an attack on such tinkering, policy pivots to walls were already common. And with the greater prosperity brought about by the Industrial Revolution, with the disruptive change and noisy competition that Smith described, battles between walls and economic change have figured prominently in American policy and politics. The immediate post–World War II period in the United States brought broadly shared prosperity, fueled in part by high productivity growth, the dominant position of American industry and labor in global markets after the war, and the massive expansion of education and skills through the G.I. Bill. Globally, the Bretton Woods international monetary system allowed some flexibility for individual economies to manage adjustments at home in the presence of structural consumer changes.

The period of elites' neglect began in the late 1970s. That period experienced a turn toward ever-greater openness and competition, accompanied by more skepticism of government social programs. Persuasive paeans to laissez-faire, or at least largely laissez-faire, ideas greatly influenced both the economics profession and economic policy. Policy in particular focused on drivers of economic growth, with less attention to guardrails to minimize the adverse effects from technological change and globalization. As frustration mounted through employment and community losses in Youngstown, Ohio, and other heartland areas, economists' neoliberal advice gained ground in both Republican and Democratic administrations. Political shifts did occur under the surface, with populist campaigns of walls against change waged by Patrick Buchanan as a Republican and Ross Perot as an independent in 1992, by Sen. Rick Santorum as a Republican in 2008, and by Donald Trump in 2016. Still other campaigns remain in the wings.

The point of raising these contrasts is not that economists got it wrong in neoliberal economic ideas, just as Smith did not get it wrong when he centered the wealth of a nation on living standards and individuals' ability to consume, not particular jobs or industries. Indeed, neoliberal emphases on openness and competition reflect economic thinking and economic success since Smith's time. Market capitalism has carried the endorsement of business leaders, many elected leaders, and most leading economists.

Mass Flourishing Requires Bridges, Not Walls

Since walls don't work in the long run, what does? We can build bridges that enable people to participate in the dynamic, competitive world economy. But building bridges requires a new engagement by economists, policymakers, and businesspeople.

In the past few decades, we've failed to develop and explain effective bridges. When walls came down after the 1970s, we weren't ready.

Without those bridges, voters chose between laissez-faire openness and walls. They've struggled with structural economic changes, without help from institutions, and they want better. The political counter-argument followed economists' advice—think Ronald Reagan or Margaret Thatcher or Bill Clinton or Tony Blair—preaching the gospel of change. The defense-of-market-forces argument is spot-on when it comes to macroeconomic gains, but it isn't persuading significant portions of the public. Doubling down on neoliberal economic messages is not winning the rhetorical war with the walls.

By contrast, bridges take individuals from the old to the new. They offer a structure for mass flourishing and a mechanism to ensure broader public support for the market system, support that isn't the confident "given" of an Econ 101 course's description.

Bridges may be harder to define and build than walls—economically, politically, and socially. But they work with economics—understanding the benefits of change, how to prepare individuals to participate in the economy as it is and will be, and how to reconnect individuals to the economy when changes break ties of participation. These steps of preparation (developing skills) and reconnection (redesigning social insurance) are also in Econ 101 and have a long lineage. Policymakers in Washington and other capitals—and economists—need to spend much more time on these ideas. Business leaders also need to think about bridge building and their role in it, and economists, while not to blame for a lack of theoretical ideas, need to *notice* social crosscurrents from change. And just as calls to build a wall do carry moral weight, sufficient to persuade many people to trade off efficiency to help dislocated individuals and communities, bridges have a moral connection to individual dignity and mass flourishing.

Technological change and globalization inflicted body blows on much of the industrial economy. Unlike cyclical difficulties, these pressures appeared quickly, were long-lasting, and were geographically concentrated.

These factors made economic adjustment unusually difficult for many workers relying on market forces and on public policies aimed at cushioning short-term, episodic losses of earnings or work. Meanwhile, neoliberal views—of economists such as Milton Friedman or Friedrich Hayek—were rising in public policy as well the economics profession. While these economists did not argue for a hands-off management of change, neither did they emphasize preparation for and reconnection to the changing economy.

Economists have—sometimes fairly—been tarred with the brush of being defenders of change, whatever the disruptive wake that accompanies it. In turn, conservative politicians often embraced these ideas as representing benefits to the economy as a whole or entrepreneurial opportunity or innovation—all true, actually—while giving much less thought to near-term economic losers from shifts in technology or global markets.

A bridge helps you get to or get back to where you want to go. It is a helpful path across a tough-to-traverse stretch. While economists have long understood that the gainers from structural change can compensate the losers, that doesn't mean requiring successful companies to carry the failures. It does mean raising taxes on successful companies to pay for investments in broader economic participation from everyone else. The key is not to blame corporations or economists for some workers' plight or to argue for walls of protection, but to enhance skills that will lead to more productive jobs now and in the future.

Queen Elizabeth's question about noticing does give a bit of pause, though. Economic *policy* has picked up the cause of broader economic participation and prosperity before. Lincoln-era assaults on barriers to economic opportunity aimed at preparing more people for connection to a changing economy. Franklin Roosevelt's commitment to social insurance offered economic reconnection to individuals whose fortunes and prospects were battered by the downturn of the Great Depression of the 1930s. These "Lincolnvelt" interventions safeguarded capitalism and were consistent with economic principles.

Toward those ends, compensation is not a check from a gainer to the loser, but a basic principle that support for preparation (opportunity) and reconnection (social insurance) must accompany market acceptance of change. It preserves both the gains of market capitalism and dynamism, and popular support for those gains.

The "how" of preparation builds on existing institutions for success in education and training. Community colleges are central players in providing skills to meet job demands of the changing economy, but in most states they are starved for resources. In contrast to calls for demand-side support—free tuition—I proposed supply-side assistance—funding through a federal block grant—for community colleges in their skill-development mission. Likewise, firms can boost on-the-job training, with support from tax subsidies to compensate for the risk of trained workers leaving for a job elsewhere. The massive retraining required in the wake of the COVID-19 pandemic only amplifies the need for this policy.

General progrowth policies can support these bridges by keeping the American economy at the forefront of dynamic change. Federal support for R&D can assist both basic science and technology and commercialization of applications. A strong public commitment to research puts the economy in a good position for new possibilities and change. Indeed, the United States should maintain global research preeminence to ensure mass flourishing.

These steps to assist preparation are meaningful tools to encourage broader economic participation. But they do not meet the need for reconnection when structural shifts disrupt income for a long period. To avoid inevitable calls for walls of protection, we need to rethink social insurance.

Current U.S. social insurance programs focus on temporary lay-offs (unemployment insurance) and the needs of older Americans (Social Security and Medicare). Trade Adjustment Assistance, launched in the 1960s, has always lacked the political support for adequate funding. A better approach would be Personal Reemployment Accounts (support for training and income for structural job losers), wage insurance for some workers (to encourage rapid reemployment and skill acquisition), and the Earned Income Tax Credit (expanded substantially, particularly for younger, childless workers). In addition, some "place-based aid" to communities can effectively subsidize employment opportunities in areas in which long-term rates of working-age unemployment are high. Changing the structure of federal tax subsidies to health insurance can help delink employment and access to health insurance and raise labor demand for low- and mid-skilled workers.

Bridges Require Intentional Business and Government Action

Companies have essential roles to play in bridge building. Especially for dislocated communities, governments alone can't lead the way in restoring the economy to dynamism. The examples of Massachusetts and Pittsburgh demonstrate that future-oriented local business leadership—supported by local and national government—makes the difference in local flourishing.

While business philanthropy can make a difference for some educational, cultural, and community recipients, philanthropy is *not* the core element of business bridge building. Rather, business's role reflects both the internal workings of the market system Adam Smith and subsequent economists championed, and the external—social and political—support for that system.

Preparation for competition today is essential and of greater significance than for the simpler economy illustrated in *The Wealth of Nations*. Collectively, the business sector should defend the process of competition. Most economic discussion of enhancing competition focuses on restraints on anticompetitive behavior through limits on market power. Classical economists supported this emphasis. But business itself should prepare for competition by arguing against policy frictions such as the entry barriers erected by occupational licensing's limits on employment mobility, zoning restrictions' adverse effects on geographic mobility, and larger-scale state tinkering through subsidies and burdensome regulation that can deter entry. This motivation was the crux of Smith's argument against the cost in living standards of mercantilist tinkering. Collectively, the business community must offer its strong voice in defense of competition. Collective business organizations can also add their voices—for example, the Business Roundtable for the largest corporations, the National Federation of Independent Business for smaller firms, and the U.S. Chamber of Commerce for business generally. The competitive process is important for the smooth functioning of the market system.

Even large, geographically sprawling businesses can help here, whether managers act in the interests of investors or of a social good. In both cases, companies benefit from local workforces capable of participating in the dynamic, competitive economy. But companies should not always step in to fill the void of dysfunctional government, because then they'll weaken their vital contribution to living standards.

Recall that this concern over a potential lack of business accountability and its consequences for the economy animated Milton Fried-

MASS FLOURISHING REQUIRES BRIDGES

man's famous essay of half a century ago, whose point is well summed up in its title—"The Social Responsibility of Business Is to Increase Its Profits." Friedman's argument was simple, powerful, and influential in corporate governance and public policy. In 1997, the Business Roundtable issued a statement firmly in line with Friedman's shareholder primacy dictum. But by 2019, the Roundtable changed its view, with a new statement arguing that the purpose of the corporation is a commitment to all stakeholders (with shareholders last on the list). Again, under its assumptions, Friedman's view leads to similar outcomes. The Roundtable's statement once again raises concerns about tinkering and accountability that worried Friedman. It also generated praise from many elected officials and business leaders, as well as some prominent investors.

But broader externalities like climate change are not addressable only by business maximization. One punch line, of course, is that these (and other) externalities can be addressed by adding policy interventions (taxation or regulation, for example) to long-term shareholder value maximization.

But, again, business must play a role. To prepare workers for economic shifts requires training and reskilling. Externalities can be mitigated by firms coming together with local community colleges, communities, and state governments. Notable examples by major corporations have benefited them and the communities in which they operate. The Business Roundtable and the Chamber of Commerce can document and explain "what works" to encourage successful replication.

Business's role in bridge building has another, more macro objective—to bolster public support for the dynamic and competitive market economy. Certain basic arguments, from Smith's defense of competition to Friedman's articulation of the purpose of the corporation, take broad public support as given. In recent decades of structural economic change, however, this support has wavered in populist rhetoric urging walls against change (largely from the right) or arguing against business's freedom to manage that change (largely from the left). Business bridge building is needed for public support. Business leaders must think of themselves as "somewheres"—concerned participants in particular communities and partners of particular people—as well as "anywheres" who think about dynamism's value. This thinking would be usefully supported by annual reports to the board of directors, shareholders, and the public on the firm's bridge-building activities.

There are positive steps individuals and businesses can take even in the face of government indifference, indecision, or inaction. But government policy must play a central role in building bridges as an alternative to walls. The failure of the familiar U.S. political debate between a neoliberal version of laissez faire and democratic socialism reflects in large part its inability to address economic preparation (opportunity) and reconnection (social insurance). "The wall" has filled the void.

As for governments at all levels today, we need leaders who can make the case for public investment in bridges rather than walls. And because of the complexity of bridges, we need creative ideas and institutional processes to implement them. Support for research and development shifts the frontier of knowledge and applications. Even federal block grant funding for community colleges, and tax credits for training, will need energetic and sustained governmental attention. Preparation support could target places as well as people, communities, and areas adversely affected by generally positive (across the nation) changes. Successful interventions will likely bring federal support together with local needs, as the history of land-grant colleges and their impacts suggest.

These policy ideas need to be accompanied by leadership and a process that ensures their execution. While leadership needs a policy champion, it also requires a policy *framing*. The neoliberal economic framing, if not completely laissez-faire, stresses the dynamism and growth in living standards from structural changes and a market economy. Changes are simply to be accepted because of net gains overall. Think of this framing as one of "outside-in." The change is valuable, and insiders as individuals or firms need to adjust to it; on average, they gain by doing so. An alternative framing, more akin to the classical mass-flourishing goal, is "inside-out." We will put in place supports, supported by taxation, to ensure preparation for and reconnection to the economy for everyone. Such a framing also recognizes the intrinsic worth of dynamism and the market economy. But it *begins* by removing barriers to economic participation, *then* encourages the changes driving dynamism and growth.

Process matters in addition to ideas, framing, and leadership. Just as the National Security Council and later the Domestic Policy Council and National Economic Council have brought together agencies with different functions to solve crosscutting problems, building bridges for economic participation and engagement requires a rethinking of public management. A cabinet-level U.S. Taskforce on Economic Engagement could deliver all-of-government advice and coordination for the White House with an annual report and required congressional testimony to engage the public broadly. Building from local experiences across the United States, business and university leaders could be called upon to serve on an advisory council with the taskforce.

A participation economy requires noticing. Economic and political elites must notice trends in the entire economy, not just on average or among similarly situated elites. A revival of national service, broadly construed, could help rebuild bridges of Smith's "national empathy" among Americans—and shift the country to a "we're all in this together" approach to mass flourishing.

The Pandemic Emphasizes the Need for Bridges

The COVID-19 pandemic of 2020–2021 took hold after the writing of this book was well underway. While it suddenly turned a strong economy into one with high unemployment, it mostly just accelerated ongoing structural changes, especially from digital technologies. Workers with fewer skills for jobs of the future are now losing out even more to people in demand on global markets. The coronavirus also laid bare workplace distinctions by skill group. Most skilled professionals could work from home, while many less-skilled people faced diminished hours in bricks-and-mortar establishments, or no work at all.

Politically, the pandemic has boosted interest in walls: against tight global integration in supply chains, and against large firms squeezing out small and midsize firms. Voters fear diminished future earnings for workers and students with limited access to digital technology. Bridges for future work have therefore become all the more important. Bridges offer much more than macroeconomic stabilization; they could strengthen public backing of the competitive market economy in a challenging period. But these efforts must not remain so modest relative to both the need and the opportunity.

With the pandemic as a backdrop, the election of Joe Biden as president fueled hopes of arresting populist pressures in America. Such hopes seem quite optimistic, though, and, of course, hope is not a strategy. Three concerns remain. First, while antiglobalization voices like that of Peter Navarro are gone from official circles, the Biden administration and the Democratic party more generally are skeptical about the benefits of trade and trade agreements. Trump-era protectionism and interest in industrial policy to favor manufacturing remain very much in place. Second, the Biden administration emphasized in its American Jobs Plan of March 2021 greater public spending on health care and public assistance, with much less discussion of skill preparation or a rethinking of social insurance programs to support work. Nor has it worked to create processes to foster bridges across the federal government, or advocated partnerships with state and local governments toward that end. Indeed, the administration's embrace of backward-looking industrial policy misses the opportunity to build bridges to the future rather than attempting to compensate those not ready to participate in it. Finally, the closely divided U.S. electorate indicates that Donald Trump's personal defeat is a far cry from a defeat of economic populism, and walls are still strong factors in politics.

Still, the news is not all discouraging. President Biden's interest in infrastructure, green or otherwise, bodes well for mid-skill jobs for many Americans and for a tighter labor market with pressure to increase wages. Rising pleas from states for federal support for higher education are a plus for skill development and retraining. The Biden administration's explicit concern for income inequality suggests an interest in raising incomes of the least well off among us. Finally, the budget cost of bridge policies may be now less daunting given a willingness to raise taxes on well-to-do Americans, though bridge policies are not yet on offer. Certainly the administration is more inclined to actively pursue supports such as bridges, following an inside-out policy approach, rather than a laissez-faire outside-in approach where market outcomes are simply accepted.

Looking ahead takes us well beyond the Biden administration's plans. Many economists and economic policymakers continue to focus on conceptual debates between neoliberalism and socialism. But the practical political back and forth is more likely to center on bridges (classical liberalism) and walls (social democratic protections from the left and antichange protections from the right). As I have argued here, bridges have the better economic foundation. Those bridges also bring together preparation for and reconnection to opportunity, emphasizing individual agency and roles for government and business as well. While bridges push the economic frontier, their flip side actually tears down walls, barriers to opportunity for more individuals. Smith's *Wealth of Nations* and *Theory of Moral Sentiments* come full circle here.

While I have focused on economic challenges and policy options for walls and bridges in the United States, the themes and arguments outlined here are certainly not unique to America. Smith's vision of a competitive market economy began in Britain, the fount of dynamism and innovism described by Edmund Phelps and Deirdre McCloskey. Historical battles between walls and bridges in response to structural economic changes dot the history of Britain and other industrial economies. Today's populism in the United States, Britain, France, Italy, Spain, Brazil, and elsewhere reflects the inability of the competitive market economy to "make the sale" that mass flourishing is possible, not just prosperity for the well-equipped.

Failing to remember mass flourishing as the objective—or putting liberal or neoliberal pieties ahead of it—left an opening for populist walls dividing elites, including economic elites, from "the people." Such divisions fail to yield policies for prosperity, but assume the mantle of inclusion. Extending the definition of Smith's competition to include being prepared to compete is about bridges to full participation in the economy. Those bridges bolster public support for capitalism. And as my teacher, Harvard economist Benjamin Friedman, noted in his book *The Moral Consequences of Economic Growth*, periods of mass flourishing carry social as well as economic benefits, with less discrimination and broader social inclusion.[1]

Beyond policymakers, economists, too, need to return to mass flourishing and bridges. As critics of liberal orthodoxy from Keynes to Polanyi have noted, the national and global competitive market economy produces long-run prosperity on average, but at the cost of disconnection for many individuals along the way. Such disconnections fuel calls for walls against change and can undermine support for the Smithian system. Powerful neoliberal economic doubling down in the decentralized market economy by economic luminaries such as Hayek or Friedman makes important contributions about the value of markets and the price system. But today's economists must be more than laissez-faire champions of markets and the price system. Economics offers the blueprints for bridges to prepare individuals for the market system, reconnect them to it, and build support for it.

Structural economic forces, like the technological change and globalization we have emphasized here, are powerful and account for significant gains in average living standards. Technological disruption promises further, if noisy, advances, with artificial intelligence and robotics representing "general purpose technology" leaps forward. While U.S. trade tensions with China and trading blocs like the European Union suggest decoupling to a degree, forces of global competition and the importance of global markets for business remain strong. But the fact that these forces are strong, and increase the wealth of the nation, does *not* imply that a body politic should passively accept their wake.

What these alternative approaches and events portend was the subject of two vignettes I used at the beginning of this book—my failure to persuade President George W. Bush to resist calls for steel tariffs, and the diverging paths for me and for many Youngstown workers in response to technological change and globalization. The steel tariffs of 2001 represented a response to cries for walls against change in a political environment that had paid far too little attention to them. Since September 1977, when I started studying economies as an undergraduate, technological change and globalization have magnified the market value of my skills and the skills of many professionals. Meanwhile, the closure of Youngstown's integrated steel mills did not lead to moon-shot efforts toward the preparation and reconnection of many workers and communities for the changing economy.

Imagine if bold support for community colleges and training would match the preparation and reconnection of the G.I. Bill as America was encouraging global integration. Imagine if leadership of bridge ideas moved political debate toward economic participation and away from the straw-man alternatives of laissez faire or socialism. Imagine a broader understanding of and support for the economic system that generates an ever-increasing wealth of the nation.

Imagine mass flourishing.

Notes

Chapter 1. Introduction

1. Glenn Hubbard and Anthony Patrick O'Brien, *Economics,* 8th edition, Hoboken, NJ: Pearson, 2021.

Chapter 2. How We Got Here

1. See, for example, the review in James McBride and Mohammed Aly Sergie, "NAFTA's Economic Impact," *Council on Foreign Relations Online,* October 1, 2018.

2. See Glenn Hubbard, "The $64,000 Question: Living in the Age of Technological Possibility or Showing Possibility's Age?," in John W. Diamond and George R. Zodrow, eds., *Prospects for Economic Growth in the United States,* Cambridge: Cambridge University Press, 2021, pages 115–131.

3. Bureau of Labor Statistics data, September 2019.

4. See, for example, Benjamin Austin, Edward Glaeser, and Lawrence H. Summers, "Jobs for the Heartland: Place-Based Policies in 21st-Century America," *Brookings Papers on Economic Activity* 1 (2018), pages 151–232.

5. See ibid.

6. See Anne Case and Angus Deaton, "Mortality and Morbidity in the 21st Century," *Brookings Papers on Economic Activity,* 2017, pages 397–443; and Anne Case and Angus Deaton, *Deaths of Despair and the Future of Capitalism,* Princeton, NJ: Princeton University Press, 2020.

7. Trade Adjustment Assistance (TAA) is the U.S. government's principal program to assist workers whose job prospects are adversely affected by foreign competition; we will discuss it further in later chapters. Proposed by President John F. Kennedy as part of a policy package to increase support for free trade instead of high tariffs, TAA consists of programs authorized under the Trade Expansion Act of 1962 and the Trade Act of 1974. No application was even accepted until 1969, and since that time, the program's low funding and bureaucratic requirements have made it

much less than a success in addressing worker dislocations from trade. The program does not address long-term structural job loss from effects of technological change. We return to problems in its design in Chapters 6 and 8.

8. See Andrew E. Clark and Andrew J. Oswald, "Unhappiness and Unemployment," *Economic Journal* 104 (1994), pages 648–659; André Hajek, "Life Satisfaction and Unemployment: The Role of Voluntariness and Job Prospects," SOEP Paper on Multidisciplinary Research No. 601, Berlin: DIW Berlin, 2013; and Rainer Winkelmann, "Unemployment and Happiness," World of Labor No. 94, Bonn Institute for the Study of Labor (IZA), 2014.

9. See David Koistinen, *Confronting Decline: The Political Economy of Deindustrialization in Twentieth-Century New England,* Gainesville: University Press of Florida, 2013, page 222.

10. See Katherine G. Abraham and Melissa S. Kearney, "Explaining the Decline in the U.S. Employment-to-Population Ratio: A Review of the Evidence," Working Paper No. 24333, National Bureau of Economic Research, February 2018.

11. See Kerwin Charles, Erik Hurst, and M. J. Notowidigdo, "The Masking of Declining Manufacturing Employment by the Housing Bubble," *Journal of Economic Perspectives* 30:2 (2016), pages 179–200.

12. See Kerwin Charles, Erik Hurst, and Mariel Swartz, "The Transformation of Manufacturing and the Decline in U.S. Employment," in Barry Eichengreen and Jonathan Parker, eds., *NBER Macroeconomics Annual* 33 (2018), pages 307–372.

13. See David H. Autor, David Dorn, and Gordon H. Hanson, "The China Syndrome: Local Labor Market Effects of Import Competition in the United States," *American Economic Review* 103:6 (2013), pages 2121–2168.

14. See David H. Autor, David Dorn, and Gordon H. Hanson, "Untangling Trade and Technology: Evidence from Local Labor Markets," *Economic Journal* 125 (2015), pages 621–646.

15. See Daron Acemoglu, David H. Autor, David Dorn, Gordon H. Hanson, and Brendan Price, "Impact Competition and the Great U.S. Employment Sag of the 2000s," *Journal of Labor Economics* 34 (2016), pages S141–S198; Nicholas Bloom, Kyle Handley, Andre Kurmann, and Philip Luck, "The Impact of Chinese Trade on U.S. Employment: The Good, the Bad, and the Apocryphal," Working Paper, Stanford University, 2019.

16. See David H. Autor, "Trade and Labor Markets: Lessons from China's Rise," World of Labor, No. 431, Bonn Institute for the Study of Labor (IZA), 2018.

17. See David H. Autor, David Dorn, and Gordon H. Hanson, "The China

Shock: Learning from Adjustment to Large Changes in Trade," *Annual Review of Economics* 8:1 (2016), pages 205–240.

18. See Autor, "Trade and Labor Markets."

19. See ibid.

20. See Abraham and Kearney, "Explaining the Decline."

21. See David H. Autor, David Dorn, Gordon H. Hanson, and Kaveh Majlesi, "Importing Political Polarization? The Electoral Consequences of Rising Trade Exposure," *American Economic Review* 110 (October 2020), pages 3139–3183.

22. See Friedrich A. Hayek, *The Road to Serfdom,* Chicago: University of Chicago Press, 1944.

23. Friedrich A. Hayek, "The Use of Knowledge in Society," *American Economic Review* 35 (September 1945), pages 519–530.

24. Milton Friedman, *Capitalism and Freedom,* Chicago: University of Chicago Press, 1962.

25. In fact, until it adopted the federal income tax in 1913, tariffs—excise taxes on individuals' and businesses' purchases of imported goods—were the federal government's largest source of revenue by far. One reason for the shift toward *income* taxation was concern that tariffs harmed low-income individuals and advantaged high-income business interests. Tax reformers viewed tariffs as costly for mass prosperity and popular support for the economic system. They believed income taxes would raise revenue more progressively.

26. The G.I. Bill also aimed at economic inclusion. World War I veterans had received about $60 and a train ticket home, not much of a bridge of preparation or reconnection to the economy they had protected. Congress tried to placate struggling veterans with a bonus in the World War Adjusted Compensation Act of 1924, but their woes continued, culminating in a tumultuous march on Washington in 1932 for advances on their bonus payments. The G.I. Bill's emphasis on education and homeownership implicitly acknowledged that access to college and owning a home had been beyond the reach of the average American. About half of the 16 million World War II veterans participated in education or training programs, and the Veterans Administration assisted in granting 2.4 million home loans in the first decade after the war. Long viewed as a policy success, the G.I. Bill was updated in 1984 and 2008 to back educational benefits for veterans. The most recent expansions came in the Harry W. Colmery Veterans Educational Assistance Act of 2018, signed by President Trump.

27. While historians have debated the reasons for the Luddite movement (for

example, antitechnology animus versus poor working-class economic conditions), the term "Luddite" entered the lexicon as a descriptor for someone who advocates building a wall to block out something new that threatens the familiar. That the term has not gone away says something about the emotional appeal of walls against risks many individuals find difficult to manage.

28. See David H. Autor, "Work of the Past, Work of the Future," *American Economic Review Papers and Proceedings* 109 (May 2019), pages 1–32.

29. See Amy Goldstein, *Janesville: An American Story,* New York: Simon & Schuster, 2017.

Chapter 3. Mass Flourishing

1. See Adam Smith, *The Theory of Moral Sentiments: An Essay Towards an Analysis of the Principles by Which Men Naturally Judge Concerning the Conduct and Character, First of their Neighbors, and Afterwards of Themselves,* London, 1759. I use *The Theory of Moral Sentiments* as shorthand.

2. See Adam Smith, *An Inquiry into the Nature and Causes of the Wealth of Nations,* London, 1776. I use *The Wealth of Nations* as shorthand.

3. He was buried at Canongate Kirkyard in Edinburgh. Some years ago, Ray Horton traveled to Edinburgh and searched for Smith's gravesite. Finding it overgrown and in disrepair, he expressed his dismay to me in a missive from his travels. I wrote the church elders offering to raise funds to refurbish the site. The elders told me my assistance was not necessary. Whether by coincidence or providence or prodding, a local benefactor was secured, and Smith's gravesite is presentable today.

4. Smith railed at the inefficiency of the British East India Company in Book V, Chapter 1 of *The Wealth of Nations.*

5. See Kenneth J. Arrow and Gerard Debreu, "Existence of an Equilibrium for a Competitive Economy," *Econometrica* 22 (July 1954), pages 265–290.

6. In this, Smith prefigured Ricardo in criticizing the Corn Laws. As noted in Chapter 2, these restrictions protected British agricultural interests, and were opposed by both workers (who objected to higher food prices) and emerging industrialists (who had to pay higher wages to compensate). Ultimately repealed, the Corn Laws prompted a political debate between Thomas Malthus (who supported the restrictions) and Ricardo.

7. Smith also identified the importance of globalization as affecting the size of the market. In particular, he identified the "discovery" of America by Christopher Columbus in 1492 and Vasco da Gama's voyage to India as significant commercial

events. And he commented on the value going forward of structural shifts away from agriculture toward manufacturing and trade. See Adam Smith, *The Wealth of Nations,* Book II, Chapter 7, Part III.

8. MIT economist and Nobel laureate Robert Solow estimated a residual in growth accounting (after input growth) as labor-augmenting technological change, arriving exogenously in the model. While a faster rate of technological change raises an economy's growth rate, the model does not explain why the rate of technological change differs over time and across countries. See Robert M. Solow, "A Contribution to the Theory of Economic Growth," *Quarterly Journal of Economics* 70 (February 1956), pages 65–94.

9. See the work of Nobel laureate Paul Romer; in particular, Paul Romer, "Endogenous Technological Change," *Journal of Political Economy* 98 (October 1990), pages S71–S102.

10. See Edmund Phelps, *Mass Flourishing,* Princeton, NJ: Princeton University Press, 2013; and Edmund Phelps, Raicho Bojilov, Hian Teck Hoon, and Gylfi Zoega, *Dynamism,* Cambridge, MA: Harvard University Press, 2020.

11. See the review in Glenn Hubbard, "The $64,000 Question: Living in the Age of Technological Possibility or Showing Possibility's Age?," in John Diamond and George Zodrow, eds., *Prospects for Economic Growth,* Cambridge: Cambridge University Press, 2021, pages 115–131.

12. See Deirdre N. McCloskey, *The Bourgeois Virtues: Ethics for an Age of Commerce,* Chicago: University of Chicago Press, 2006; *Bourgeois Equality: How Ideas, Not Capital, Enriched the World,* Chicago: University of Chicago Press, 2016; and *Why Liberalism Works,* New Haven: Yale University Press, 2020.

13. See Mihaly Csikszentmihalyi, *Flow: The Psychology of Optimal Experience,* New York: Harper Penguin Modern Classics, 1990.

14. See, for example, Edmund Phelps, *Rewarding Work,* Cambridge: Harvard University Press, 2007; and Glenn Hubbard, "Supporting Work, Inclusion, and Mass Prosperity," in Michael R. Strain, ed., *The U.S. Labor Market: Questions and Challenges for Public Policy,* Washington, DC: AEI Press, 2016, pages 96–105.

15. See Karl Polanyi, *The Great Transformation: The Political and Economic Origins of Our Time,* New York: Farrar and Rinehart, 1944. It appeared the same year as Friedrich Hayek's *The Road to Serfdom,* but met far less acclaim, partly because it was not serialized in *Reader's Digest* like Hayek's classic.

16. Smith's throwing down the gauntlet, in *The Wealth of Nations,* attacked the prevailing economic orthodoxy. He argued that mercantilists had the wrong foun-

dation—the "wealth of a nation" lay not in gold and silver, but in the living standard of its people. He attacked mercantilists' very economic engine—walls of protection and special-interest tinkering by government—and replaced it with competition and the invisible hand, with government securing the integrity of market forces.

Chapter 4. Adam Smith Schools Today's Commentators

1. See David Koistinen, *Confronting Decline: The Political Economy of Twentieth Century New England,* Gainesville: University Press of Florida, 2013. We return to Massachusetts's efforts in Chapter 8. A cautionary tale: As textile manufacturing experienced competitive pressures in southern states decades later, those states had a more mixed record in casting aside retrenchment and economic arguments for walls in favor of bridges of economic development.

2. See Oren Cass, *The Once and Future Worker: A Vision for the Renewal of Work in America,* New York: Encounter Books, 2018.

3. More recent economists have emphasized that this decentralized mechanism promotes liberty as well as economic growth. See, for example, Friedrich A. Hayek, "The Use of Knowledge in Society," *American Economic Review* 35 (September 1945), highlighted in Chapter 3.

4. See David H. Autor, Anna Salomons, and Bryan Seegmiller, "New Frontiers: The Origins and Content of New Work, 1940–2018," Working Paper, MIT, 2020.

5. See Daron Acemoglu and Pascual Restrepo, "The Race Between Man and Machine: Implications of Technology for Growth, Factor Shares, and Employment," *American Economic Review* 108 (2018), pages 1488–1542.

6. See David H. Autor, "Why Are There Still So Many Jobs? The History and Future of Workplace Automation," *Journal of Economic Perspectives* 29 (2015), pages 3–30. The ratio of employment to population has declined in the United States in the twenty-first century owing in large part to population aging and increases in retirement.

7. See Raghuram Rajan and Luigi Zingales, *Saving Capitalism from the Capitalists,* Princeton, NJ: Princeton University Press, 2003.

8. See Luigi Zingales, *A Capitalism for the People: Recapturing the Lost Genius of American Prosperity,* New York: Basic Books, 2012. See also Luigi Zingales, "Capitalism After the Crisis," *National Affairs* 1 (2009), pages 22–35.

9. I once wrote a book with Navarro, with a somewhat different take on America's recent economic challenges. See Glenn Hubbard and Peter Navarro, *Seeds of*

Destruction: Why the Path to Economic Ruin Runs through Washington and How to Reclaim American Prosperity, Upper Saddle River, NJ: FT Press, 2011.

10. My successor as chair of the President's Council of Economic Advisers, Gregory Mankiw, pointed out that "there is a lot of evidence that inward-looking economic policies that isolate a country from the rest of the world are bad for that country. You could make a list of the 100 most prominent economists in the world, and Peter Navarro wouldn't be on it. His views are very, very far from the mainstream" (quoted in Molly Ball, "Peter Navarro Used to Be a Democrat. Now He's the Mastermind Behind Trump's Trade War," *Time,* August 23, 2018). But is this the best economic response? Adam Smith shredded Thomas Mun's mercantilism two centuries ago, but without personal invective.

11. A bit more algebra breaks this down. Household income equals the amount of funds received from the sale of goods and services (GDP), plus what is received from the government as transfer payments (Transfers) such as Social Security payments or unemployment insurance payments. With this breakdown in mind and letting "Taxes" stand for households' (on their own and as owners of businesses) tax payments, domestic saving is given by:

Domestic saving = (Household saving) + (Government saving) = [(GDP + Transfers - Taxes) - Consumption)] + [Taxes - (Government Purchases + Transfers)]. Saving supplied by foreigners = (Exports - Imports). Saving supplied by foreigners, then, equals the excess of national investment over national saving.

12. Among contemporary popular commentators see, for example, the criticism of economists' views in Binyamin Appelbaum, *The Economists' Hour: False Prophets, Free Markets, and the Fracture of Society,* New York: Little Brown and Company, 2019; and Nicholas Lemann, *Transaction Man: The Rise of the Deal and the Decline of the American Dream,* New York: Farrar, Straus and Giroux, 2019.

13. See Colin Mayer, *Prosperity: Better Business Makes the Greater Good,* Oxford: Oxford University Press, 2018.

14. See Martin Lipton, "The New Paradigm: A Roadmap to an Implicit Corporate Governance Partnership Between Corporations and Investors to Achieve Sustainable Long-Term Investment and Growth," World Economic Forum, 2019.

15. We will return to this idea in Chapter 7 in considering Milton Friedman's argument that the purpose of a corporation should be to maximize value for its shareholders.

16. See Leo Strine, Jr., "Corporate Governance 'Counter-narratives': On Corporate Purpose and Shareholder Value(s)," Remarks at Columbia Law School, March 1, 2019.

17. See "Tom Enders," *European CEO,* January 28, 2013.

18. See Rajan and Zingales, *Saving Capitalism from the Capitalists.*

19. See Milton Friedman, "The Social Responsibility of Business Is to Maximize Its Profits," *New York Times Sunday Magazine,* September 13, 1970. We return to Friedman's points in Chapter 7.

20. Management thinker and University of Toronto professor emeritus Roger Martin makes this point forcefully in *When More Is Not Better: Overcoming America's Obsession with Economic Efficiency,* Boston: Harvard Business Review Press, 2020.

Chapter 5. Why Walls Are Still Attractive

1. William Bunting, "Reagan in Youngstown," *The Ripon Forum,* August–September 2008, https://riponsociety.org/article/reagan-in-youngstown-2/.

2. Casey Mulligan, "I'm a Tariff Man: Comparing Presidents Reagan and Trump," *National Review,* October 19, 2020, https://www.nationalreview.com/2020/10/i-am-a-tariff-man-comparing-presidents-reagan-and-trump/.

3. See Robert W. Crandall, "Import Quotas and the Automobile Industry," *Brookings Review* 2:4 (1984), pages 8–16.

4. See Kimberly Clausing, "The Progressive Case Against Protectionism," *Foreign Affairs* 58 (November–December 2019), pages 109–120.

5. See Mary Amiti, Stephen J. Redding, and David E. Weinstein, "The Impact of the 2018 Tariffs on Prices and Welfare," *Journal of Economic Perspectives* 33:4 (Fall 2019), pages 187–210.

6. See Pablo D. Fajgelbaum, Pinelopi K. Goldberg, Patrick J. Kennedy, and Amit K. Khandelwal, "The Return to Protectionism," Working Paper No. 25638, National Bureau of Economic Research, 2019; *Quarterly Journal of Economics,* forthcoming.

7. See Aaron Flaaen and Justin Pierce, "Disentangling the Effects of the 2018–2019 Tariffs on a Globally Connected U.S. Manufacturing Sector," Working Paper No. 2019-086. Board of Governors of the Federal Reserve System, 2019.

8. See Michael R. Strain, "The American Dream Is Alive and Well," *Wall Street Journal,* February 1–2, 2020.

9. See, for example, Chris Matthews, "Here's Why the Middle Class Is Disappearing All Around the World," *Fortune,* July 13, 2016; Pew Research Center,

America's Shrinking Middle Class: A Close Look at Changes Within Metropolitan Areas, 2016; Alex Morris, "American Middle Class: Why Is It Disappearing?," *Rolling Stone,* November 13, 2018; and Stephen Rose, "Squeezing the Middle Class," Working Paper, Brookings Institution, 2020.

10. See Pew Research Center, *Majorities Say Government Does Too Little for Older People, the Poor and the Middle Class,* 2018.

11. See David H. Autor, Lawrence F. Katz, and Melissa S. Kearney, "The Polarization of the U.S. Labor Market," *American Economic Review* 96 (May 2006), pages 189–194.

12. See David H. Autor, "Work of the Past, Work of the Future," *American Economic Review* 109 (May 2019), pages 1–32.

13. See Adam Looney, Jeff Larrimore, and David Splinter, "Middle-Class Redistribution: Tax and Transfer Policy for Most Americans," Working Paper, Aspen Institute Economic Strategy Group, 2020.

14. See Raicho Bojilov and Edmund S. Phelps, "The Effects of Two Different Cultures," Working Paper 78, Center on Capitalism and Society, Columbia University, September 2012.

15. See William D. Nordhaus, "Schumpeterian Profits in the American Economy: Theory and Measurement," Working Paper No. 10433, Cambridge, MA: National Bureau of Economic Research, 2004.

16. See, for example, Milton Friedman, *A Theory of the Consumption Function,* Princeton, NJ: Princeton University Press, 1957; Albert Ando and Franco Modigliani, "The 'Life Cycle' Hypothesis of Saving: Aggregate Implications and Tests," *American Economic Review* 53 (March 1963), pages 55–84; and Robert E. Hall, "Stochastic Implication of the Life Cycle—Permanent Income Hypothesis: Theory and Evidence," *Journal of Political Economy* 86 (December 1978), pages 971–987.

17. See, for example, Christopher D. Carroll, "Buffer Stock Saving and the Life Cycle/Permanent Income Hypothesis," *Quarterly Journal of Economics* 112 (February 1997), pages 1–55; and R. Glenn Hubbard, Jonathan Skinner, and Stephen P. Zeldes, "The Importance of Precautionary Motives in Explaining Individual and Aggregate Saving," *Carnegie-Rochester Conference Series on Public Policy* 40 (1994), pages 59–125.

18. The story becomes a bit more complicated when individuals face borrowing restrictions—"liquidity-constrained" consumers may experience significant consumption declines when earnings fall. See R. Glenn Hubbard and Kenneth L. Judd, "Liquidity Constraints, Fiscal Policy, and Consumption," *Brookings Papers on Economic Activity,* 1986, pages 1–59.

19. See R. Glenn Hubbard, Jonathan Skinner, and Stephen P. Zeldes, "Precautionary Saving and Social Insurance," *Journal of Political Economy* 103 (April 1995), pages 360–399.

20. See the analysis of Social Security Administration individual earnings records from 1979 to 2011 by Fatih Guvenen, Serdar Ozkan, and Jae Song, "The Nature of Countercyclical Income Risk," *Journal of Political Economy* 122 (June 2014), pages 621–660. Note: We focus on male workers here because of major shifts in the labor supply related to childbirth and child-rearing that were concentrated among women.

21. See Jason DeBacker, Bradley Heim, Vasia Panousi, Shanthi Ramnath, and Ivan Vidangos, "Rising Inequality: Transitory or Persistent? New Evidence from a Panel of U.S. Tax Returns," *Brookings Papers on Economic Activity*, Spring 2013, pages 67–142.

22. Again, see Hubbard and Judd, "Liquidity Constraints."

23. Such social insurance will reduce total saving, but increase individuals' well-being. See, for example, R. Glenn Hubbard and Kenneth L. Judd, "Social Security and Individual Welfare: Precautionary Saving, Borrowing Constraints, and the Payroll Tax," *American Economic Review* 77 (September 1987), pages 630–646. Indeed, thinking of social insurance benefits as "wealth" significantly reduces measured wealth inequality across individuals focusing only on individually held assets. For an example with Social Security "wealth," see Sylvain Catherine, Max Miller, and Natasha Sarin, "Inequality Has Increased Far Less Than You Think (If You Consider Social Security Benefits)," *Promarket*, University of Chicago Booth School of Business, Stigler Center, April 16, 2020.

Chapter 6. Bridges

1. Slavery, of course, was the greatest barrier to mass flourishing in America. Lincoln died before he could do much to help build bridges for freedmen, but the land-grant colleges eventually opened up to Black students.

2. This application of "bridge" has a rich history in American jurisprudence as well. In an important U.S. Supreme Court case decided in 1837, a principle was established that community rights going forward are a complement to private property rights. Allowing owners of a bridge to monopolize transportation over a route, as argued by the Charles River Bridge Company, would limit bridges to the future, the Supreme Court decided. Chief Justice Roger Taney argued that canals and railroads were efficiently taking away business from highways and that granting monop-

olies to legacy corporations would limit future transportation improvements (*Charles River Bridge v. Warren Bridge*, 36 U.S. [11.Pet.] 420 [1837]). Adam Smith would surely have agreed.

3. See Gary Clyde Hufbauer and Zhiyao (Lucy) Lu, "The Payoff to America from Globalization: A Fresh Look with a Focus on Costs to Workers," Policy Brief PB17-16, Peterson Institute for International Economics, 2017.

4. See the analysis in Alan S. Blinder, "The Free-Trade Paradox: The Bad Politics of a Good Idea," *Foreign Affairs Online,* December 11, 2018.

5. Enter Adam Smith once more, who pointed out in *The Wealth of Nations* that the obvious case for free trade would be opposed by "the interested sophistry of merchants and manufacturers." Left unsaid in this tug of war is a bridge, a connection to a new opportunity or a reconnection to the productive economy. That connection and reconnection are the flesh on the bones of the idea that "the gainers can compensate the losers."

6. See David H. Autor, "Work of the Past, Work of the Future," *American Economic Review* 109 (May 2019), pages 1–32.

7. See Anna Stansbury and Lawrence H. Summers, "Productivity and Pay: Is the Link Broken?," Working Paper No. 18-5, Peterson Institute for International Economics, 2018. The authors measure "productivity" as total economy real output per hour; they measure "average compensation" as total economy real compensation per hour, deflated by the CPI-U-RS price deflator.

8. See ibid.

9. See Autor, "Work of the Past, Work of the Future,"

10. Indeed, as I argue later, a "mass flourishing" concept of opportunity for many more Americans is needed to keep the social consensus for the innovative market system.

11. And there's more: Some economists have suggested that underlying economic forces are concentrating highly productive and highly skilled workers in successful "superstar" firms: John Van Reenen and Christina Patterson, "Research: The Rise of Superstar Firms Has Been Better for Investors Than for Employees," *Harvard Business Review Online,* May 11, 2017.

12. See Oren Cass, *The Once and Future Worker: A Vision for the Renewal of Work in America,* New York: Encounter Books, 2018.

13. See Scott Winship, "What's Behind Declining Male Labor Force Participation: Fewer Good Jobs or Fewer Men Seeking Them?," Working Paper, Mercatus Center, George Mason University, 2017.

14. See Claudia Goldin and Lawrence F. Katz, *The Race Between Education and Technology,* Cambridge, MA: Harvard University Press, 2008. They build on previous work such as Jan Tinbergen, "Substitution of Graduate by Other Labor," *Kyklos* 27 (1974), pages 217–226.

15. See David H. Autor, Claudia Goldin, and Lawrence F. Katz, "Extending the Race Between Education and Technology," National Bureau of Economic Research Working Paper No. 26705, January 2020.

16. See Florian Hoffmann, David S. Lee, and Thomas Lemieux, "Growing Income Inequality in the United States and Other Advanced Economies," *Journal of Economic Perspectives* 34 (2020), pages 52–78.

17. See ibid.

18. Comparing data across OECD countries on average gross (that is, pretax) hourly earnings reveals that low-skilled U.S. workers earn much less than their counterparts in Germany, Canada, or the United Kingdom. See https://stats.oecd.org/Index.aspx?QueryId=82334. Also see Autor, Goldin, and Katz, "Extending the Race Between Education and Technology."

19. See Paul Osterman, "Skill Training for Adults," MIT Work of the Future Research Brief, October 2020.

20. See MIT Work of the Future, *The Work of the Future: Building Better Jobs in an Age of Intelligent Machines,* November 2020, page 52.

21. See Amy Ganz, Austan Goolsbee, Glenn Hubbard, and Melissa Kearney, "A Policy Agenda to Develop Human Capital for the Modern Economy," in Melissa Kearney and Amy Ganz, eds., *Expanding Economic Opportunity for More Americans,* Aspen, CO: Aspen Institute, 2018.

22. See Rajashri Chakrabarti, Nicole Gorton, and Michael F. Lovenheim, "State Investment in Higher Education: Effects on Human Capital Formation, Student Debt, and Long-Term Financial Outcomes of Students," Working Paper 27885, National Bureau of Economic Research, October 2020.

23. See National Science Foundation, *National Center for Science and Engineering Statistics,* "National Patterns of R&D Resources," annual series.

24. Countries with higher levels of R&D spending typically enjoy higher incomes. See Charles Jones, "The Facts of Economic Growth," in John B. Taylor and Harald Uhlig, eds., *Handbook of Macroeconomics,* vol. 2A, Amsterdam: North-Holland, 2018. Economists focus on knowledge spillovers as generating high social returns, starting with Zvi Griliches, "Research Costs and Social Returns: Hybrid Corn and Related Innovations," *Journal of Political Economy* 66 (October 1958),

pages 419–432. See, more recently, Brian Lucking, Nicholas Bloom, and John van Reenen, "Have R&D Spillovers Declined in the 21st Century?," *Fiscal Studies* 40 (December 2019), pages 561–590.

25. See *Statement on the Purpose of a Corporation,* Washington, DC: Business Roundtable, 2019; Martin Lipton, *The New Paradigm,* Davos, Switzerland: World Economic Forum, 2016; and Leo E. Strine, Jr., "Toward Fair and Sustainable Capitalism," University of Pennsylvania Institute for Law and Economic Research Paper No. 19-39, October 2019.

26. Roosevelt was a pragmatist who initially tried to reduce competition, with the National Recovery Administration setting prices for many industries. This wall-based strategy soon collapsed, and FDR pivoted to bridges. But the New Deal did increase regulation throughout the economy, most of which ended only in the 1970s and 1980s.

27. See, for example, Christopher J. O'Leary and Randall W. Eberts, "Personal Reemployment Accounts," *Upjohn Institute Employment Research Newsletter* 11:1 (2004).

28. See, for example, the review in Katherine Lucas McKay, "Bridging the Gap: How Wage Insurance Can Address Unemployment-Related Income Volatility," EPIC Report, Aspen Institute, July 2017.

29. In 2020, the average EITC payment nationwide was $2,605. But this figure is skewed by payments to workers with children. For single, childless workers, the maximum EITC payment in 2020 was $538. See https://eitc.irs.gov.

30. See Jason Furman, Timothy Geithner, Glenn Hubbard, and Melissa Kearney, "Promoting Economic Recovery After COVID-19," Aspen Economic Strategy Group, June 2020.

31. See the discussion in Glenn Hubbard, "Supporting Work, Inclusion, and Mass Prosperity," in Michael R. Strain, ed., *The U.S. Labor Market: Questions and Challenges for Public Policy,* Washington, DC: AEI Press, 2016, pages 96–105. A temporary expansion of the EITC for childless workers was included in the 2021 federal American Rescue Plan Act.

32. See Hilary Hoynes and Jesse Rothstein, "Tax Policy Toward Low-Income Families," in Alan J. Auerbach and Kent Smetters, eds., *Economics of Tax Policy,* Oxford: Oxford University Press, 2017.

33. The calculation computes the real minimum wage by adjusting the minimum wage for changes in the Consumer Price Index, Urban Consumers: All Items in U.S. City Average. Data are from the U.S. Bureau of Labor Statistics and fred.stlouisfed.org.

34. See Benjamin Austin, Edward Glaeser, and Lawrence H. Summers, "Saving the Heartland: Place-based Policy in 21st-Century America," *Brookings Papers on Economic Activity,* 2018:1, pages 151–232.

35. See Kristina Huttunen, Jarle Møen, and Kjell G. Salvanes, "Job Loss and Regional Mobility," *Journal of Labor Economics* 36 (2018), pages 479–509. Public policy may also play unintended adverse roles. Occupational licensing costs and restrictions in some states make moving within an occupation type more difficult. And the structure of unemployment insurance benefits can cause individuals to lose certain extended benefits when they move from one state to another.

36. See calculations from the Current Population Survey Historical Migration/ Geographic Mobility Tables reported in Kelsey Berkowitz, "Stuck in Place: What Lower Geographic Mobility Means for Economic Opportunity," *Third Way Report,* January 28, 2019.

37. See Nick Schulz, "Mobility Matters: Understanding the New Geography of Jobs," American Enterprise Institute, July 25, 2012.

38. See the analysis in Raj Chetty, Nathaniel Hendren, Patrick Kline, and Emmanuel Saez, "Where Is the Land of Opportunity? The Geography of Intergenerational Mobility in the United States," *Quarterly Journal of Economics* 129 (November 2014), pages 1553–1623.

39. Other programs have had more success with larger incentives. See Marco Caliendo, Steffen Künn, and Robert Mahlstedt, "The Return to Labor Market Mobility: An Evaluation of Relocation Assistance for the Unemployed," *Journal of Public Economics* 148 (2017), pages 136–151.

40. This term is used generally in such discussions. See, for example, International Labor Organization, *Guidelines for a Just Transition Towards Environmentally Sustainable Economics and Societies for All,* Geneva, Switzerland, 2015; and Blue Green Alliance, *Solidarity for Climate Action,* Report, 2020.

41. See, for example, the review of studies in Daniel Raimi, Wesley Look, Molly Robertson, and Jake Higdon, *Economic Development Policies to Enable Fairness for Workers and Communities in Transition,* Report 20-08, Resources for the Future and Environmental Defense Fund, August 2020.

42. See ibid.

43. See Timothy J. Bartik, "Using Place-Based Jobs Policies to Help Distressed Communities," *Journal of Economic Perspectives* 34 (Summer 2020), pages 99–127.

44. By reducing the reliance on employer-provided health insurance, we can also reduce inefficient health care spending and increase wages. John F. Cogan, Glenn

Hubbard, and Daniel Kessler, *Healthy, Wealthy, and Wise: Five Steps to a Better Health Care System,* Stanford, CA: Hoover Institution Press, 2011.

Chapter 7. Business as a Bridge Builder

1. Missteps after early innovation in digital photography led Kodak to file for federal bankruptcy in 2012. Selling many of its successful patents, it emerged from bankruptcy a year later, and recently made headlines when it received a federal loan to commence production of pharmaceuticals during the COVID-19 pandemic. Mike Dickinson, "Kodak's Decades of Decline," *Rochester Business Journal,* September 13, 2017, https://rbj.net/2017/09/13/kodaks-decades-of-decline/.

2. A secondary rationale (and perhaps primary for some employers) for welfare capitalism was to discourage workers from joining unions. See, for example, Stuart Brandes, *American Welfare Capitalism, 1880–1940,* Chicago: University of Chicago Press, 1976.

3. Eastman also gave to what eventually became the Rochester Institute of Technology. He died by suicide in 1932 after two years of a painful illness.

4. See Darren Walker, "Uncomfortable Questions," *New York Times Sunday Review,* July 5, 2020.

5. See George Shultz, Michael Boskin, John Cogan, and John Taylor, "Some Thoughts on the Business Roundtable's Statement of Corporate Purpose," *RealClearMarkets,* February 5, 2020.

6. See Milton Friedman, "The Social Responsibility of Business Is to Increase Its Profits," *New York Times Sunday Magazine,* September 13, 1970, for this and subsequent references.

7. See Sanjai Bhagat and Glenn Hubbard, "Should the Modern Corporation Maximize Shareholder Value?," *Economic Perspectives,* Washington, DC: American Enterprise Institute, September 2020.

8. See Friedman, "The Social Responsibility of Business Is to Increase Its Profits."

9. See Bhagat and Hubbard, "Should the Modern Corporation Maximize Shareholder Value?"

10. Oliver Hart and Luigi Zingales, "Companies Should Maximize Shareholder Welfare, Not Market Value," *Journal of Law, Finance, and Accounting* 2 (2017), pages 247–274.

11. Investors play a role, too. Shareholders could exercise their voting power to require corporate managers to be sensitive to workforce training or effects of climate

change on long-term value. Large institutional shareholders—like BlackRock, State Street, and Vanguard—with index holdings in almost all large firms can play and are playing a constructive role here.

12. See William R. Kerr and Jordan Bach-Lombardo, "Walmart's Workforce of the Future," Harvard Business School Case, 9-819-042, July 30, 2019.

13. See National Skills Coalition, "United States' Forgotten Middle," https://www.nationalskillscoalition.org/resources/publications/file/middle-skill-fact-sheets-2014/NSC-United-States-MiddleSkillFS-2014.pdf.

14. See William Kerr, Michael Norris, and Manjari Raman, "CEWD: Closing the Skills Gap," Harvard Business School Case, 9-818-081, May 6, 2019.

15. See Peter Q. Blair, Tomas G. Castagnino, Erica L. Groshen, Papia Debroy, Byron Auguste, Shad Ahmed, Fernando Garcia Diaz, and Cristian Bonavida, "Searching for STARS: Work Experience as a Job Market Signal for Workers Without Bachelor's Degrees," Working Paper No. 26844, National Bureau of Economic Research, March 2020.

16. See W. N. Evans, Melissa S. Kearney, B. C. Perry, and James X. Sullivan, "Increasing Community College Completion Rates Among Low-Income Students: Evidence from a Randomized Controlled Trial Evaluation of a Case Management Intervention," *Journal of Policy Analysis and Management* 39 (2020), pages 930–965.

17. See Marianne Bertrand, K. Hallberg, K. Hofmeister, B. Morgan, and E. Shirey, "Increasing Academic Progress Among Low-Income Community Students: Early Evidence from a Randomized Controlled Trial," Chicago: University of Chicago Poverty Lab, 2019.

18. See Joseph Fuller, Harvard Business School Podcast on Managing the Future of Work interview with Ardine Williams, vice president of workforce development at Amazon, January 8, 2020.

19. See Louis Soares, "The Power of the Education-Industry Partnership," Center for American Progress, October 4, 2010.

Chapter 8. Governments and Bridges

1. Early scholarship on land-grant colleges focused more on their role in democratizing access to education than on their role in advancing skill development in an economy experiencing structural changes. See, for example, Earle D. Ross, *Democracy's College: The Land Grant Movement in the Formative Stage,* Ames: Iowa State University Press, 1942; and Allan Nevins, *The State Universities and Democracy,* Ames: Iowa State University Press, 1962.

2. See Nathan M. Sorber, *Land-Grant Colleges and Popular Revolt: The Origins of the Morrill Act and the Reform of Higher Education,* Ithaca, NY: Cornell University Press, 2018, Introduction.

3. See "An Act Donating Public Lands to the Several States and Territories Which May Provide Colleges for the Benefit of Agriculture and the Mechanic Arts, July 2, 1862," in *A Century of Lawmaking for a New Nation: U.S. Congressional Documents and Debates, 1774–1875, 37th Congress, 2nd Session,* http://memory.loc.gov.

4. See Sorber, Introduction to *Land-Grant Colleges and Popular Revolt.*

5. This framing follows the approach of scholars in development economics such as the late Gustav Ranis of Yale University.

6. The monetary analogy is useful because the successor to the gold standard, largely abandoned in the 1930s, after World War II was the Bretton Woods system, which gave individual governments more of a safety valve to set domestic economic policy. In contrast to the outside-in orientation of the gold standard, Bretton Woods pursued an inside-out approach, focusing on domestic needs and political concerns, while still accepting the market system broadly. The work of John Maynard Keynes directly and Karl Polanyi indirectly highlights that point. That system facilitated a large expansion of trade and globalization with that flexibility.

7. For example, the popular home mortgage interest deduction is more generous to higher-income buyers (whose higher marginal tax rates make the deduction more valuable) than to lower-income buyers. It could be replaced by a tax credit more relatively beneficial to lower-income homebuyers. Tax preferences for saving for retirement and financial flexibility should not be valuable only for higher-income individuals. Tax credits can bolster the saving of low-income households and foster prosperity more broadly.

8. Under a cash flow tax, corporations would deduct as expenses wages, all purchases from other firms, and the full cost of capital investment. Compared with the current corporate income tax, the cash flow approach would exempt from taxation the normal return on capital. As a consequence, the tax would fall on returns above the competitive return—say, from rents or high returns from innovation or intellectual property protection. Tax contributions would effectively be higher, then, from firms prospering from structural disruptions.

It is useful to note that this tax mechanism offers a better way to fund programs for workers than trying to encourage gain sharing with employees firm by firm. Most firms in the economy are competitive, making it difficult to raise wages or training expenses relative to the current level. And many firms with returns well above the competitive rate—think Apple or Google—already have mostly well-trained and highly compensated workers. The cash flow tax mechanism allows high profits generally to help fund bridge programs.

9. See Chapter 2 on the "China shock" to employment and communities, with its economic and political consequences. Harvard sociologist William Julius Wilson saw the same problem in linking a decline in manufacturing and blue-collar jobs to crime and addiction: *When Work Disappears,* New York: Random House Vintage Books, 1996.

10. A helpful antecedent program here is the successful Project QUEST (Quality Employment through Skills Training), founded in San Antonio, Texas in 1992 in response to a wave of plant closures. Workers lacked skills for new good jobs in information technology, health care, and other sectors. The project worked with firms and community colleges to ascertain new job opportunities and skill pathways, *and* to nurture a group of high-risk learners with near-term financial burdens. Among its leaders were retired military officers with a background in and commitment to workforce development. Counseling was ongoing and rigorous. As this successful program evolved, community colleges provided more of the services to individual students. A similar program is the Accelerated Study in Associate Program (ASAP) of the City University of New York. See Mark R. Warren, *Dry Bones Rattling: Community Building to Revitalize American Democracy,* Princeton, NJ: Princeton University Press, 2011; and Anne Roder and Mark Elliott, *Nine Year Gains: Project QUEST's Continuing Impact,* New York: Economic Mobility Corporation, 2019.

11. See Government Accountability Office, "Department of Labor Should Assess Efforts to Coordinate Services Across Programs," March 28, 2019, https://www .gao.gov/products/GAO-19-200.

12. See Mason M. Bishop, *Landscape Study of Federal Employment and Training Programs,* Washington, DC: American Enterprise Institute, January 28, 2020, https:// www.aei.org/research-products/report/landscape-study-of-federal-employment-and -training-programs/.

13. See Jason Furman, Timothy Geithner, Glenn Hubbard, and Melissa S. Kearney, "Promoting Economic Recovery After COVID-19," Aspen Economic Study Group, June 2020.

14. See Timothy J. Bartik, "Using Place-Based Jobs Policies to Help Distressed Communities," *Journal of Economic Perspectives* 34 (Summer 2020), pages 99–127; Benjamin Austin, Edward Glaeser, and Lawrence H. Summers, "Saving the Heart-

land: Place-Based Policies in 21st-Century America," *Brookings Papers on Economic Activity* (Spring 2018), pages 151–232.

15. Adam Smith, *The Wealth of Nations,* Book I, Chapter 8.

16. See David H. Autor, David Dorn, and Gordon Hanson, "The China Syndrome: Local Labor Market Effects of Import Competition in the United States," *American Economic Review* 103 (October 2013), pages 2121–2168; Timothy J. Bartik, "Should Place-Based Jobs Policies Be Used to Help Distressed Communities?," Upjohn Institute Working Paper 19-308, Kalamazoo, MI: W. E. Upjohn Institute for Employment Research.

17. See Harry J. Holzer, Richard N. Block, Marcus Cheatham, and Jack H. Knott, "Are Training Subsidies for Firms Effective?," *Industrial and Labor Relations Program* 46 (1993), pages 625–636; and Ronald S. Jarmin, "Evaluating the Impact of Manufacturing Extension on Productivity Growth," *Journal of Policy Analysis and Management* 18 (1999), pages 99–119.

18. See Roger S. Ahlbrandt, Jr., "The Revival of Pittsburgh—A Partnership Between Business and Government," *Long-Range Planning* 23 (1990), pages 31–40; and John P. Hoerr, *And the Wolf Finally Came: The Decline of the American Steel Industry,* Pittsburgh: University of Pittsburgh Press, 1988.

19. See the analysis in Sean Safford, *Why the Garden Club Couldn't Save Youngstown,* Cambridge, MA: Harvard University Press, 2009.

20. See the description in Ben Armstrong, "Industrial Policy and Local Economic Transformation: Evidence from the Rustbelt," Working Paper, Brown University, 2020.

21. See Timothy J. Bartik, "What Works to Help Manufacturing—Intensive Local Economies?," Upjohn Technical Report No. 18-305, Kalamazoo, MI: W. E. Upjohn Institute for Employment, 2018.

22. See Timothy J. Bartik, "Bringing Jobs to People: Improving Local Economic Development Policies," in Melissa S. Kearney and Amy Ganz, eds., *Securing Our Economic Future,* Aspen, CO: Aspen Economic Strategy Group, 2020.

23. Based on 2018 data, workers with full-time jobs over a year with a bachelor's degree earn 114 percent more than workers with a high school degree; full-time, full-year workers with an associate's degree (community college) earn 25 percent more. See 2018 data from the American Community Survey, cited in Rachel Fulcher Dawson, Melissa S. Kearney, and James X. Sullivan, "Comprehensive Approaches to Increasing Student Completion in Higher Education: A Survey of the Land-

scape," Working Paper No. 28046, National Bureau of Economic Research, November 2020.

24. Federal funding can go a long way to improving degree completion rates at community colleges. See Dawson, Kearney, and Sullivan, "Comprehensive Approaches to Increasing Student Completion in Higher Education."

25. See the discussion in E. Jason Brown, Shawn Kantor, and Alexander Whalley, "Extending the Reach of Research Universities: A Proposal for Productivity Growth in Lagging Communities," Policy Proposal 2018-11, Washington, DC: Brookings Institution, The Hamilton Project, 2018.

26. See, for example, the analyses in James D. Adams, "Comparative Localization of Academic and Industry Spillovers, "*Journal of Economic Geography* 2 (2002), pages 253–278; and Edward L. Glaeser, *Triumph of the City: How Our Greatest Invention Makes Us Richer, Smarter, Greener, Healthier, and Happier,* London: Penguin, 2012.

27. Economic effects of universities on local growth are not simply theoretical speculation. Economists have found that the founding of a university increases local GDP growth, corporate patenting, and growth of local industrial pharmaceutical labs. See Anna Valero and John van Reenen, "The Economic Impact of Universities: Evidence from Across the Globe," *Economics of Education* 68 (2019), pages 53–67; Adam Jaffe, "Real Effects of Academic Research," *American Economic Review* 79 (December 1989), pages 957–990; Naomi Hausman, "University Innovations and Local Economic Growth," Working Paper, Hebrew University, 2018; and Jeffrey Furman and Megan MacGarvie, "Academic Science and the Birth of Industrial Research Laboratories in the U.S. Pharmaceutical Industry," *Journal of Economic Behavior and Organization* 63 (2007), pages 756–776. Spillovers estimated in this body of research bore fruit in large part in partnerships with local firms.

28. See Eva Klein and James K. Woodell, *Higher Education Engagement in Economic Development: Foundations for Strategy and Practice,* Washington, DC: Association of Public and Land-Grant Universities, 2015.

29. See Jorge H. Atiles, Chris Jenkins, Patricia Rayas-Duarte, Randal K. Taylor, and Hailin Zhang, "Service, Cooperative Extension, and Community Engagement," in R. J. Sternberg, ed., *The Modern Land-Grant University,* West Lafayette, IN: Purdue University Press, 2014, pages 59–81.

30. See also the arguments for decentralized presence of federal applied research support to broaden growth-raising effects of useful knowledge across regions of the country in Jonathan Gruber and Simon Johnson, *Jump-Starting America: How Break-*

through Science Can Revive Economic Growth and the American Dream, New York: Public Affairs, 2019.

31. See Anna Fife, Hilary Greenberg, and Alastair Fitzpayne, "Supporting Employer-Provided Training in the COVID-19 Recovery," *Policy Brief,* Aspen Institute Future of Work Institutions, December 2020.

32. Isabel Sawhill and John Bridgeland, "Here's a Cost-Effective National Service Proposal That Could Bridge Our Deep Divisions," *Washington Post,* February 21, 2020.

33. See the discussion in Robert D. Putnam and Shaylyn Romney Garrett, *The Upswing: How America Came Together a Century Ago and How We Can Do It Again,* New York: Simon & Schuster, 2020.

34. See, for example, Suzanne Mettler, *Soldiers to Citizens: The G.I. Bill and the Making of the Greatest Generation,* Oxford: Oxford University Press, 2006. Historian Kathleen Frydl has observed that the G.I. Bill shared with another contemporary policy, the Marshall Plan for Europe, not only federal funding but also flexibility among recipients (educational institutions and European governments in those cases) in putting funds to use. She also noted this feature as one for the land-grant colleges. See Kathleen J. Frydl, *The G.I. Bill,* Cambridge: Cambridge University Press, 2009, Chapter 7 and Conclusion.

Chapter 9. Mass Flourishing Requires Bridges

1. Benjamin M. Friedman, *The Moral Consequences of Economic Growth,* New York: Random House, 2005.

Index

Abraham, Katherine, 28
absolute advantage, 86
Advanced Research Projects Agency-
    Energy (ARPA-E), 161
agriculture, 23, 62, 77, 151–153, 161,
    171–172
Airbus, 81–82
alcohol abuse, 22, 165
Allegheny Conference on Commu-
    nity Development, 166
Alphabet Inc., 81
Amazon, 81, 146
American Rescue Plan Act (2021),
    126
American Revolution, 42, 86
Amiti, Mary, 89
antitrust policy, 43, 123, 146, 184
Appelbaum, Binyamin, 107
Apple Computer, 37
Arizona State University, 144
Arrow, Kenneth, 44
artificial intelligence, 5, 23, 35, 70, 90,
    108, 170, 197
Association for Talent Development,
    119
AT&T, 142
Austin, Benjamin, 21, 127
Australia, 77
Austrian School, 29

automation, 20, 26, 63, 64, 161;
    robotic, 5, 6, 22–23, 28, 35, 49–50,
    90, 197
automobile industry, 5, 34, 49–50, 80,
    87, 88
Autor, David, 26, 27, 28, 36, 63–64,
    93, 115

Back to School (film), 107
BAE Systems, 81
bailouts, 67
Bartik, Timothy, 129
Berlin Wall, ix, 19
Bezos, Jeff, 99
Bhagat, Sanjai, 140
Biden, Joe, xi, 17, 67, 97, 130, 183,
    194–195
Blair, Tony, 186
Boeing Company, 71, 81
Bojilov, Raicho, 98
Bolsonaro, Jair, 3
Bolten, Joshua, 137
Boskin, Michael, 138
Brazil, 3
Bretton Woods system, 184, 215n6
Brexit, 3, 11, 28, 132–133
Bridgeland, John, 176
bridges, 15–16; businesses' role in,
    135–150, 189–190; characteristics of,

bridges (*continued*)
37–38, 106; COVID-19 pandemic
and, xi, 194–198; educational,
33–34, 116, 151–152; financing of,
69; governments and, x–xi, 151–177,
188, 192; Lincoln's, 105, 133, 151, 154;
making the case for, 3, 133, 157–158,
192; mass flourishing linked to,
viii–ix, 4, 178–198; as moral imperative, 38, 54–55, 59, 100, 186;
need for, 18, 54–55; Polanyi's views
and, 55, 56; preparation through,
viii–ix, 3, 7, 18, 37, 55, 57, 69,
115–120, 131, 133, 137, 179, 182, 186,
196; proposals for, 124–130, 159–160;
for reconnection, viii–ix, 7, 18, 37,
55, 57, 69, 120–132, 133, 137, 179,
186, 196; requirements for, 154–162;
risks aggregated by, 100, 102–103,
106–109, 111, 124; Roosevelt's, 121,
154; social connection from, 100;
social insurance programs as,
101–103; types of, 131. *See also*
preparation; reconnection
British East India Company, 43, 79
Buchanan, James, 67
Buchanan, Patrick, 31, 85, 185
Buckham, Matthew, 152
Bush, George H. W., xiii, 19, 31, 85,
87, 123
Bush, George W., ix, xiii, 17, 123;
China's WTO membership backed
by, 26–27, 87; Personal Reemployment Accounts proposed by, 124;
steel tariffs imposed by, 1–2, 64, 66,
84, 88, 182, 197–198
Bush, Vannevar, 170
business cycle, 5–6, 22, 24, 38, 94,
121–122, 179

Business Roundtable (BRT), 79,
137–140, 144, 145, 184, 190, 191

Canada, 77, 87, 126
Capitalism and Freedom (Friedman),
30
A Capitalism for the People (Zingales),
68
Carnegie Foundation, 173
Case, Anne, 21–22
Casey, Bob, 120
Cass, Oren, 60–69, 77, 111, 113, 114,
126, 182–183
Center for Energy Workforce Devel-
opment (CEWD), 142–143
Chakrabarti, Rajashri, 118
Cheney, Dick, 1
China, 63, 165, 197; economic boom
in, 20, 24, 26, 35, 90, 108, 178;
exports from, 25–26, 28, 72, 76;
political backlash against, 70–71,
75, 155–156; retaliation by, 76–77;
tariffs aimed at, 76, 89; unfair trad-
ing practices by, 75, 156; in World
Trade Organization, 20, 24, 25, 27,
75, 76–77, 87
Clausing, Kimberly, 89
Cleveland, 168
climate change, 62, 128, 129, 147, 155,
191
Clinton, Bill, 9, 17, 20, 26, 29, 87,
186
Clinton, Hillary, 9, 10, 11, 28
Cogan, John, 130, 138
Colorado, 164, 174
Columbia University, 145
Columbus, Christopher, 202–203n7
The Communist Manifesto (Marx and
Engels), 95

community colleges, 127, 129, 198;
completion rates at, 169–170; declining state-level support for, 117,
188; enrollment figures for, 117;
government grants to, 117–118, 162,
165, 168–169, 172–173, 188, 192;
private partnerships with, 119–120,
143–144, 145–146, 169, 191
comparative advantage, 45, 77, 86,
109–110
competition: assumptions underlying, 153–154; benefits of, 42–43;
efficiency from, 42–44, 62; government policing of, 30, 53–54;
"invisible hand" linked to, 42, 45,
54, 67, 68, 80, 180; living standards
linked to, 43, 180; policing of, 155;
public support for, 69; Smith's
stress on, 42, 44, 52, 56, 59, 67,
78, 80, 148, 153, 180, 190
Comprehensive and Progressive
Agreement for Trans-Pacific Partnership, 77
computing, 5, 20, 35, 49, 90, 94, 108,
170
Connecticut, 120, 174
construction industry, 25
Consumer Technology Association,
70
consumption smoothing, 102–103
contracts, 46, 149
Corn Laws, 32, 45
corporate purpose, 79, 139, 140
corporations, 78–79
Cotton, Tom, 66
Council of Economic Advisers, 1, 27,
119, 123
COVID-19 pandemic, 37, 83, 91, 94,
119, 124, 144, 154, 188; bridges and,

xi, 194–198; corporate and government spending during, 132, 139,
157; economic disruption from,
17–18, 67, 116, 118, 133, 139, 147,
169; inequality worsened by, 21; job
lock during, 129; unemployment
insurance during, 122; wall proposals inspired by, 17–18, 133, 194
Crandall, Robert, 88
creative destruction, 35, 90, 94, 109
Csikszentmihalyi, Mihaly, 53
current account balance, 73–74, 85

Dalio, Ray, 94
data analytics, 5, 70
Dawson, Rachel, 169
"deaths of despair," 22
Deaton, Angus, 21–22
DeBartolo Holdings, 15
Debreu, Gerard, 44
decarbonization, 127–128, 129, 147
Declaration of Independence, 43
Defense Advanced Research Projects
Agency (DARPA), 160–161
Deng Xiaoping, 20
deregulation, 62
Dimon, Jamie, 94, 137
disability benefits, 27
division of labor, 44, 45, 52
Dorn, David, 26
drug abuse, 22, 165
Dutch East India Company, 43, 79
dynamism, 17, 57, 61; disruption
linked to, 22, 24, 80, 91, 99, 178,
182; neoliberalism linked to, viii,
28, 59, 193; Phelps's view of, 50–52;
protectionist risk to, x; public support for, viii, ix, 16, 52, 69, 82, 101,
104, 150, 178, 183, 192; as social

dynamism (*continued*)
construct, 16, 148; social insurance
compatible with, 56, 92, 96, 103,
125, 188

earmarks, 67
Earned Income Tax Credit (EITC),
125–126, 131, 156, 189
Eastman, George, 134, 149
Eastman Kodak, 134, 136, 149
Eastman School of Music, 134
Economic Development Administration, 128
Economics (Hubbard and O'Brien),
6–7
education, 46, 49, 55, 115–116. *See also*
job training
EdX, 144
efficiency, 73, 154; absolute vs. relative, 86; from competition, 42–44,
62; from globalization, 5; from
mechanization, 23, 34, 90; protectionist loss of, x, 6, 17, 29, 45, 52–53,
59–60, 64, 69, 182, 184, 186; from
specialization, 86, 109–110; tax policy and, 130. *See also* productivity
electrification, 35, 90, 91
electronics industry, 58–59
Elizabeth I, queen of England, 34–35
Elizabeth II, queen of Great Britain,
12, 175, 187
"empowerment zones," 128
Enders, Thomas, 81–82
endogenous growth, 49–50
Engels, Friedrich, 95
England's Treasure by Foreign Trade
(Mun), 39
European Union, 11, 19, 77, 133, 197
exogenous growth, 49–50

Fajgelbaum, Pablo, 89
Fannie Mae, 67
Federal Reserve, 67
Feldstein, Martin, 175
feudalism, 56, 96
financial account balance, 74
financial crisis of 2007–2009, 67,
147
Fink, Laurence, 79, 137
First National Bank of Boston, 58
Five Star movement, 3
Flaanen, Aaron, 89
flow, in psychology, 53, 181
Ford, Henry, 33
foreign exchange, 25
Foxconn, 37
France, 3, 11, 81, 133
Franklin, Benjamin, 41
Freddie Mac, 67
Friedman, Benjamin, 196–197
Friedman, Milton, 29, 148, 149, 153,
187, 197; as public intellectual,
30; shareholder value maximiza-
tion stressed by, 82, 138–140, 142,
190–191; universal basic income
backed by, 130
Frydl, Kathleen, 219n34
Furman, Jason, 126, 163

gainers compensating losers, 6,
99–100, 109–114, 122, 126, 183,
187
Gama, Vasco da, 202–203n7
Ganz, Amy, 117
Gates, Bill, 99, 138
Geithner, Timothy, 126, 163
General Agreement on Tariffs and
Trade (GATT, 1947), 33, 87
Germany, 73–74

G.I. Bill (Servicemen's Readjustment
    Act, 1944), x, 33–34, 87, 96, 157,
    179, 184
Glaeser, Edward, 21, 127
globalization, 3, 34, 79, 87, 96;
    employment and earnings buffeted
    by, 21, 88, 111, 115, 143; mass pros-
    perity disrupted by, 95–96; popu-
    list opposition to, 31; productivity
    gains from, 5, 25; structural changes
    from, 50, 94, 107, 147, 148, 172,
    186–187, 197
global warming, 62, 128, 129, 147, 155,
    191
Goldberg, Pinelopi, 89
Goldin, Claudia, 114, 115
gold standard, 111, 155
Goldstein, Amy, 38
Google, 144, 169
Goolsbee, Austan, 117
Gordon, Robert, 36, 91
Gorsky, Alex, 137
Gorton, Nicole, 118
Grand Rapids, Michigan, 168
Grange (Patrons of Husbandry), 152
Graziosi, Graig, 9, 14
Great Depression, 33, 96, 121, 188
The Great Transformation (Polanyi),
    55–56
Greece, 3
Greeley, Horace, 165
guilds, 43
Gutenberg, Johannes, 35

Hadrian, emperor of Rome, viii, 4,
    31–32
Hanson, Gordon, 26
Harris, Kamala, xi
Hart, Oliver, 141

Hawley, Josh, 66
Hayek, Friedrich, 4, 29–30, 187, 197
health care, 94, 129–130, 135, 189, 195
homeownership, 156–157, 201n26
Homestead Act (1862), 105
Hoover, Herbert, 33
Horton, Ray, 8–9, 10, 13
housing: bubble in (2007), 25–26;
    cost of, 23; employment in, 25
Hoynes, Hilary, 126
Hufbauer, Gary Clyde, 108
human capital, 5, 49
Hume, David, 39, 40, 86

IBM Corporation, 70, 144, 169
India, 20, 24, 35, 90, 108, 178
indigenous innovation, 92
Industrial Revolution, 35, 45, 48, 52,
    90, 92, 184
Industry Resilience Program, 128
inequality, 36–37, 95, 111–113, 116, 195
information technology, 64
innovism, 51, 52, 59, 61, 91
International Monetary Fund, 20
internet, 35, 90, 170
"invisible hand," 155, 181; competition
    linked to, 42, 45, 54, 67, 68, 80,
    180; laissez distinguished from, 149;
    reconnecting linked to, 70; social
    ties linked to, 55
iPhone, 37
Italy, 3, 133

Japan, 21, 34, 77
job training, x, 7, 23–25, 101–102,
    162, 179; by community colleges,
    117–118, 119, 129, 143, 169, 172,
    173, 188, 198; corporate bridges of,
    141–147; mixed results of, 156, 163;

job training (*continued*)
public and private incentives for,
49–50, 82, 116, 119–120, 125; risk
to employers and communities of,
161, 174; skills mismatch remedied
by, 28; statistics on, 117; tax incentives proposed for, 120, 124, 145,
192; in Youngstown, 14, 167
Johnson, Lyndon B., 122
joint stock companies, 79

Kaldor, Nicholas, 6, 110, 183
Katz, Lawrence, 93, 115
Kearney, Melissa, 28, 93, 117, 126, 163,
169
Kennedy, John F., 122, 199–200n7
Kennedy, Patrick, 89
Kessler, Daniel, 130
Keynes, John Maynard, 29, 36, 91
Khan, Sadiq, xi
Khandelwal, Amit, 89
Kissinger, Henry, 159
Knight, Frank, 161
Krishnamoorthi, Raja, 120

labor force participation, 22, 25, 26,
64, 114
laissez faire, 5, 64, 103; criticisms of,
7, 56; globalization linked to, 111;
insufficiency of, 17, 98, 101, 104,
108, 132, 153, 178, 185, 186, 192, 193,
195, 197, 198; invisible hand distinguished from, 149; physiocratic
origins of, 41; Smith's misgivings
about, 43, 45, 153; unwarranted
optimism linked to, 3–4
Lamont, Thomas, 33
land-grant colleges, x, 96, 105, 106,
154, 162, 179; agriculture vs. manu-

facturing and, 152, 172; lessons of,
151, 172–174
land-use regulation, 23
Larrimore, Jeff, 93
Lawrence, Robert, 112
Lazear, Edward, 112
Lee, William, 35
Lemann, Nicholas, 107
limited liability, 79
Lincoln, Abraham, x, 96, 105, 120–121,
133, 151, 154, 187–188
LinkedIn, 169
Lipton, Martin, 78, 120, 184
living standards, 62, 197; competition
linked to, 43, 180; Industrial Revo-
lution and, 48, 178; prosperity
equated with, 42, 54, 185; special-
ization linked to, 44
Locke, John, 86
Lockheed Corporation, 81
Looney, Adam, 93
Lovenheim, Michael, 118
Lu, Lucy, 108
Luddites, 34–35, 90

Malthus, Thomas, 202n6
Mankiw, Gregory, 63, 205n10
manufacturing: in China, 20, 152;
computer-aided, 49–50, 70; Corn
Laws' inhibition of, 32; cyclical
employment in, 25–26; in Great
Britain, 85; idealized view of,
60–61, 63, 65, 167, 182, 195; in
Midwest, 8, 15, 23, 168; productivity in, 62, 63, 161; public–private
partnerships for, 166–168, 171–172,
174; supply chains in, 5, 9, 18, 21,
71–72, 89, 194; tariffs and, 89, 110;
uncertain outlook for, 65; U.S.

decline in, 24, 25–26, 63, 75, 84–85, 108, 114
Manufacturing Extension Partnerships, 171–172
Marshall Plan, 149, 219n34
Marx, Karl, 95
Maryland, 174
Maslow, Abraham, 130
Massachusetts, 58–59, 65, 174, 189
Massachusetts Institute of Technology (MIT), 135, 149
Masser, Alpha, 152
mass flourishing, ix, x, 156; bridges required for, viii–ix, 4, 178–198; as classical economists' goal, 4, 6, 16, 196; core element of, 103–104; employee engagement linked to, 144–145; as moral imperative, xi, 17, 69, 180–185; psychology of, 53; Smith's embrace of, 4, 46–48, 52–53, 54–55, 57, 59, 69–70, 78, 80, 136; social insurance linked to, 103
Mass Flourishing (Phelps), 50
Mayer, Colin, 77–80, 82, 120, 126, 184
McAnaney, Florence, 135
McCloskey, Deirdre, 4, 50, 51, 52, 55, 91, 181, 196
McDonnell Douglas, 81
McKinley, William, 33
McKinsey & Company, 144
McMillon, Doug, 142
Medicaid, 27, 163–164
Medicare, 121, 158–159, 189
Mellon, Richard King, 166
mercantilism, 72–73, 85–86, 96; Mun's defense of, 39–40; productivity threatened by, 77, 83, 88; Smith's opposition to, viii, 6, 32, 40, 41–45,

52–53, 56–57, 60, 61, 65, 66, 85, 88, 148, 180, 181
Mexico, 71, 88
Microsoft Corporation, 138, 144
middle class, 92–93
migration, 23, 31
minimum wage, 126, 129
mobility, 12, 23, 24, 28, 127, 165, 190
monopolies, 42, 43, 155
Monthly Economic Report, 62
The Moral Consequences of Economic Growth (Friedman), 196–197
Morrill, Justin, 152
Morrill Land Grant Act (1862), 105, 118, 151, 173
mortality, 21–22
most-favored-nation status, 87
Moving the Opportunity program, 127
Mun, Thomas, 39–40, 60, 77
Murray, Charles, 130

National Federation of Independent Business, 190
national income accounting, 73
National Institutes of Health, 170
National Recovery Administration, 35, 211n26
National Science Foundation, 170
National Urban League, 144
Navarro, Peter, 70–73, 75–76, 77, 183–184, 194
Navigation Acts, 32, 86
neoliberalism, 30, 155, 161, 178, 185, 187, 197; dynamism linked to, viii, 28, 59, 193; openness linked to, 28, 29, 31, 34, 185; tariffs contrary to, 34
New Deal, 157
New England Council, 58

newspaper publishing, 5
Nissan, 34
Nixon, Richard, 10, 130
Nordhaus, William, 99–100
North American Free Trade Agreement (NAFTA, 1993), 19–20, 76, 87
Northrop Grumman, 146
Nucor Steel, 119

Obama, Barack, 10, 17, 88, 102, 123
occupational licensing, 23, 190, 212n35
The Once and Future Worker (Cass), 60–63, 113
One Million Degrees (educational program), 143–144
openness, 35, 36, 49–51, 57, 87, 90, 160, 184, 186; bridges linked to, ix, 106; communist collapse linked to, 19, 33; inequality linked to, 112–113; neoliberalism linked to, 28, 29, 31, 34, 185; public support for, 97, 98, 106, 109, 123, 182–183; risks of, 12–13, 22, 28–29, 30, 61, 88, 97–99, 103–104, 108, 111, 132, 153; Smith's embrace of, x, 4, 52, 59, 78, 80, 135
opportunity policy, 95
opportunity zones, 127–128
outsourcing, 24

Peel, Robert, 32
Perot, Ross, 20, 31, 185
Personal Reemployment Accounts, 124, 125, 131, 156, 189
Phelps, Edmund, 4, 55, 98, 181; employer subsidies backed by, 126; openness and innovation linked by, 50–51, 52, 92, 97, 196

physiocrats, 41
Pierce, Justin, 89
Pittsburgh, 166–167, 189
place-based aid, 126–129, 131, 162, 164–166, 168, 173, 189, 192
Polanyi, Karl, 55–56, 75
pollution, 155
populism, viii, ix, 25; walls linked to, ix, 36–38, 55, 66, 69, 71, 75, 111, 133, 153, 155, 178, 185, 192, 195, 196
preparation, viii; bridges needed for, 7, 16, 100. 115; economic basis for, 53–56; through existing institutions, 188; "inside-out" approach to, 155, 193; place-based aid for, 127, 162, 165, 192; public goods for, 16; Smith's support for, 46, 54–55, 78, 180, 181; social insurance for, 16, 100; types of, 131; U.S. failures in, x, 25, 75, 94–95
President's Working Group on Financial Markets, 159
price-fixing, 43
prime-age males, employment of, 21
"productive pluralism," 114
productivity, 22, 42, 108, 184; in agriculture, 62; compensation commensurate with, 112, 123; from division of labor, 44, 49; from globalization, 5; local investment linked to, 82; in manufacturing, 62, 63, 161; mercantilist threat to, 77, 83, 88; in service sector, 161; by skill level, 113; from technology, 5, 14, 21, 35, 64, 97. *See also* efficiency
property rights, 30, 46, 149
Prosperity (Mayer), 78–79
public goods, 16, 30; Smith's advocacy of, 46, 78, 148

public works, 46
Putnam, Robert, 177

Quesnay, François, 41
QUEST (Quality Employment
through Skills Training), 171,
216n10

railroads, 105, 106
Rajan, Raghuram, 65–66, 68
Reagan, Ronald, 87, 88, 186; at Berlin
Wall, 19; as neoliberal, 29, 30, 34,
186; steel tariffs imposed by, 84
recessions, 5–6, 13, 121, 132, 164
reconnection, 59, 88, 91, 98; bridges
for, viii–ix, 7, 18, 37, 55, 57, 69,
120–132, 133, 137, 179, 186, 196;
COVID-19 pandemic and, 154;
economic basis for, 53–56; in
European reconstruction, 149;
health care and, 129–130; "inside-
out" approach to, 155, 193; place-
based aid for, 128; through social
insurance, 8, 16, 56, 100, 103, 121,
124, 156, 186, 188–189, 192; U.S.
failures in, x, 25, 75, 94–95
Redding, Stephen, 89
Re-entry Acceleration Program, 145
rent seeking, 51, 80
research and development, 118–120,
123–124, 129, 188
retaliation, in trade wars, 33, 71,
76–77
Rework America Alliance, 144
Ricardo, David, 4, 36, 45, 85, 86, 91,
109
risk pooling, 103
The Road to Serfdom (Hayek), 29
robotics, 5, 22–23, 28, 35, 49–50, 197

Rochester, N.Y., 134–135, 149
Romer, Christina, 63
Rometty, Virginia, 70
Romney, Mitt, 10, 124
Roosevelt, Franklin D., x, 35, 96, 121,
133, 154, 188
Rothstein, Jesse, 126
Rubio, Marco, 66, 138
Rural Cooperative Service, 128
Rural Development Programs, 128
Rural Utility Service, 128

Salomons, Anna, 63–64
San Antonio, Texas, 171, 216n10
Santorum, Rick, 185
savings: household, 102; national,
73–74, 76
Sawhill, Isabel, 176
Schumpeter, Joseph, 4, 35, 90, 92, 97
Scottish Enlightenment, 6
Second Treatise on Civil Government
(Locke), 86
Seegmiller, Bryan, 63–64
Serve America Act (2009), 176
Servicemen's Readjustment Act (G.I.
Bill, 1944), x, 33–34, 87, 96, 157,
179, 184
service sector, 62, 63, 94, 114, 161
Shiller, Robert, 175–176
Shultz, George, 138
Simon Property Group, 15
skill bias, 22
Skillful State Network, 164
Small Business Administration, 128,
167
smartphones, 108, 170
Smith, Adam, 29, 31, 165, 184; compe-
tition and prosperity linked by, x,
78, 79–80, 86, 135, 148, 153, 180–181,

Smith, Adam (*continued*)
191; consumption stressed by, 42,
111, 113; early years of, 40; government role backed by, 45–46, 54, 55,
64, 65, 69; markets championed
by, 42, 44, 52, 56, 59, 67, 78, 80,
148, 153, 180, 190; mass flourishing
embraced by, 4, 46–48, 52–53,
54–55, 57, 59, 69–70, 78, 80, 136;
mercantilism opposed by, viii, 6,
32, 40, 41–45, 52–53, 56–57, 60, 61,
65, 66, 85, 88, 148, 180, 181; preparation to compete embraced by, 46,
54–55, 78, 180, 181; progress and
disruption linked by, viii, 92; universal education backed by, 46, 55
Smoot-Hawley Tariff (1930), 33
social insurance, x, 7, 24, 27, 30, 95;
as bridge, 101–103; dynamism
compatible with, 56, 92, 96, 103,
125, 188; for preparation, 16, 100;
proposal for, 189; for reconnecting,
8, 16, 56, 100, 103, 121, 124, 156,
186, 188–189, 192
socialism, 29, 56, 192
social media, 5
Social Security, 27, 96, 103, 121, 154,
158–159, 179, 189
Society for Human Resource Management, 119
Sokolov, Rick, 15
Solow, Robert, 203n8
Soviet Union, 19, 97, 160, 170
Spain, 81
specialization, 4, 44, 45, 52, 77, 86,
153
Splinter, David, 93
Stabenow, Debbie, 120
stagflation, 29

stakeholder capitalism, 120, 137–141,
184, 191
standard of living. *See* living standards
Stansbury, Anna, 112
Stay the Course (educational program), 143
steel, 5, 80; public–private partnerships and, 119, 166–167; tariffs on,
1–3, 9, 32, 64, 76, 85, 88, 110, 182,
197–198; in Youngstown, vii, 9, 14,
21, 23, 25, 34, 84, 87, 91, 110, 198
Stigler, George, 67
Strain, Michael, 92, 112
Strine, Leo, Jr., 80, 82, 120
Strong, Henry, 134
substance abuse, 22
sugar, 88
suicide, 22
Sullivan, James, 169–170
Summers, Lawrence, 21, 112, 127
supply chains, 5, 9, 18, 21, 71–72, 89,
194
Sweden, 160
Syriza (Greek political party), 3

Tamer Center for Social Enterprise,
145
Taney, Roger, 208–209n2
tariffs: agreements to limit, 19, 33,
87, 122; appeal of, 6; on Chinese
imports, 71–72, 75, 88, 89; Great
Depression worsened by, 33; in-
effectiveness of, 2, 9, 45, 76, 89;
neoliberal opposition to, 34; Smith's
opposition to, 45; on steel, 1–3, 9,
32, 64, 76, 85, 88, 110, 182, 197–198
tax base, 24, 46
Tax Cut and Jobs Act (2017), 128, 132,
158

taxes: on carbon, 157; corporate, 146–147, 157–158; on estates, 158; progressive vs. regressive, 46, 93, 201n25, 215n7; reductions in, 61, 76; refundable credits against, 126; training-related credits against, 120, 124, 145, 192

Taylor, John, 138

technology, 3, 4, 79; artificial intelligence, 5, 23, 35, 70, 90, 108, 170, 197; automative, 20, 26, 63, 64, 115; gainers and losers from, 99; mass prosperity disrupted by, 95–96; productivity gains from, 5, 14, 21, 35, 64, 97; risks from, 88, 91; robotic, 5, 22–23, 28, 35, 49–50, 197; structural changes from, 50, 91, 94, 107, 147, 148, 172, 186–187, 197; walls against, 34–36, 90–91, 104, 136

textile industry, 58, 65

Thatcher, Margaret, 29, 186

The Theory of Moral Sentiments (Smith), viii, x, 39–42, 56, 59, 181, 196

Toyota, 34, 119

Trade Act (1974), 199–200n7

Trade Adjustment Assistance (TAA), 23, 27, 34, 88, 122–123, 125, 156

Trade Expansion Act (1962), 122, 199–200n7

Traficant, Jim, 9

training programs. *See* job training

transfer payments, xi, 92–93, 97, 103, 130, 205n11

transition costs, 107, 123

Trans-Pacific Partnership (TPP), 77

Truman, Harry, 170

Trump, Donald, viii, 3, 8, 11, 13, 37, 70, 132; economic stagnation deplored by, 92; economists maligned by, 107; job losses linked to support for, 28; precursors of, 31; as protectionist, 9, 10, 20, 66, 71, 75–76, 84, 85, 183, 185, 195; public's view of, 14; research budget cut by, 171

unemployment, 21, 25, 89, 94, 122, 163

unemployment insurance, x, 23, 24, 103, 121–122, 163–164, 189, 212n35

unfair competition, 65

United Kingdom, 32, 81; Brexit vote in, 3, 11, 28, 132–133; Industrial Revolution in, 35, 45, 48, 52, 90, 92, 184; mercantilism in, 85–86; Working Tax Credit in, 126

U.S. Chamber of Commerce, 150, 190, 191

United States-Mexico-Canada Agreement, 20, 76

U.S. Steel, 167

Universal Basic Income (UBI), 130

University of Rochester, 134, 135

University of Vermont, 151–152

urbanization, 23

"The Use of Knowledge in Society" (Hayek), 29–30

Utah, 163

Vallourec Star, 14, 23

Vespasian, emperor of Rome, 34–35

Volcker Alliance, 170

wage insurance, 125, 131, 156, 189

wage subsidies, 69, 156

Walker, Darren, 138

walls: agriculture protected by, 172; appeal of, viii, 3, 6, 7–8, 15, 54, 84–104, 106–107, 154, 186; bipartisan support for, 9, 184; corporate governance reforms likened to, 82–83, 98, 120; COVID-19 pandemic linked to, 17–18, 133, 194; dynamism threatened by, x, 51, 60, 99, 183; ebb and flow of, 37–38; elites' opposition to, 87–89; throughout history, 4, 31–34; neoliberal assault on, 19–20, 24, 28–31, 56, 84, 185; populist demands for, ix, 36–37, 55, 66, 69, 71, 75, 111, 133, 153, 155, 178, 185, 192, 195, 196; Smith's opposition to, 52–53, 59, 88, 181–182; taxes likened to, 162; against technological change, 34–36, 90–91, 104, 136; types of, 101. *See also* mercantilism; tariffs

Wall Street (film), 18

Walmart, 5, 142

Walton, Sam, 99

Warner, Mark, 120

Warren, Elizabeth, 92, 138

The Wealth of Nations (Smith), 40, 42–43, 148, 184, 190, 196; economy as moral system in, viii; as foundational text, 39; mass flourishing in, 4, 48, 181; openness and competition in, x; pin factory described in, 44; specificity of, 46; success of, 41, 59

Weinberger, Mark, 137

Weinstein, David, 89

"welfare capitalism," 135

Wilson, William Julius, 216n9

Winship, Scott, 112, 114

Workday Inc., 144

Workforce Innovation and Opportunity Act (2014), 174

World Bank, 20

World Trade Organization (WTO), 33; China's membership in, 20, 24, 25, 27, 75, 76–77, 87

World War Adjusted Compensation Act (1924), 201n26

Yang, Andrew, 130, 176

Yellow Vests movement, 3

Youngstown, Ohio, vii, 8–10, 12–15, 38; automobile manufacturing near, 110; elites mistrusted in, 31; Japanese imports and, 21, 25; job training in, 14, 167; long-term unemployment in, 122; protectionist demands in, 84; public–private partnerships in, 105–106, 167; steel industry in, vii, 9, 13–14, 21, 23, 25, 34, 84, 87, 91, 110, 198

Youngstown Business Incubator, 14, 15, 106, 167

Youngstown Sheet & Tube Company, 9

Zingales, Luigi, 65–66, 68, 141

zoning, 190